HIDDEN SOCIETY

WRITTEN BY
RAFAEL SCAVONE

ART, COVER, AND CHAPTER BREAKS BY
RAFAEL ALBUQUERQUE

COLORS BY
MARCELO COSTA

LETTERS BY
BERNARDO BRICE

HIDDEN SOCIETY CREATED BY
RAFAEL SCAVONE AND RAFAEL ALBUQUERQUE

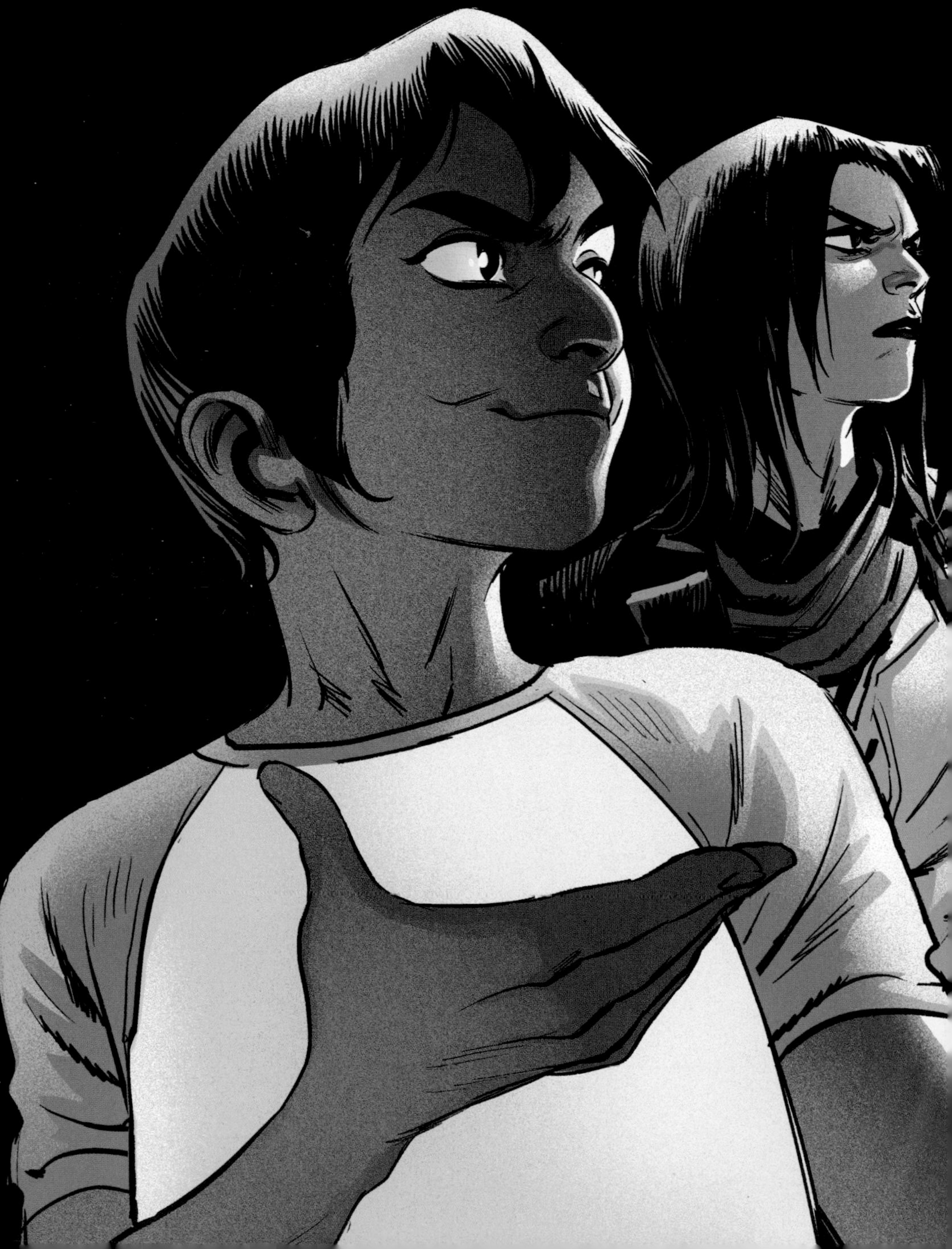

HIDDEN SOCIETY™

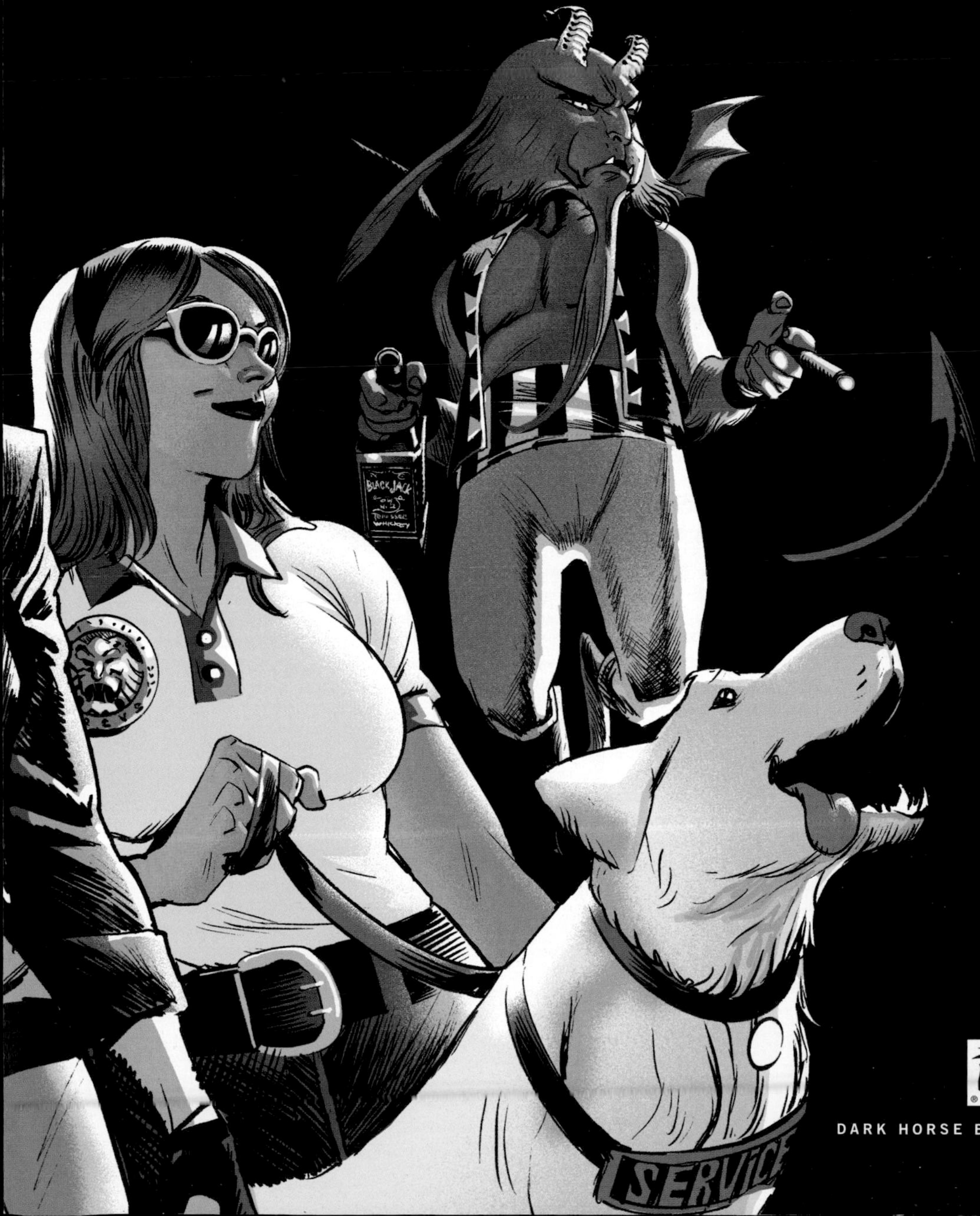

DARK HORSE BOOKS

PUBLISHER
MIKE RICHARDSON

EDITOR
DANIEL CHABON

ASSISTANT EDITOR
CHUCK HOWITT

DESIGNER
BRENNAN THOME

DIGITAL ART TECHNICIAN
JOSIE CHRISTENSEN

HIDDEN SOCIETY

Collects issues #1–#4 of the Dark Horse Comics series *Hidden Society*

Published by Dark Horse Books / A division of Dark Horse Comics LLC
10956 SE Main Street / Milwaukie, OR 97222

DarkHorse.com

To find a comics shop in your area, visit comicshoplocator.com

First edition: October 2020
Ebook ISBN 978-1-50671-718-0
Trade paperback ISBN 978-1-50671-717-3

1 2 3 4 5 6 7 8 9 10
Printed in China

Names: Scavone, Rafael, writer. | Albuquerque, Rafael, 1981- artist. | Costa, Marcelo (Colorist), colourist. | Brice, Bernardo, letterer.
Title: Hidden society / written by Rafael Scavone ; art, cover, and chapter breaks by Rafael Albuquerque ; colors by Marcelo Costa ; letters by Bernardo Brice.
Description: First edition. | Milwaukie, OR : Dark Horse Books, 2020. | "Hidden Society created by Rafael Scavone and Rafael Albuequerque" | Summary: "Ulloo, the last wizard from the Hidden Society, enlists the aid of a blind girl and her demon, a young magician, and a cursed bounty hunter in order to stop a group of nihilist warlocks ending the world"-- Provided by publisher.
Identifiers: LCCN 2020027398 (print) | LCCN 2020027399 (ebook) | ISBN 9781506717173 (trade paperback) | ISBN 9781506717180 (ebook other)
Subjects: LCSH: Comic books, strips, etc.
Classification: LCC PN6728.H526 S36 2020 (print) | LCC PN6728.H526 (ebook) | DDC 741.5/973--dc23
LC record available at https://lccn.loc.gov/2020027398
LC ebook record available at https://lccn.loc.gov/2020027399

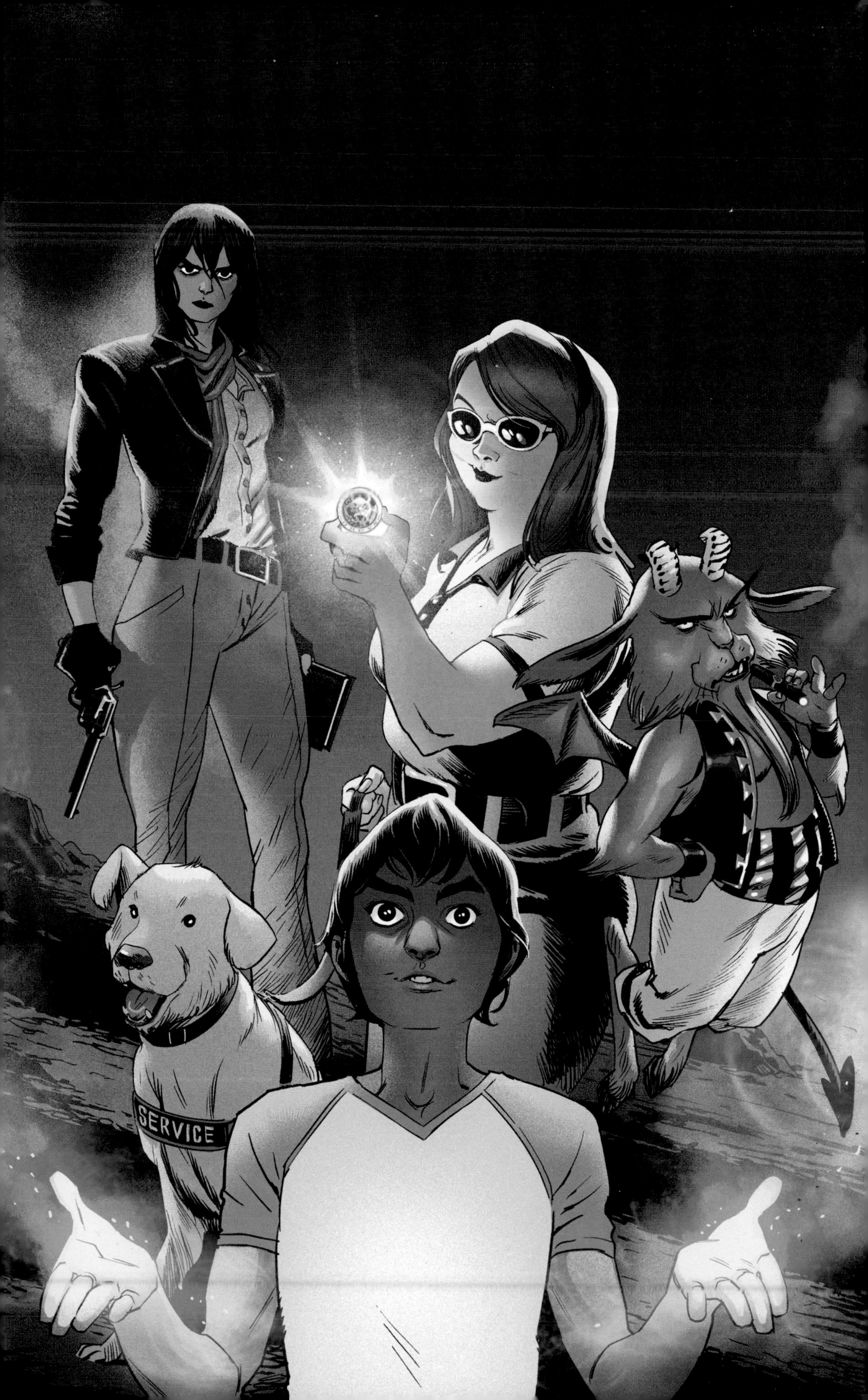
SERVICE

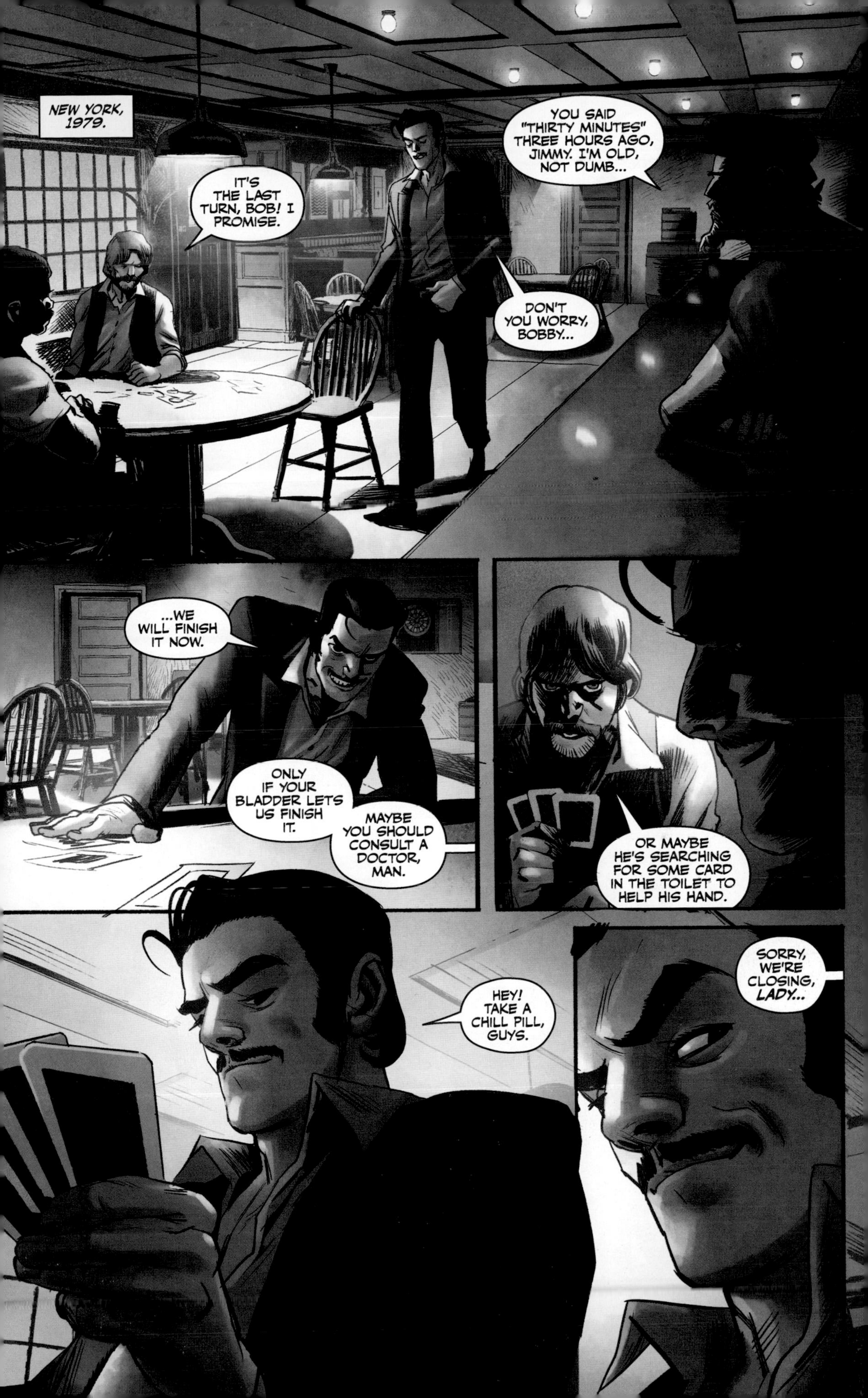
NEW YORK, 1979.
IT'S THE LAST TURN, BOB! I PROMISE.
YOU SAID "THIRTY MINUTES" THREE HOURS AGO, JIMMY. I'M OLD, NOT DUMB...
DON'T YOU WORRY, BOBBY...
...WE WILL FINISH IT NOW.
ONLY IF YOUR BLADDER LETS US FINISH IT.
MAYBE YOU SHOULD CONSULT A DOCTOR, MAN.
OR MAYBE HE'S SEARCHING FOR SOME CARD IN THE TOILET TO HELP HIS HAND.
HEY! TAKE A CHILL PILL, GUYS.
SORRY, WE'RE CLOSING, *LADY*...

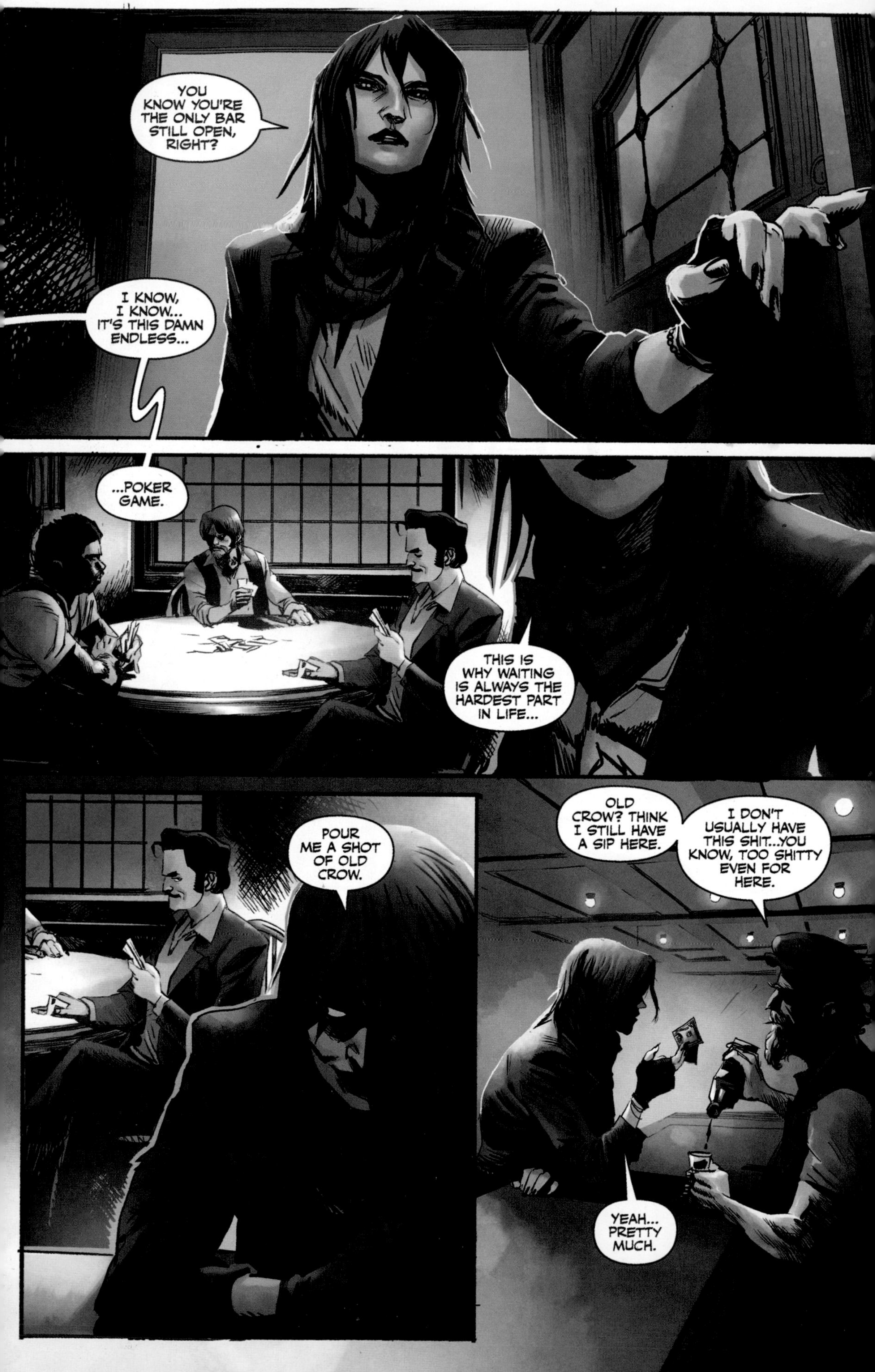
YOU KNOW YOU'RE THE ONLY BAR STILL OPEN, RIGHT?
I KNOW, I KNOW... IT'S THIS DAMN ENDLESS...
...POKER GAME.
THIS IS WHY WAITING IS ALWAYS THE HARDEST PART IN LIFE...
POUR ME A SHOT OF OLD CROW.
OLD CROW? THINK I STILL HAVE A SIP HERE.
I DON'T USUALLY HAVE THIS SHIT...YOU KNOW, TOO SHITTY EVEN FOR HERE.
YEAH... PRETTY MUCH.

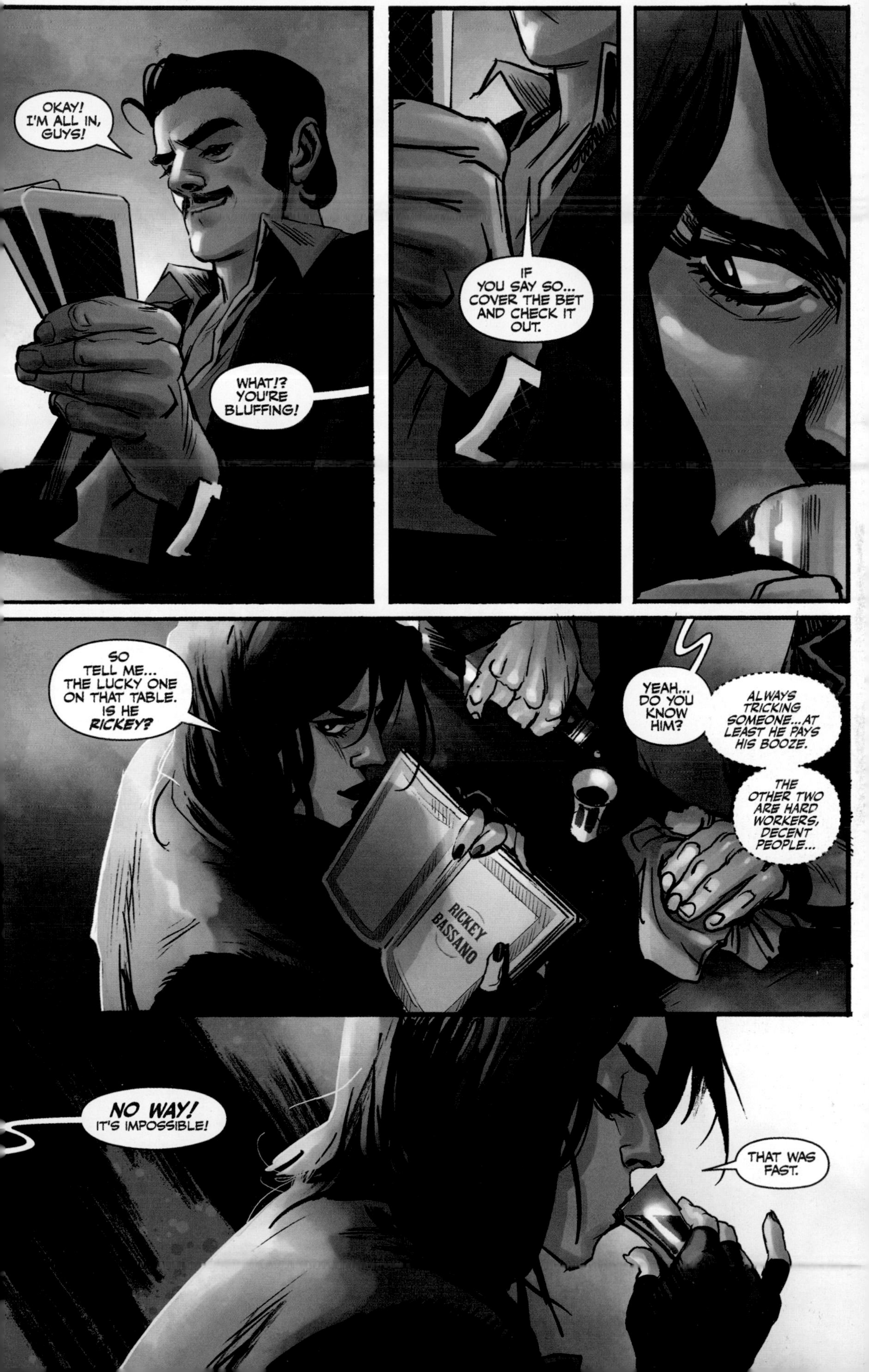
OKAY! I'M ALL IN, GUYS!
WHAT!? YOU'RE BLUFFING!
IF YOU SAY SO... COVER THE BET AND CHECK IT OUT.
SO TELL ME... THE LUCKY ONE ON THAT TABLE. IS HE RICKEY?
YEAH... DO YOU KNOW HIM?
ALWAYS TRICKING SOMEONE...AT LEAST HE PAYS HIS BOOZE.
THE OTHER TWO ARE HARD WORKERS, DECENT PEOPLE...
RICKEY BASSANO
NO WAY! IT'S IMPOSSIBLE!
THAT WAS FAST.

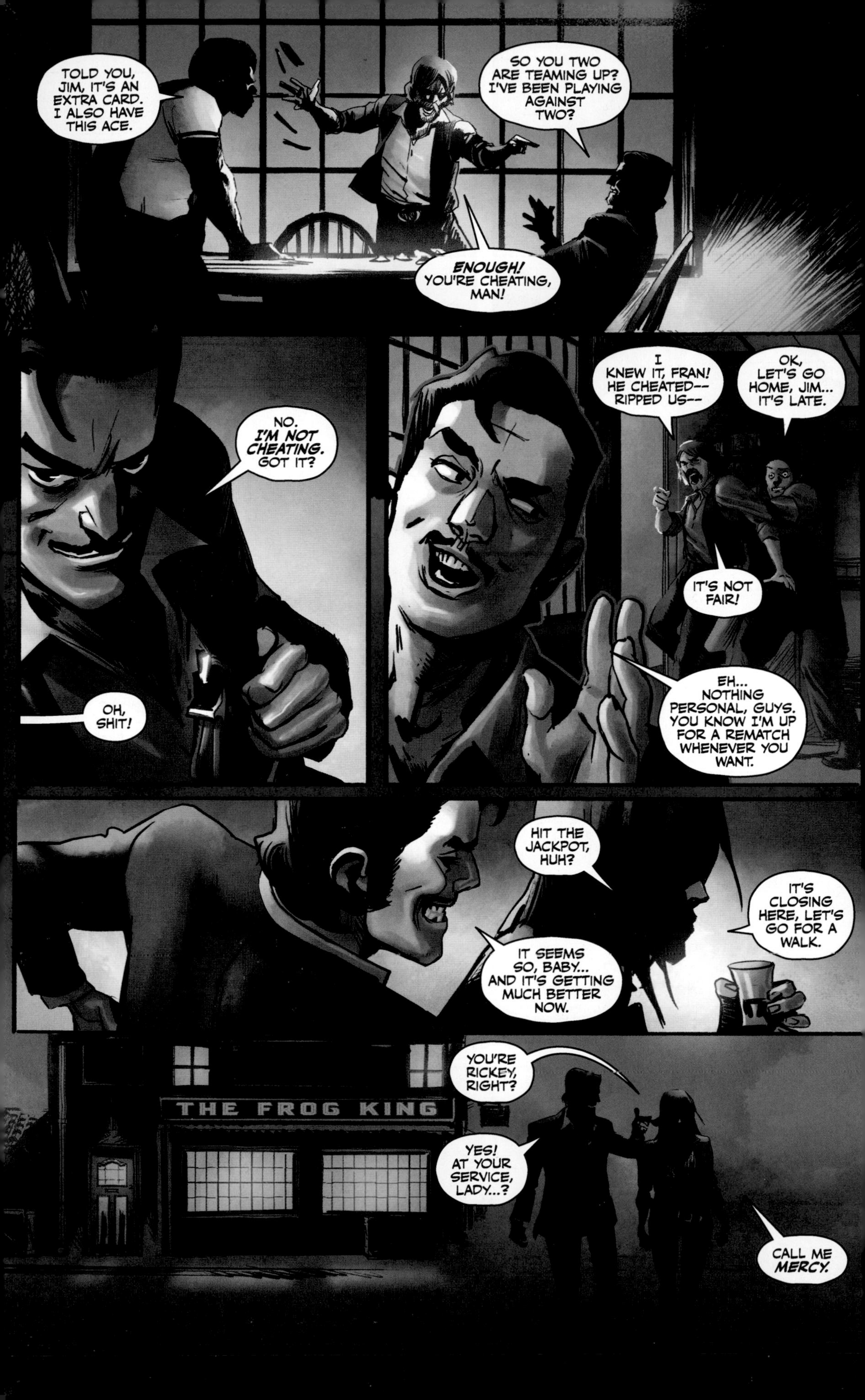
TOLD YOU, JIM, IT'S AN EXTRA CARD. I ALSO HAVE THIS ACE.
SO YOU TWO ARE TEAMING UP? I'VE BEEN PLAYING AGAINST TWO?
ENOUGH! YOU'RE CHEATING, MAN!
NO. *I'M NOT CHEATING.* GOT IT?
OH, SHIT!
I KNEW IT, FRAN! HE CHEATED-- RIPPED US--
OK, LET'S GO HOME, JIM... IT'S LATE.
IT'S NOT FAIR!
EH... NOTHING PERSONAL, GUYS. YOU KNOW I'M UP FOR A REMATCH WHENEVER YOU WANT.
HIT THE JACKPOT, HUH?
IT SEEMS SO, BABY... AND IT'S GETTING MUCH BETTER NOW.
IT'S CLOSING HERE, LET'S GO FOR A WALK.
THE FROG KING
YOU'RE RICKEY, RIGHT?
YES! AT YOUR SERVICE, LADY...?
CALL ME *MERCY.*

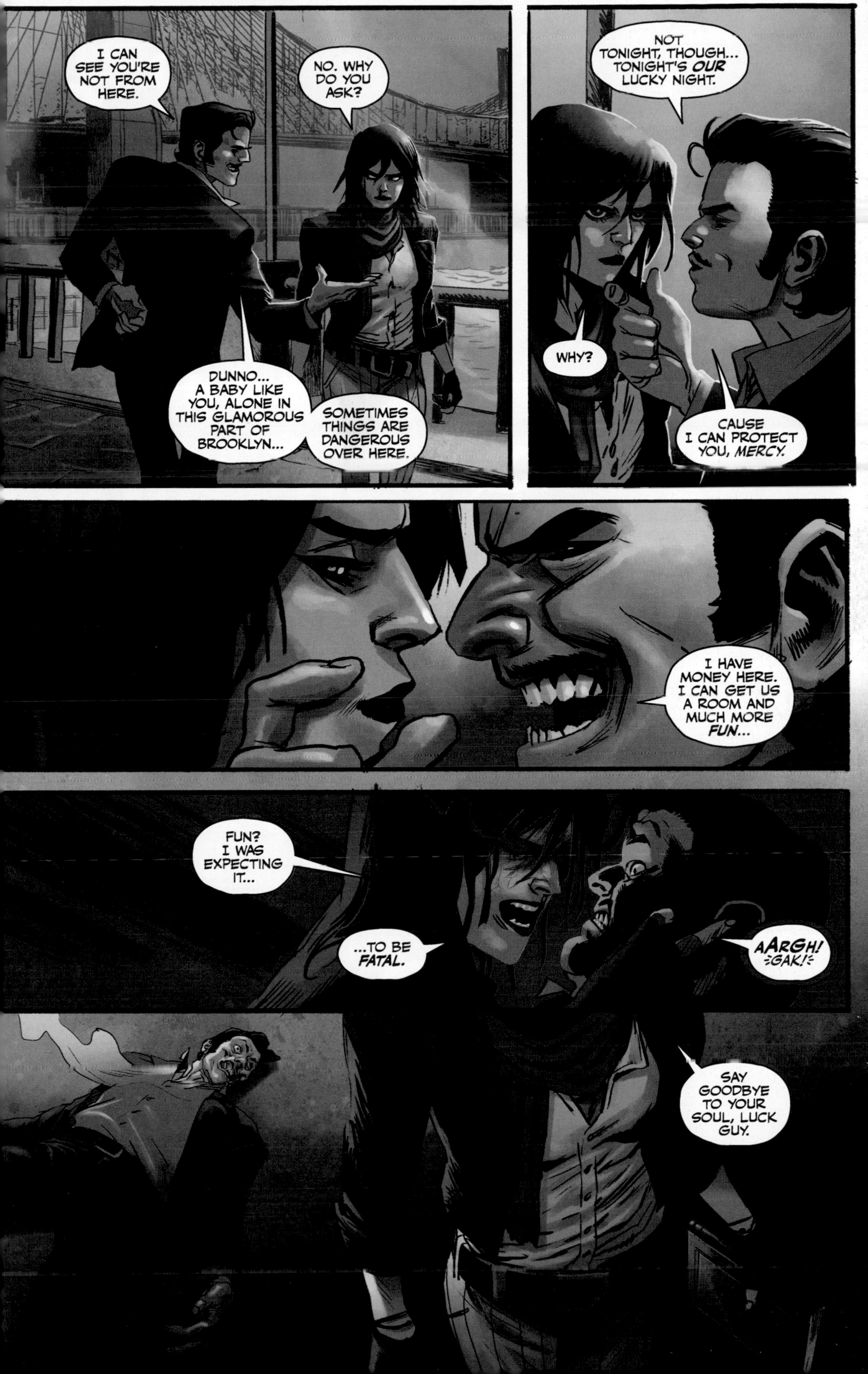
I CAN SEE YOU'RE NOT FROM HERE.
NO. WHY DO YOU ASK?
DUNNO... A BABY LIKE YOU, ALONE IN THIS GLAMOROUS PART OF BROOKLYN...
SOMETIMES THINGS ARE DANGEROUS OVER HERE.
NOT TONIGHT, THOUGH... TONIGHT'S *OUR* LUCKY NIGHT.
WHY?
CAUSE I CAN PROTECT YOU, *MERCY.*
I HAVE MONEY HERE. I CAN GET US A ROOM AND MUCH MORE *FUN*...
FUN? I WAS EXPECTING IT...
...TO BE *FATAL.*
AARGH! GAK!
SAY GOODBYE TO YOUR SOUL, LUCK GUY.

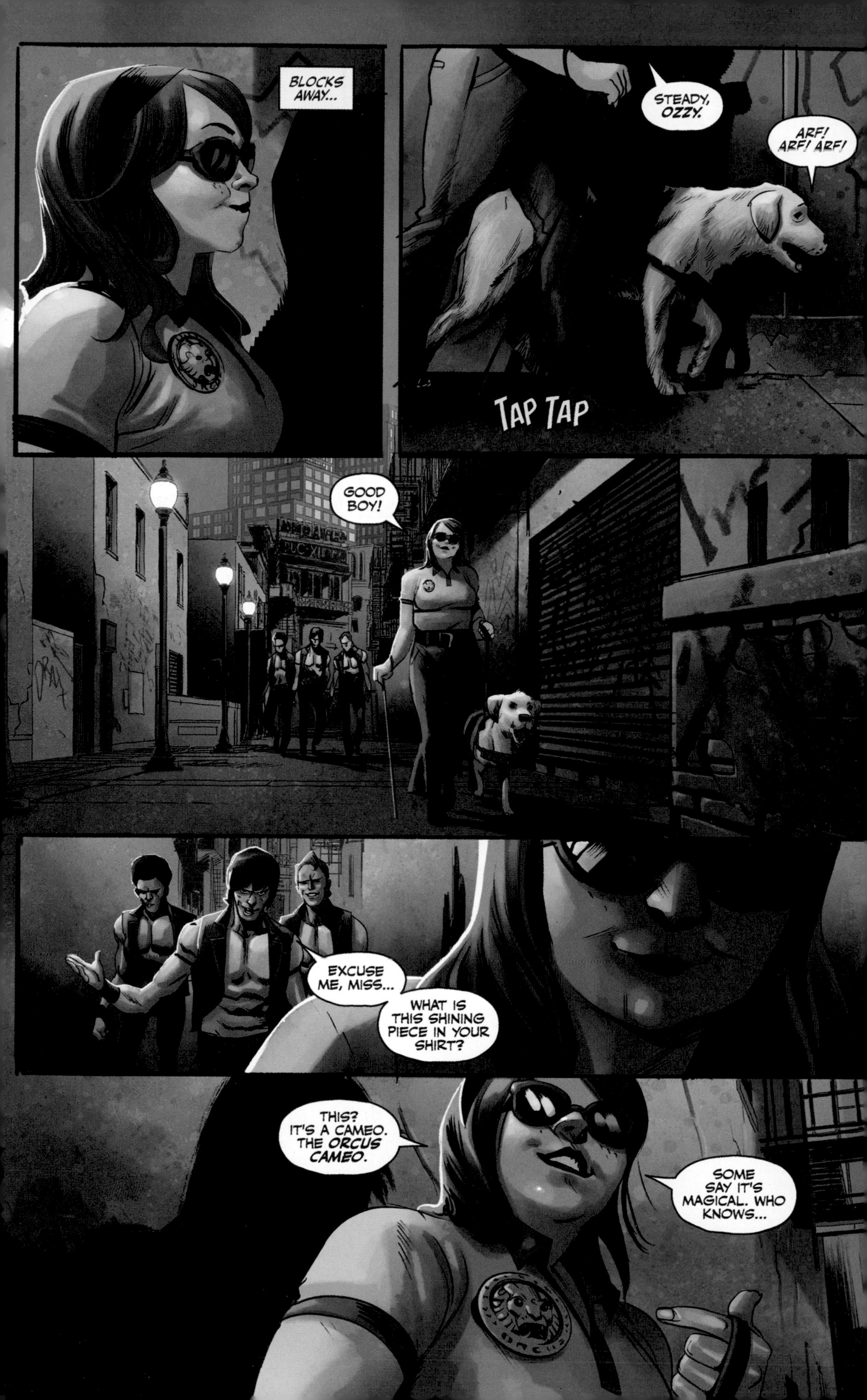
BLOCKS AWAY...
STEADY, OZZY.
ARF! ARF! ARF!
TAP TAP
GOOD BOY!
EXCUSE ME, MISS...
WHAT IS THIS SHINING PIECE IN YOUR SHIRT?
THIS? IT'S A CAMEO. THE ORCUS CAMEO.
SOME SAY IT'S MAGICAL. WHO KNOWS...

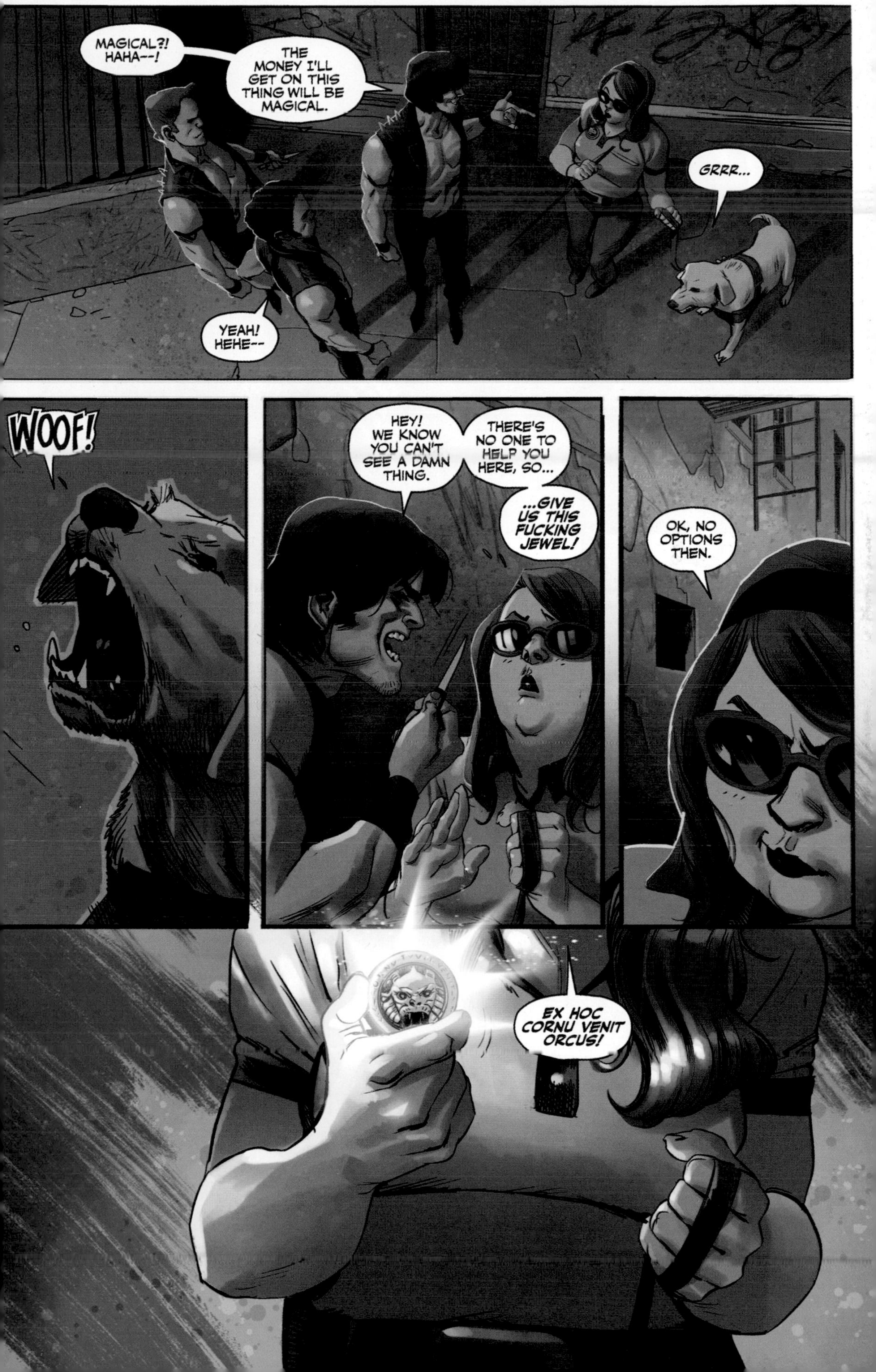
MAGICAL?! HAHA--!
THE MONEY I'LL GET ON THIS THING WILL BE MAGICAL.
GRRR...
YEAH! HEHE--
WOOF!
HEY! WE KNOW YOU CAN'T SEE A DAMN THING.
THERE'S NO ONE TO HELP YOU HERE, SO...
...GIVE US THIS FUCKING JEWEL!
OK, NO OPTIONS THEN.
EX HOC CORNU VENIT ORCUS!

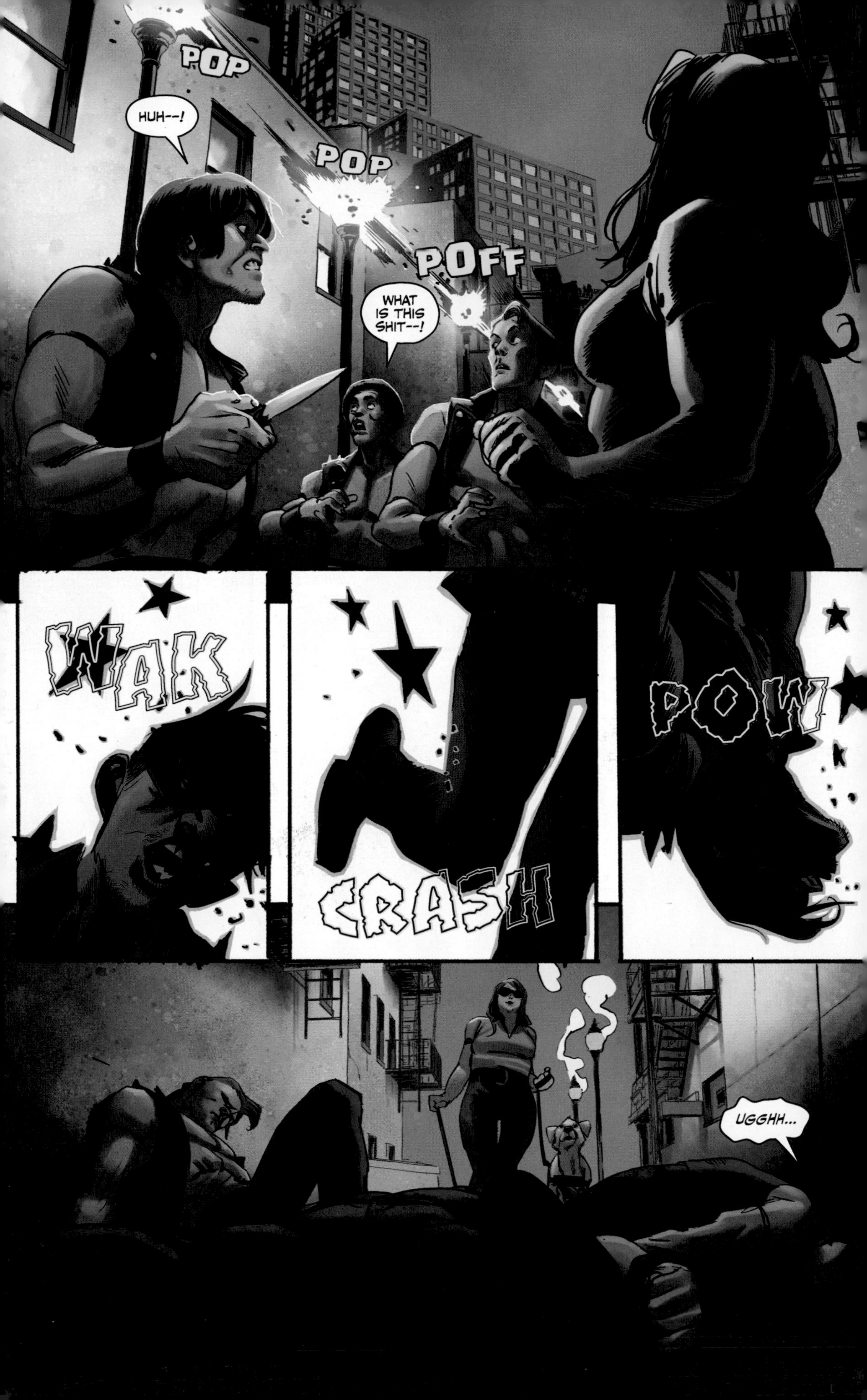
POP
HUH--!
POP
POFF
WHAT IS THIS SHIT--!
WAK
CRASH
POW
UGGHH...

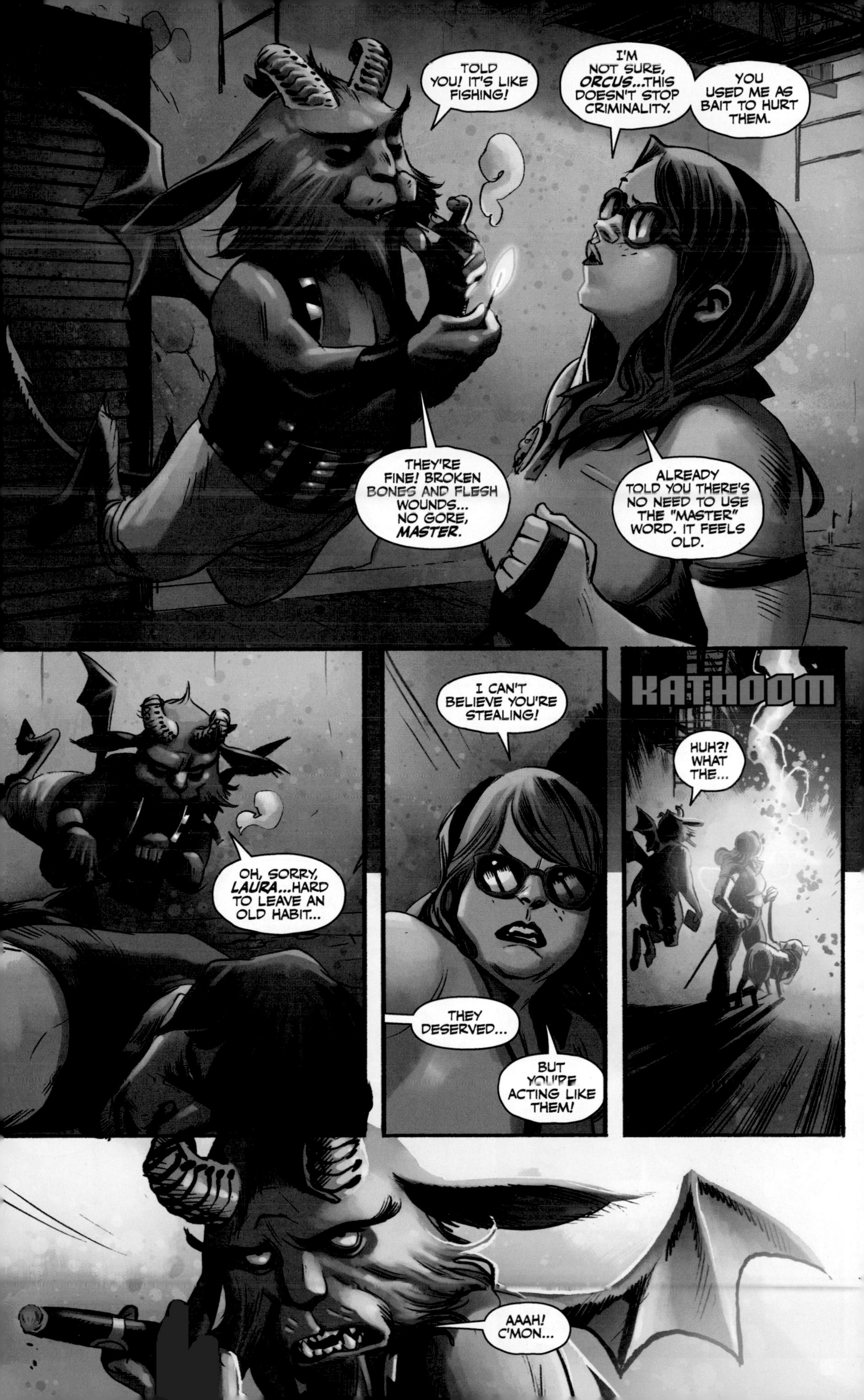

TOLD YOU! IT'S LIKE FISHING!
I'M NOT SURE, ORCUS...THIS DOESN'T STOP CRIMINALITY.
YOU USED ME AS BAIT TO HURT THEM.
THEY'RE FINE! BROKEN BONES AND FLESH WOUNDS... NO GORE, MASTER.
ALREADY TOLD YOU THERE'S NO NEED TO USE THE "MASTER" WORD. IT FEELS OLD.
OH, SORRY, LAURA...HARD TO LEAVE AN OLD HABIT...
I CAN'T BELIEVE YOU'RE STEALING!
THEY DESERVED...
BUT YOU'RE ACTING LIKE THEM!
KATHOOM
HUH?! WHAT THE...
AAAH! C'MON...

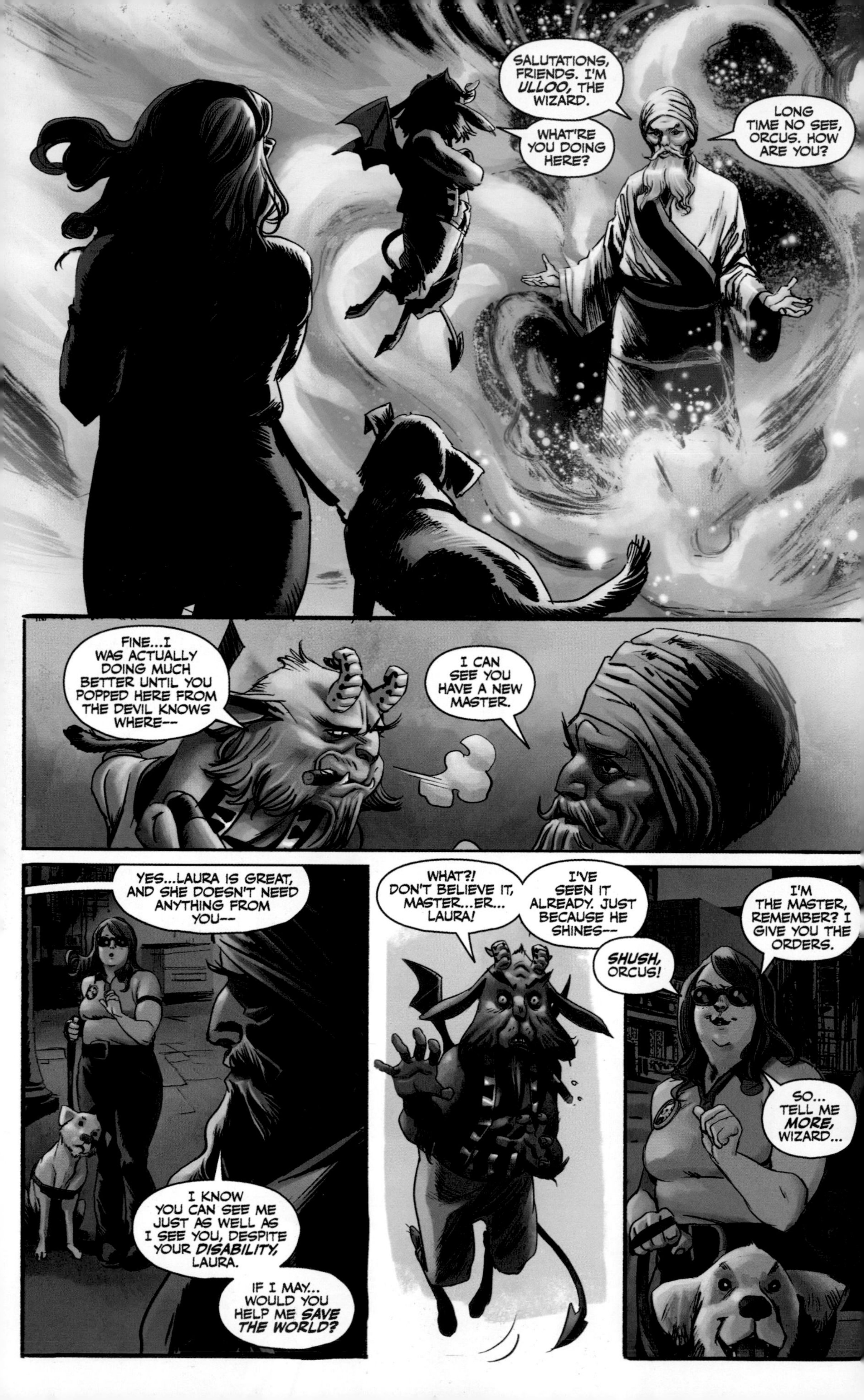
SALUTATIONS, FRIENDS. I'M *ULLOO,* THE WIZARD.
WHAT'RE YOU DOING HERE?
LONG TIME NO SEE, ORCUS. HOW ARE YOU?
FINE...I WAS ACTUALLY DOING MUCH BETTER UNTIL YOU POPPED HERE FROM THE DEVIL KNOWS WHERE--
I CAN SEE YOU HAVE A NEW MASTER.
YES...LAURA IS GREAT, AND SHE DOESN'T NEED ANYTHING FROM YOU--
I KNOW YOU CAN SEE ME JUST AS WELL AS I SEE YOU, DESPITE YOUR *DISABILITY,* LAURA.
IF I MAY... WOULD YOU HELP ME *SAVE THE WORLD?*
WHAT?! DON'T BELIEVE IT, MASTER...ER... LAURA!
I'VE SEEN IT ALREADY. JUST BECAUSE HE SHINES--
SHUSH, ORCUS!
I'M THE MASTER, REMEMBER? I GIVE YOU THE ORDERS.
SO... TELL ME *MORE,* WIZARD...

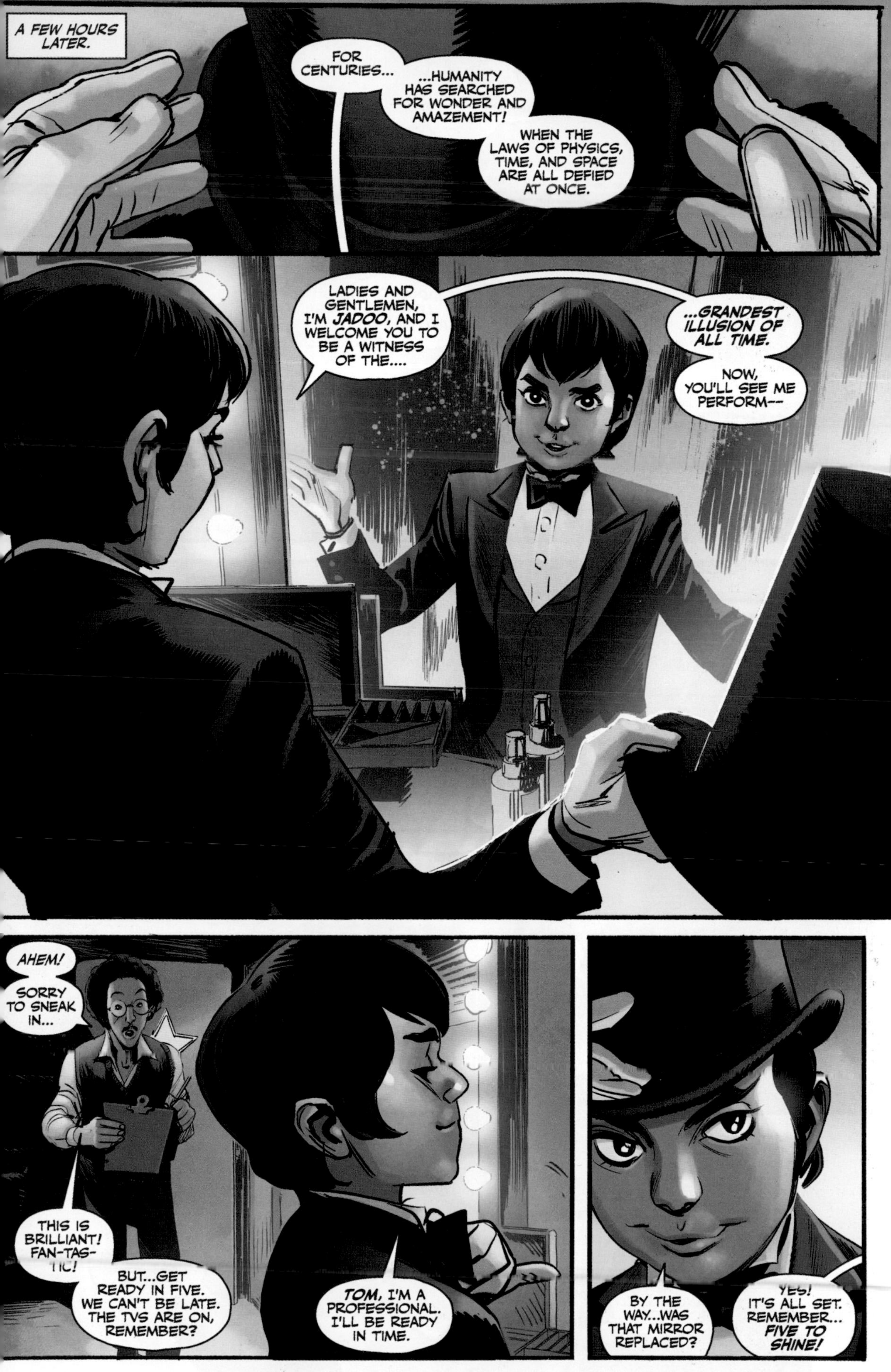
A FEW HOURS LATER.
FOR CENTURIES...
...HUMANITY HAS SEARCHED FOR WONDER AND AMAZEMENT!
WHEN THE LAWS OF PHYSICS, TIME, AND SPACE ARE ALL DEFIED AT ONCE.
LADIES AND GENTLEMEN, I'M JADOO, AND I WELCOME YOU TO BE A WITNESS OF THE....
...GRANDEST ILLUSION OF ALL TIME.
NOW, YOU'LL SEE ME PERFORM--
AHEM!
SORRY TO SNEAK IN...
THIS IS BRILLIANT! FAN-TAS-TIC!
BUT...GET READY IN FIVE. WE CAN'T BE LATE. THE TVS ARE ON, REMEMBER?
TOM, I'M A PROFESSIONAL. I'LL BE READY IN TIME.
BY THE WAY...WAS THAT MIRROR REPLACED?
YES! IT'S ALL SET. REMEMBER... FIVE TO SHINE!

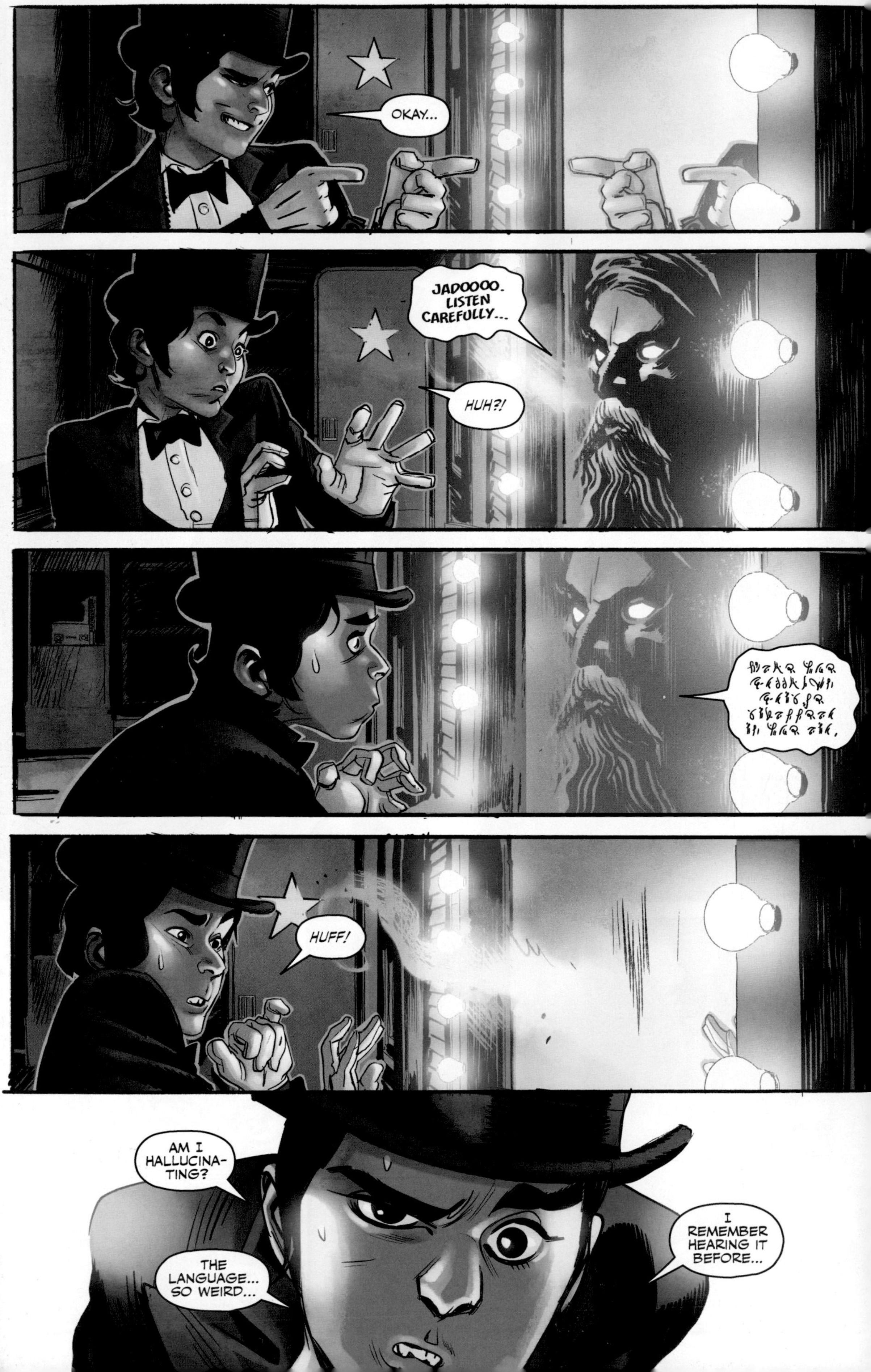

OKAY...
JADOOOO. LISTEN CAREFULLY...
HUH?!
HUFF!
AM I HALLUCINA-TING?
THE LANGUAGE... SO WEIRD...
I REMEMBER HEARING IT BEFORE...

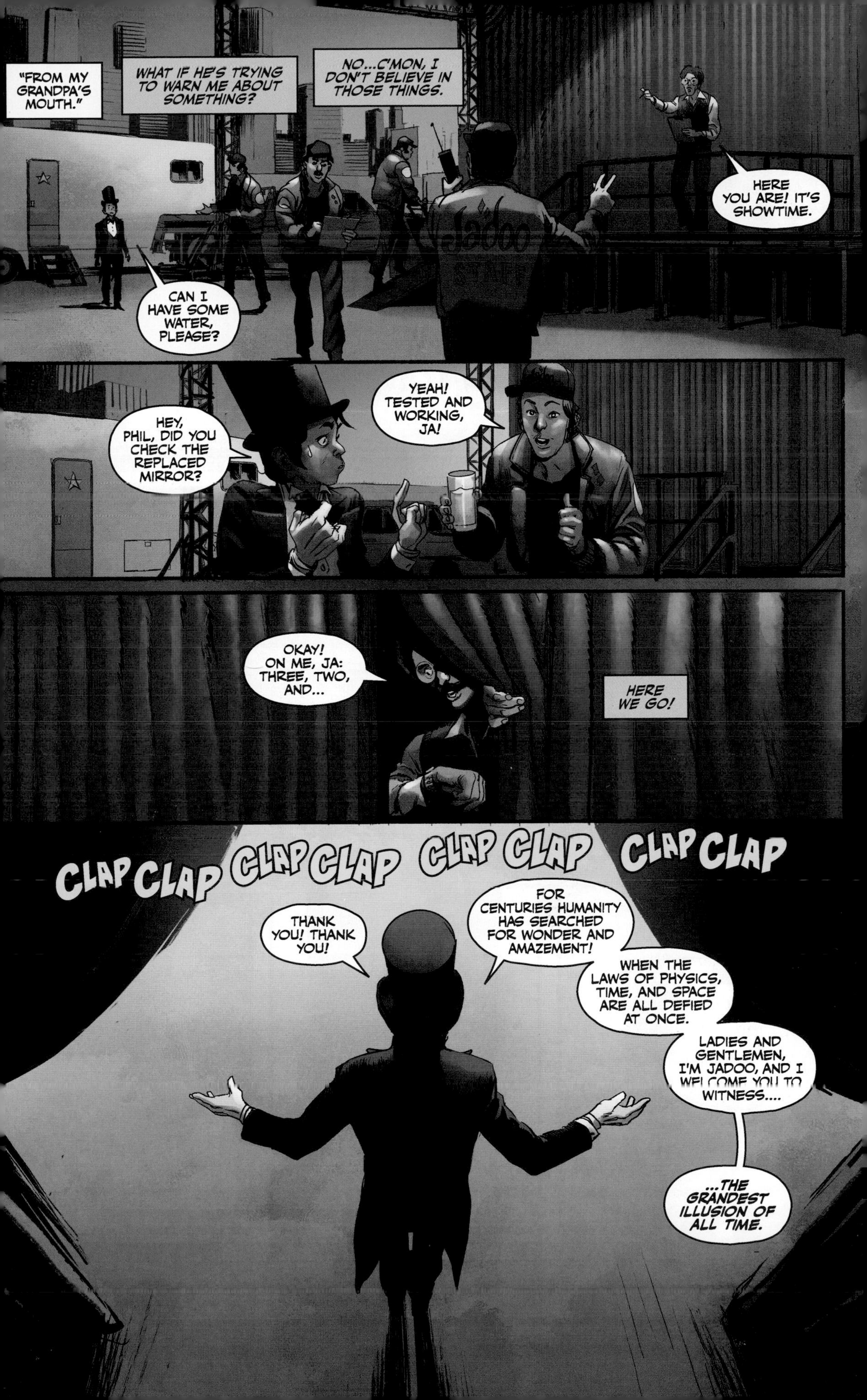

"FROM MY GRANDPA'S MOUTH."
WHAT IF HE'S TRYING TO WARN ME ABOUT SOMETHING?
NO...C'MON, I DON'T BELIEVE IN THOSE THINGS.
HERE YOU ARE! IT'S SHOWTIME.
CAN I HAVE SOME WATER, PLEASE?
HEY, PHIL, DID YOU CHECK THE REPLACED MIRROR?
YEAH! TESTED AND WORKING, JA!
OKAY! ON ME, JA: THREE, TWO, AND...
HERE WE GO!
CLAP CLAP CLAP CLAP CLAP CLAP CLAP CLAP
THANK YOU! THANK YOU!
FOR CENTURIES HUMANITY HAS SEARCHED FOR WONDER AND AMAZEMENT!
WHEN THE LAWS OF PHYSICS, TIME, AND SPACE ARE ALL DEFIED AT ONCE.
LADIES AND GENTLEMEN, I'M JADOO, AND I WELCOME YOU TO WITNESS....
...THE GRANDEST ILLUSION OF ALL TIME.

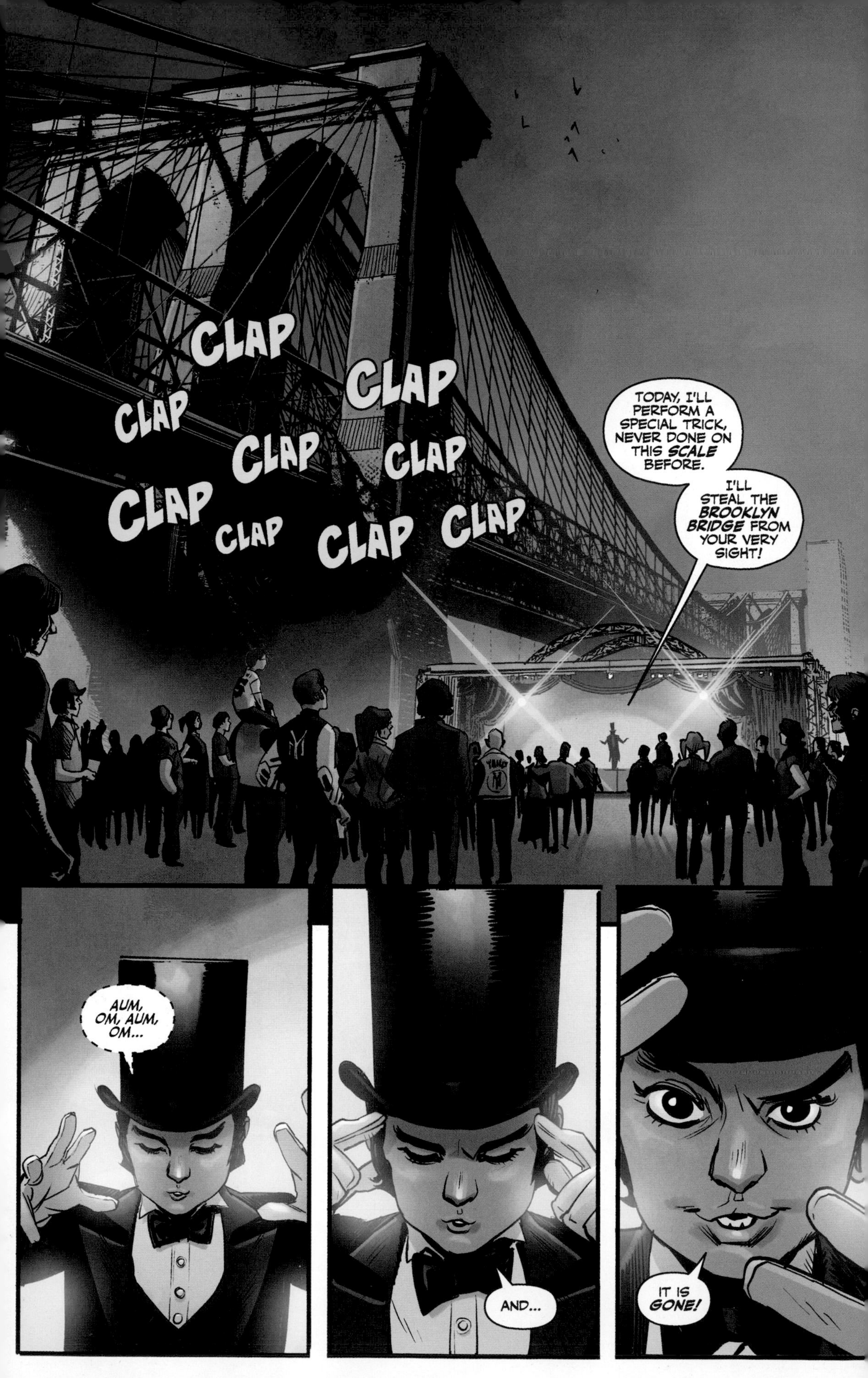
CLAP CLAP CLAP CLAP CLAP CLAP CLAP CLAP CLAP
TODAY, I'LL PERFORM A SPECIAL TRICK, NEVER DONE ON THIS SCALE BEFORE.
I'LL STEAL THE BROOKLYN BRIDGE FROM YOUR VERY SIGHT!
AUM, OM, AUM, OM...
AND...
IT IS GONE!

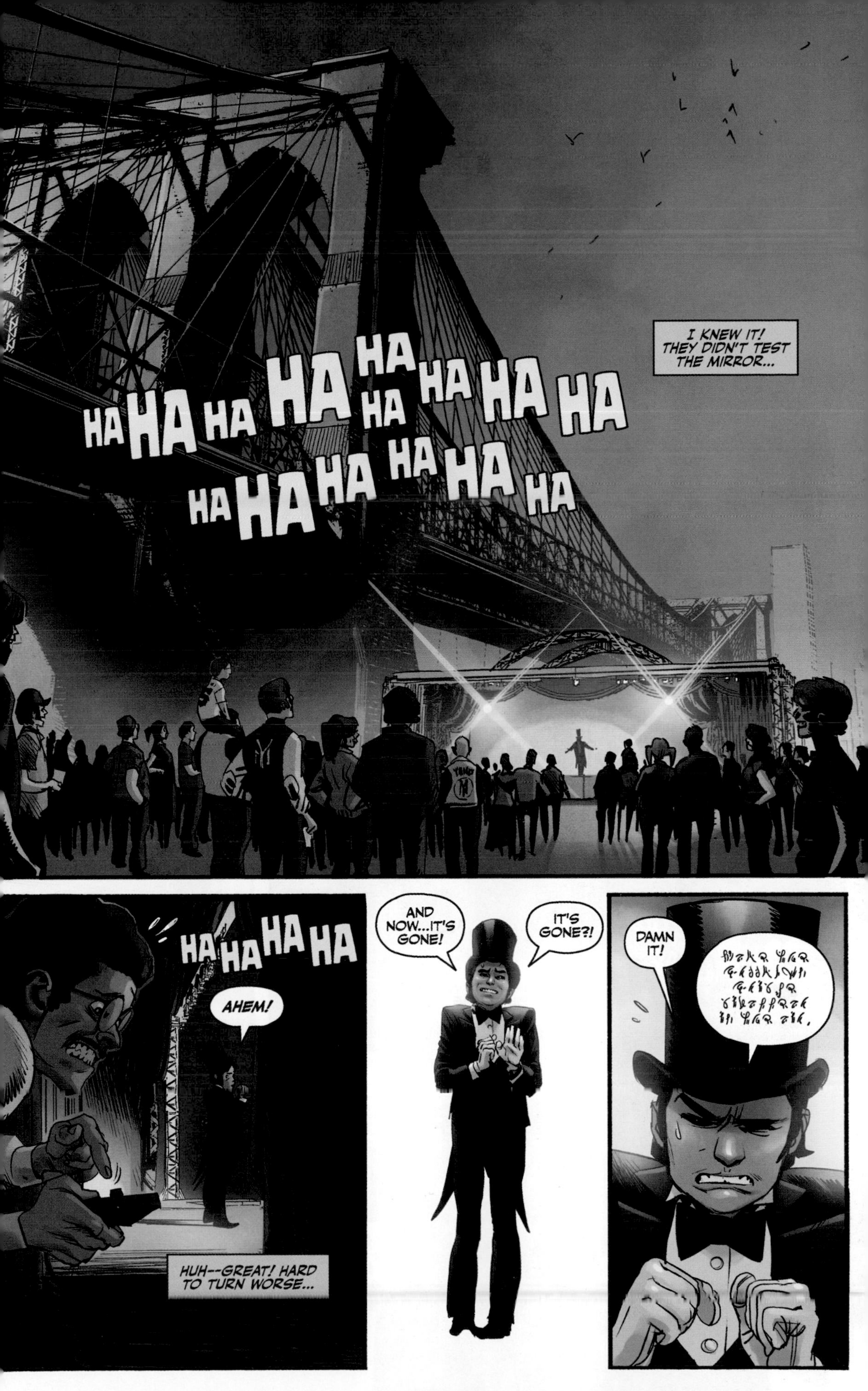

I KNEW IT! THEY DIDN'T TEST THE MIRROR...
HA HA HA HA HA HA HA HA HA
HA HA HA HA HA HA
HA HA HA HA HA
AHEM!
HUH--GREAT! HARD TO TURN WORSE...
AND NOW...IT'S GONE!
IT'S GONE?!
DAMN IT!

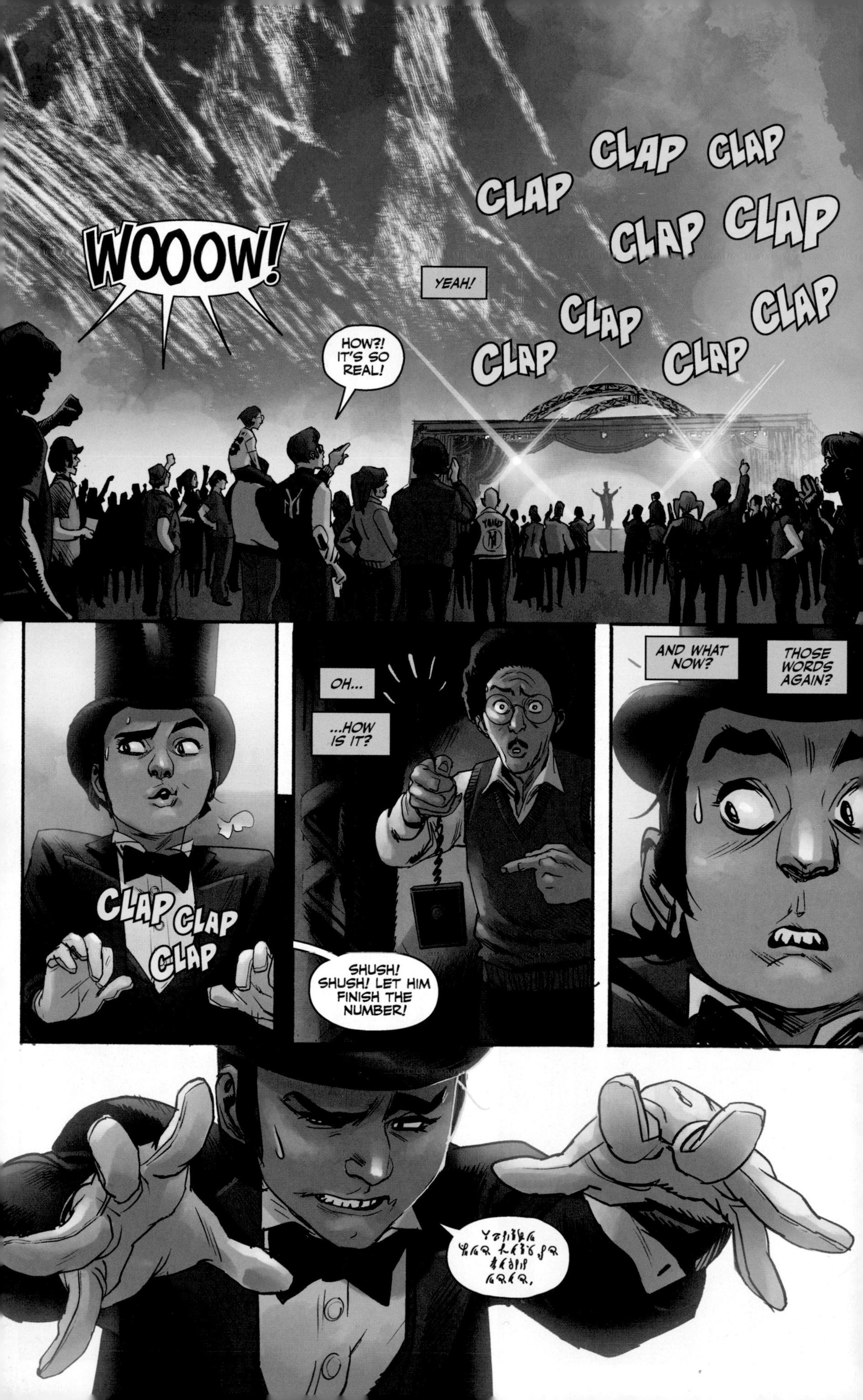
WOOOW!
HOW?! IT'S SO REAL!
YEAH!
CLAP CLAP CLAP
CLAP CLAP
CLAP CLAP CLAP CLAP CLAP
CLAP CLAP CLAP
OH...
...HOW IS IT?
SHUSH! SHUSH! LET HIM FINISH THE NUMBER!
AND WHAT NOW?
THOSE WORDS AGAIN?

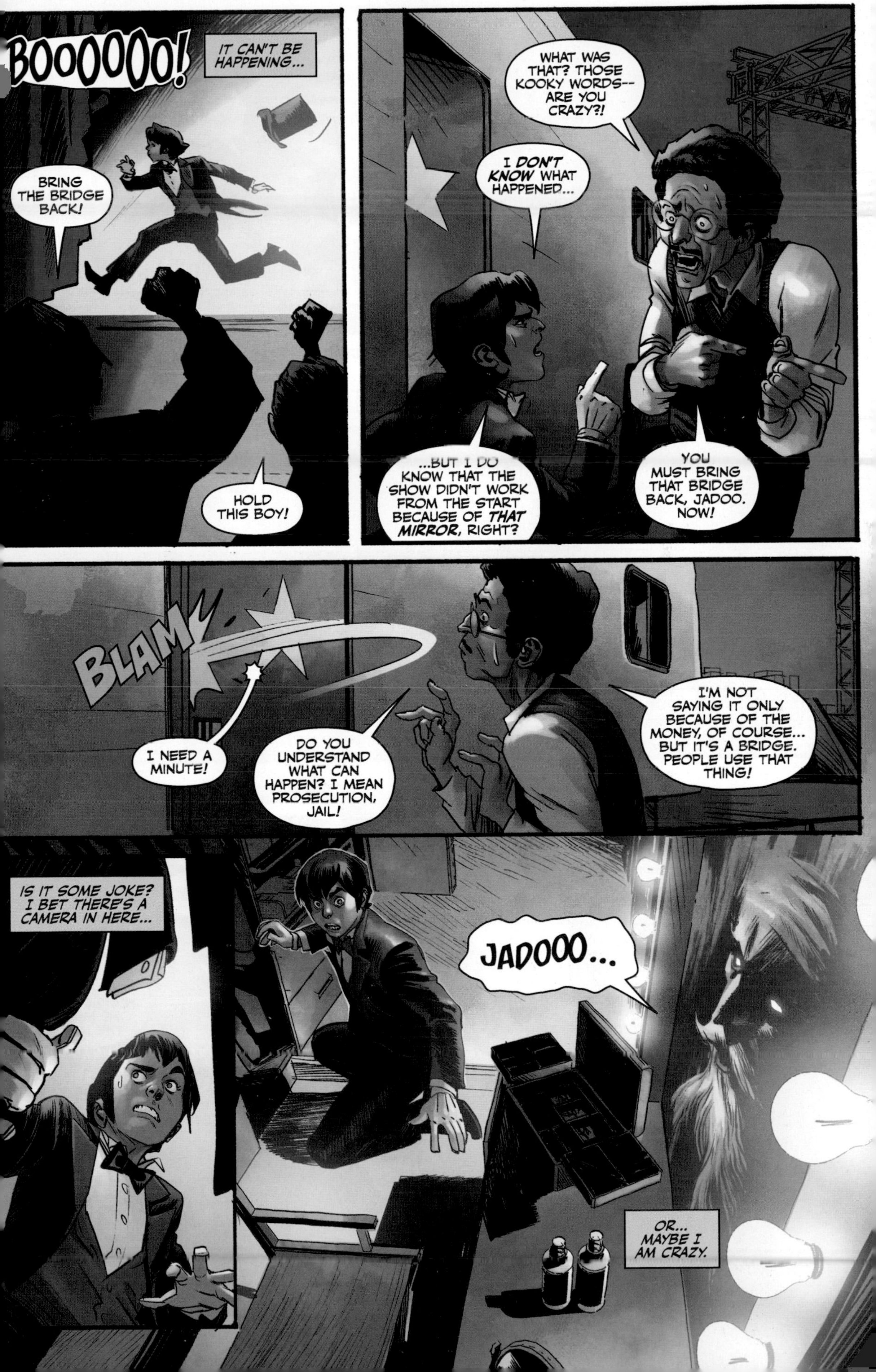
BOOOOOO!
IT CAN'T BE HAPPENING...
BRING THE BRIDGE BACK!
HOLD THIS BOY!
WHAT WAS THAT? THOSE KOOKY WORDS-- ARE YOU CRAZY?!
I DON'T KNOW WHAT HAPPENED...
...BUT I DO KNOW THAT THE SHOW DIDN'T WORK FROM THE START BECAUSE OF THAT MIRROR, RIGHT?
YOU MUST BRING THAT BRIDGE BACK, JADOO. NOW!
BLAM
I NEED A MINUTE!
DO YOU UNDERSTAND WHAT CAN HAPPEN? I MEAN PROSECUTION, JAIL!
I'M NOT SAYING IT ONLY BECAUSE OF THE MONEY, OF COURSE... BUT IT'S A BRIDGE. PEOPLE USE THAT THING!
IS IT SOME JOKE? I BET THERE'S A CAMERA IN HERE...
JADOOO...
OR... MAYBE I AM CRAZY.

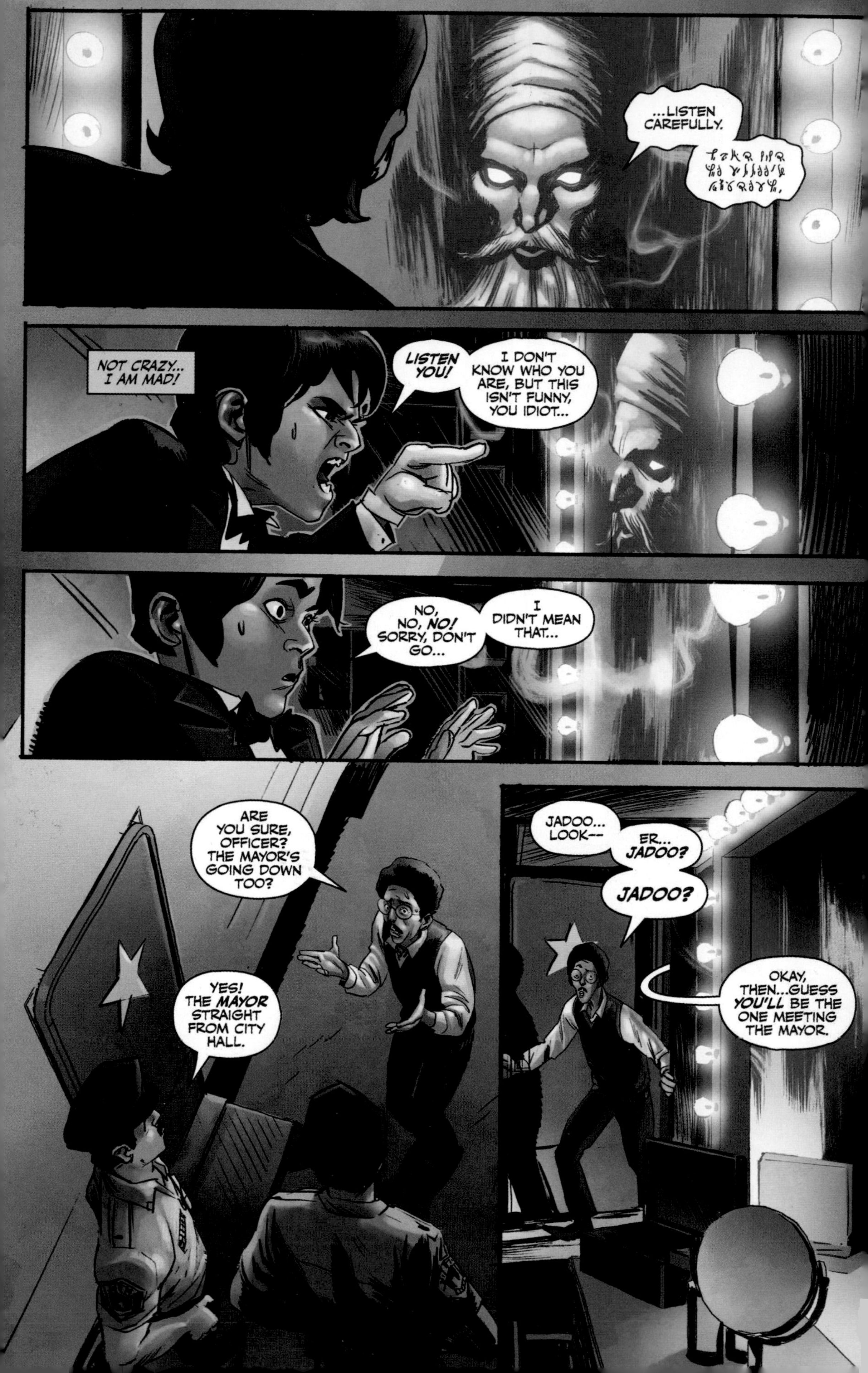

...LISTEN CAREFULLY.
NOT CRAZY... I AM MAD!
LISTEN YOU!
I DON'T KNOW WHO YOU ARE, BUT THIS ISN'T FUNNY, YOU IDIOT...
NO, NO, NO! SORRY, DON'T GO...
I DIDN'T MEAN THAT...
ARE YOU SURE, OFFICER? THE MAYOR'S GOING DOWN TOO?
YES! THE MAYOR STRAIGHT FROM CITY HALL.
JADOO... LOOK--
ER... JADOO?
JADOO?
OKAY, THEN...GUESS YOU'LL BE THE ONE MEETING THE MAYOR.

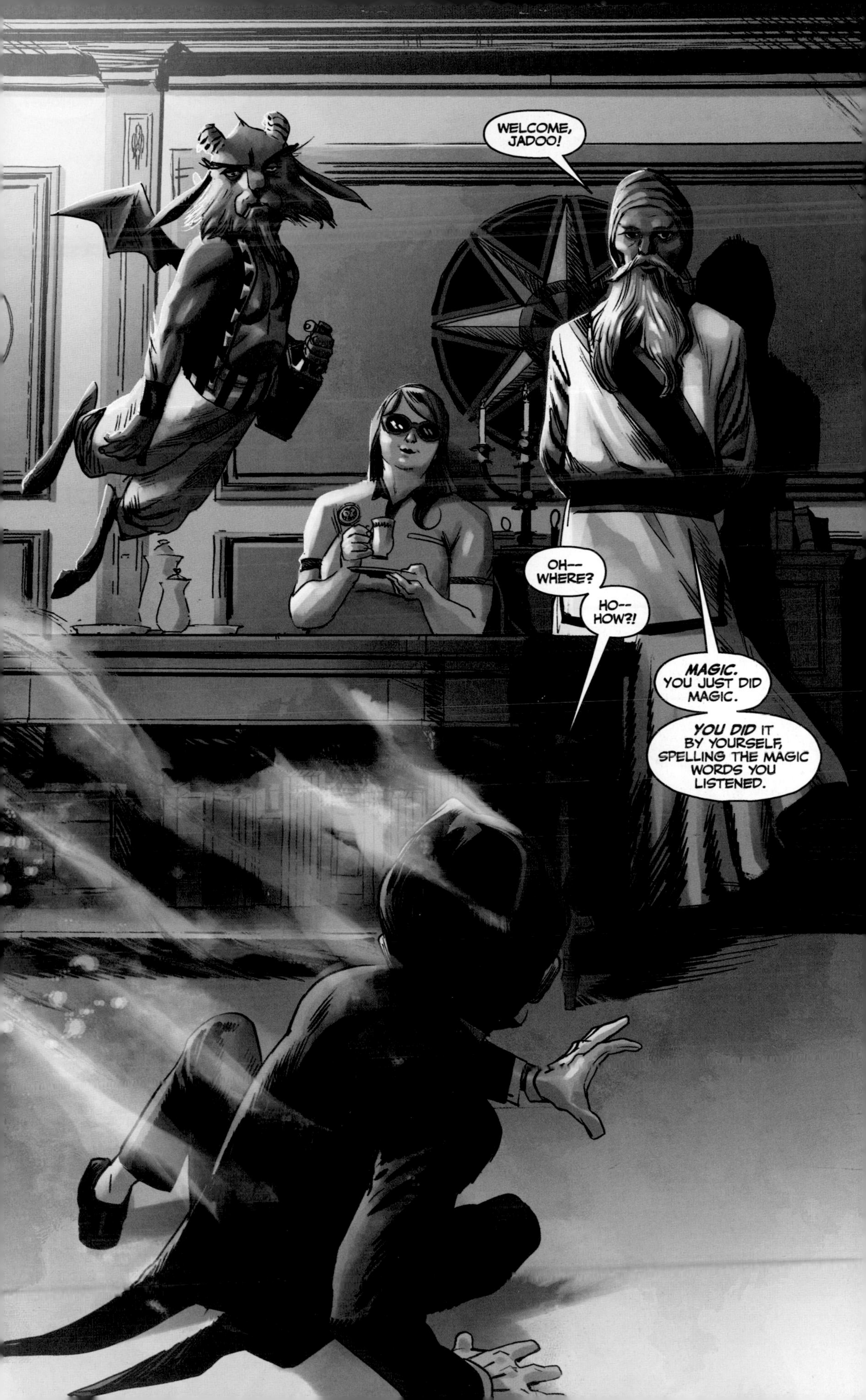
WELCOME, JADOO!
OH-- WHERE?
HO-- HOW?!
MAGIC. YOU JUST DID MAGIC.
YOU DID IT BY YOURSELF, SPELLING THE MAGIC WORDS YOU LISTENED.

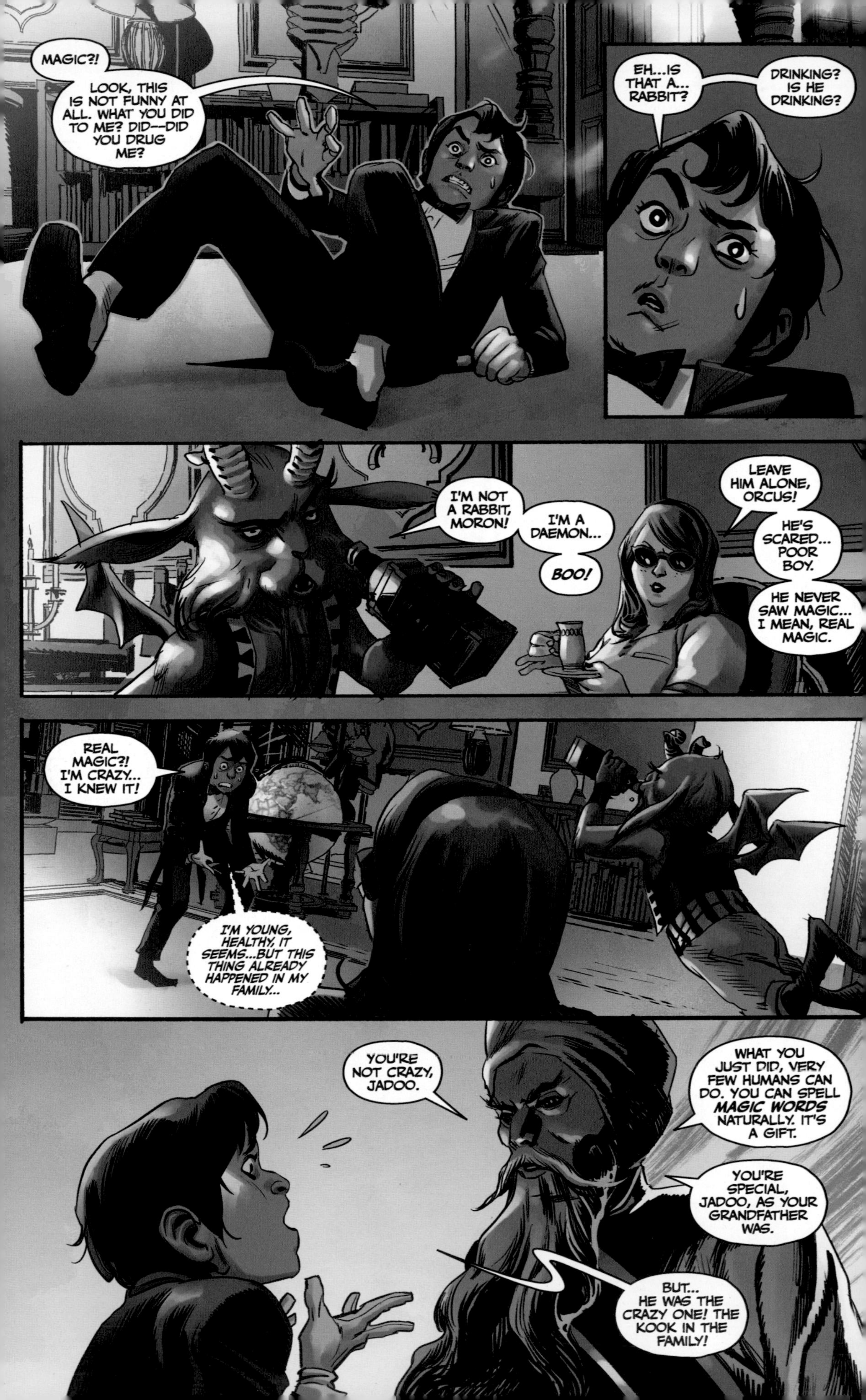
MAGIC?!
LOOK, THIS IS NOT FUNNY AT ALL. WHAT YOU DID TO ME? DID--DID YOU DRUG ME?
EH...IS THAT A... RABBIT?
DRINKING? IS HE DRINKING?
I'M NOT A RABBIT, MORON!
I'M A DAEMON...
BOO!
LEAVE HIM ALONE, ORCUS!
HE'S SCARED... POOR BOY.
HE NEVER SAW MAGIC... I MEAN, REAL MAGIC.
REAL MAGIC?! I'M CRAZY... I KNEW IT!
I'M YOUNG, HEALTHY, IT SEEMS...BUT THIS THING ALREADY HAPPENED IN MY FAMILY...
YOU'RE NOT CRAZY, JADOO.
WHAT YOU JUST DID, VERY FEW HUMANS CAN DO. YOU CAN SPELL MAGIC WORDS NATURALLY. IT'S A GIFT.
YOU'RE SPECIAL, JADOO, AS YOUR GRANDFATHER WAS.
BUT... HE WAS THE CRAZY ONE! THE KOOK IN THE FAMILY!

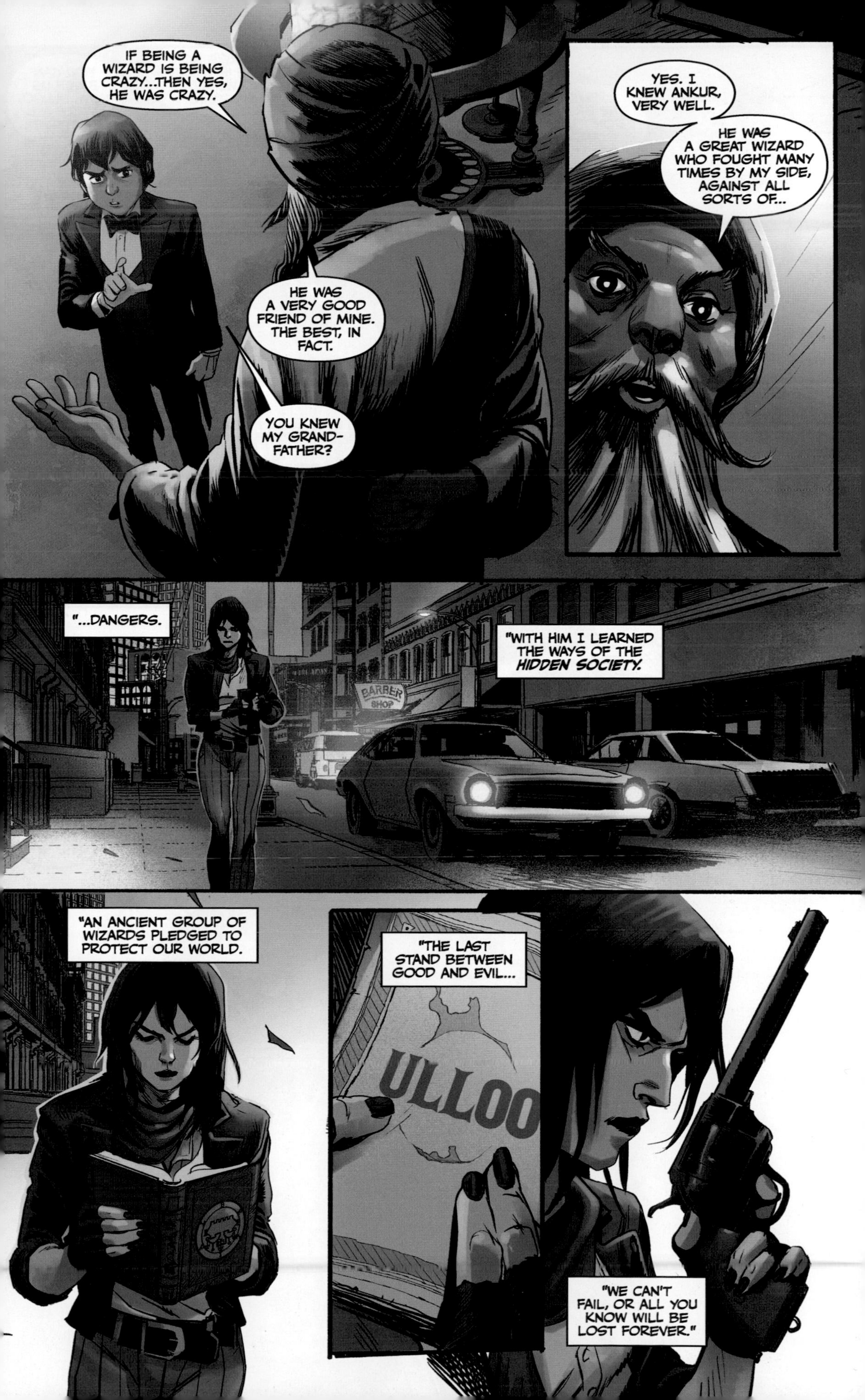

IF BEING A WIZARD IS BEING CRAZY...THEN YES, HE WAS CRAZY.
HE WAS A VERY GOOD FRIEND OF MINE. THE BEST, IN FACT.
YOU KNEW MY GRAND-FATHER?
YES. I KNEW ANKUR, VERY WELL.
HE WAS A GREAT WIZARD WHO FOUGHT MANY TIMES BY MY SIDE, AGAINST ALL SORTS OF...
"...DANGERS.
"WITH HIM I LEARNED THE WAYS OF THE *HIDDEN SOCIETY.*
BARBER SHOP
"AN ANCIENT GROUP OF WIZARDS PLEDGED TO PROTECT OUR WORLD.
"THE LAST STAND BETWEEN GOOD AND EVIL...
ULLOO
"WE CAN'T FAIL, OR ALL YOU KNOW WILL BE LOST FOREVER."

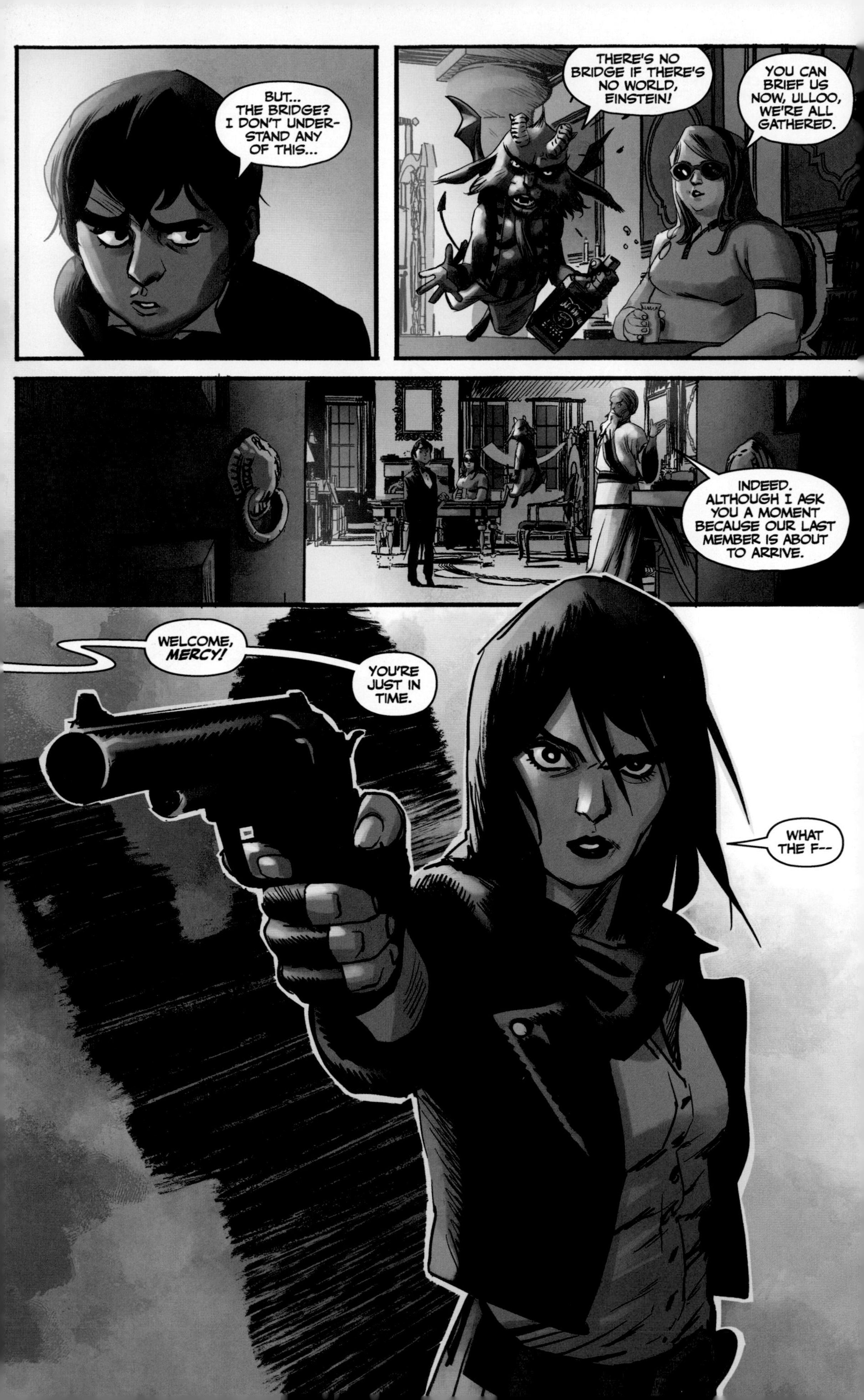
BUT... THE BRIDGE? I DON'T UNDER-STAND ANY OF THIS...
THERE'S NO BRIDGE IF THERE'S NO WORLD, EINSTEIN!
YOU CAN BRIEF US NOW, ULLOO, WE'RE ALL GATHERED.
INDEED. ALTHOUGH I ASK YOU A MOMENT BECAUSE OUR LAST MEMBER IS ABOUT TO ARRIVE.
WELCOME, *MERCY!*
YOU'RE JUST IN TIME.
WHAT THE F--

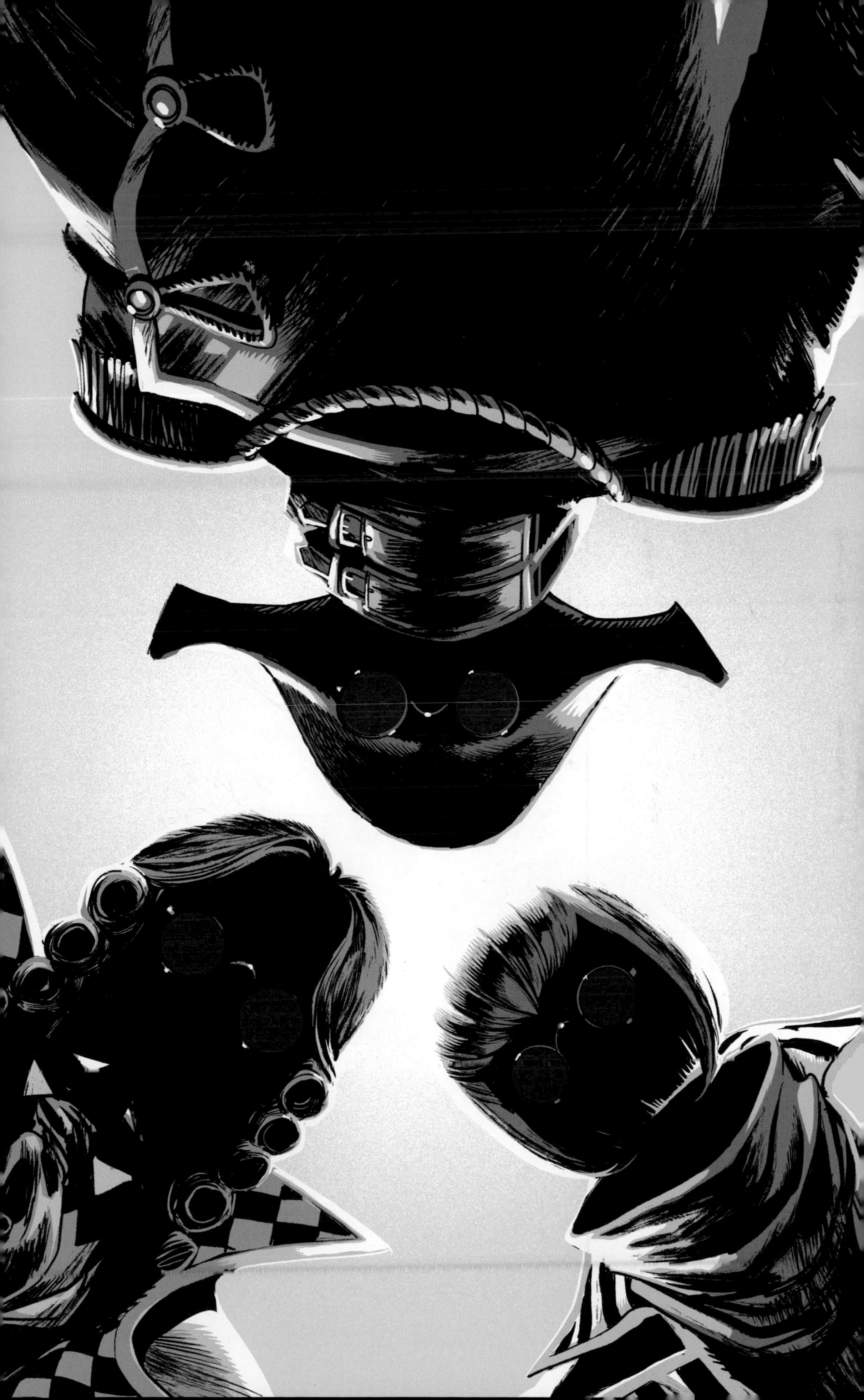

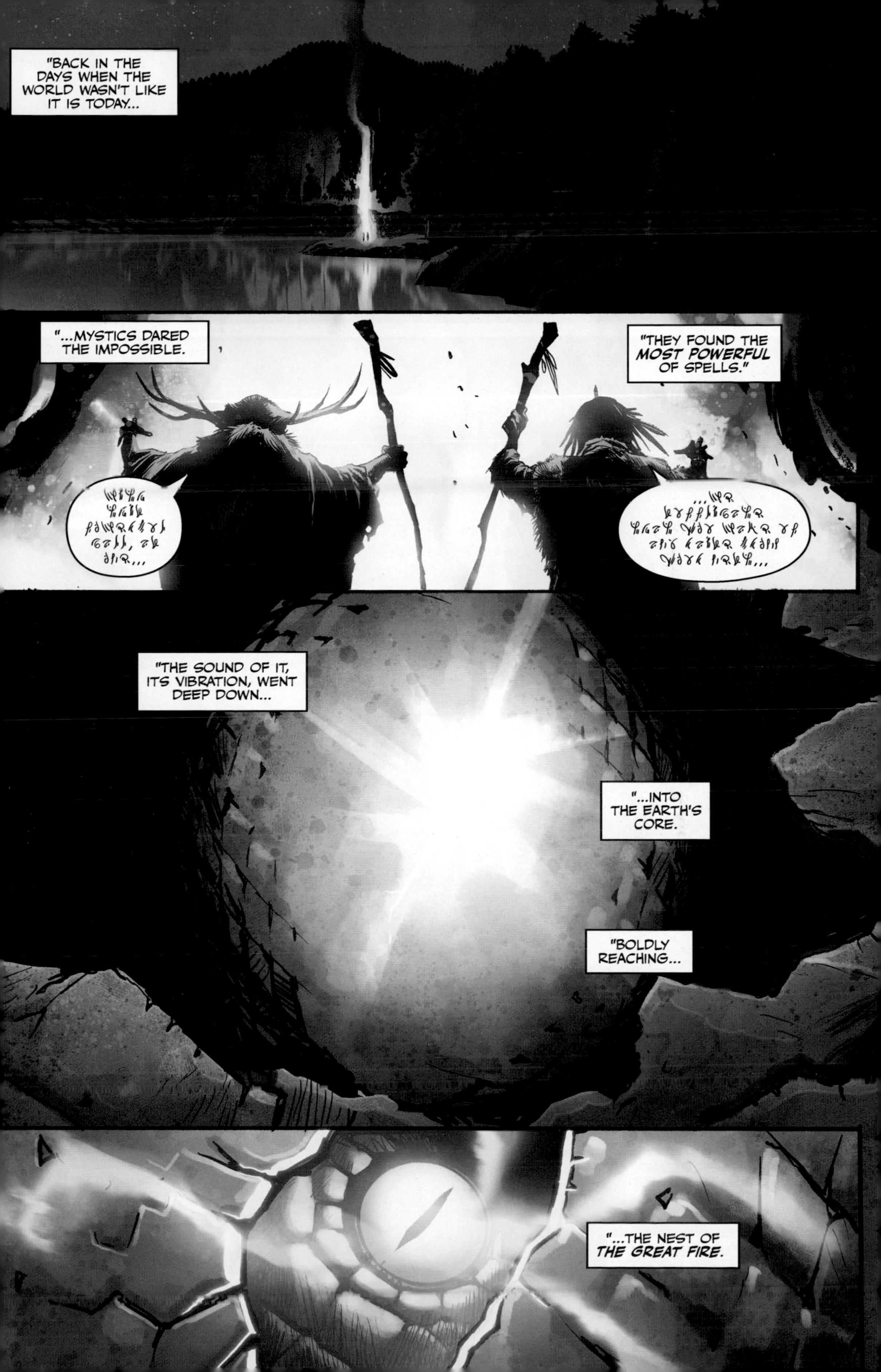
"BACK IN THE DAYS WHEN THE WORLD WASN'T LIKE IT IS TODAY...
"...MYSTICS DARED THE IMPOSSIBLE.
"THEY FOUND THE MOST POWERFUL OF SPELLS."
"THE SOUND OF IT, ITS VIBRATION, WENT DEEP DOWN...
"...INTO THE EARTH'S CORE.
"BOLDLY REACHING...
"...THE NEST OF THE GREAT FIRE.

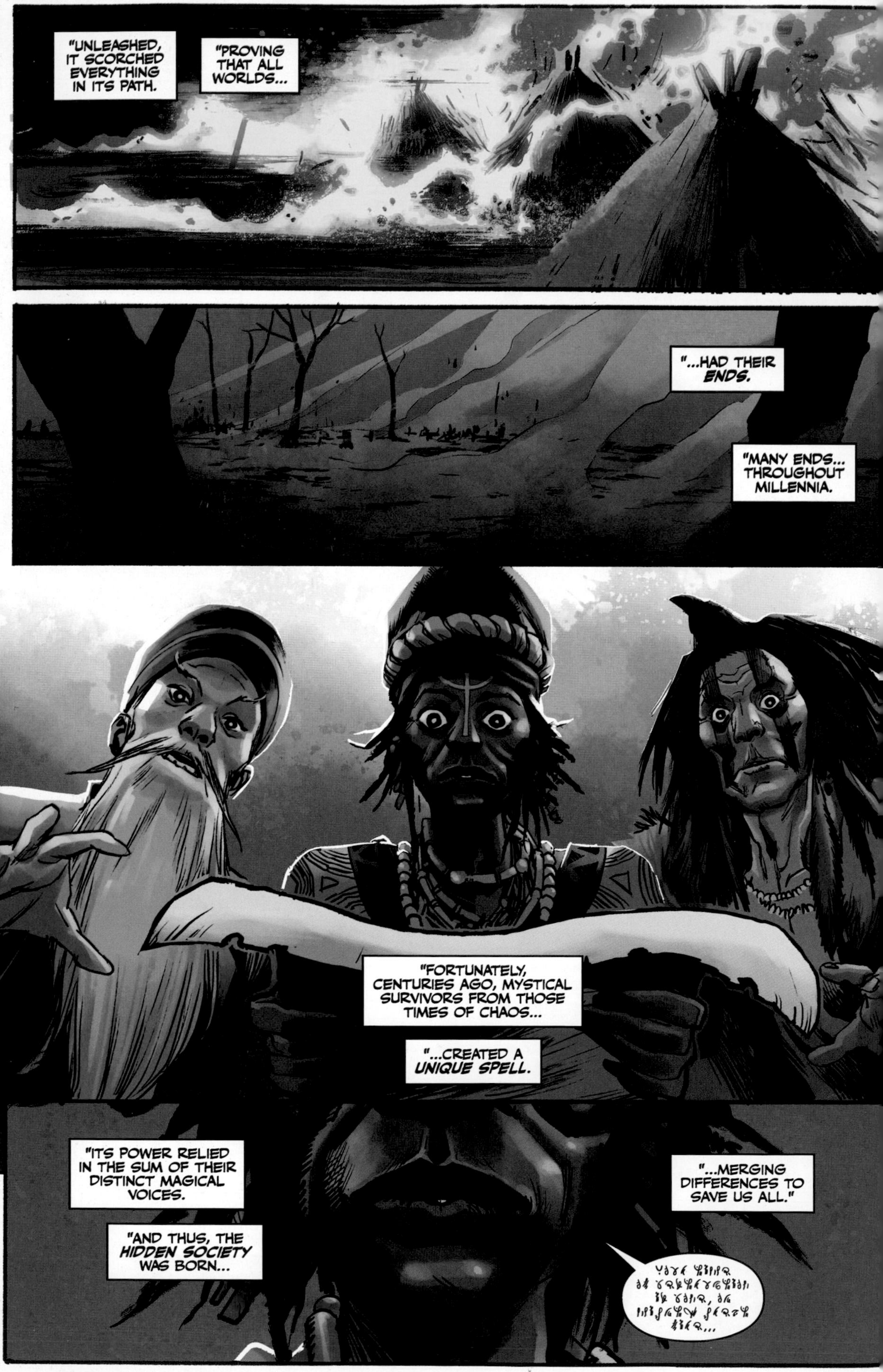
"UNLEASHED, IT SCORCHED EVERYTHING IN ITS PATH.
"PROVING THAT ALL WORLDS...
"...HAD THEIR *ENDS.*
"MANY ENDS... THROUGHOUT MILLENNIA.
"FORTUNATELY, CENTURIES AGO, MYSTICAL SURVIVORS FROM THOSE TIMES OF CHAOS...
"...CREATED A *UNIQUE SPELL.*
"ITS POWER RELIED IN THE SUM OF THEIR DISTINCT MAGICAL VOICES.
"AND THUS, THE *HIDDEN SOCIETY* WAS BORN...
"...MERGING DIFFERENCES TO SAVE US ALL."

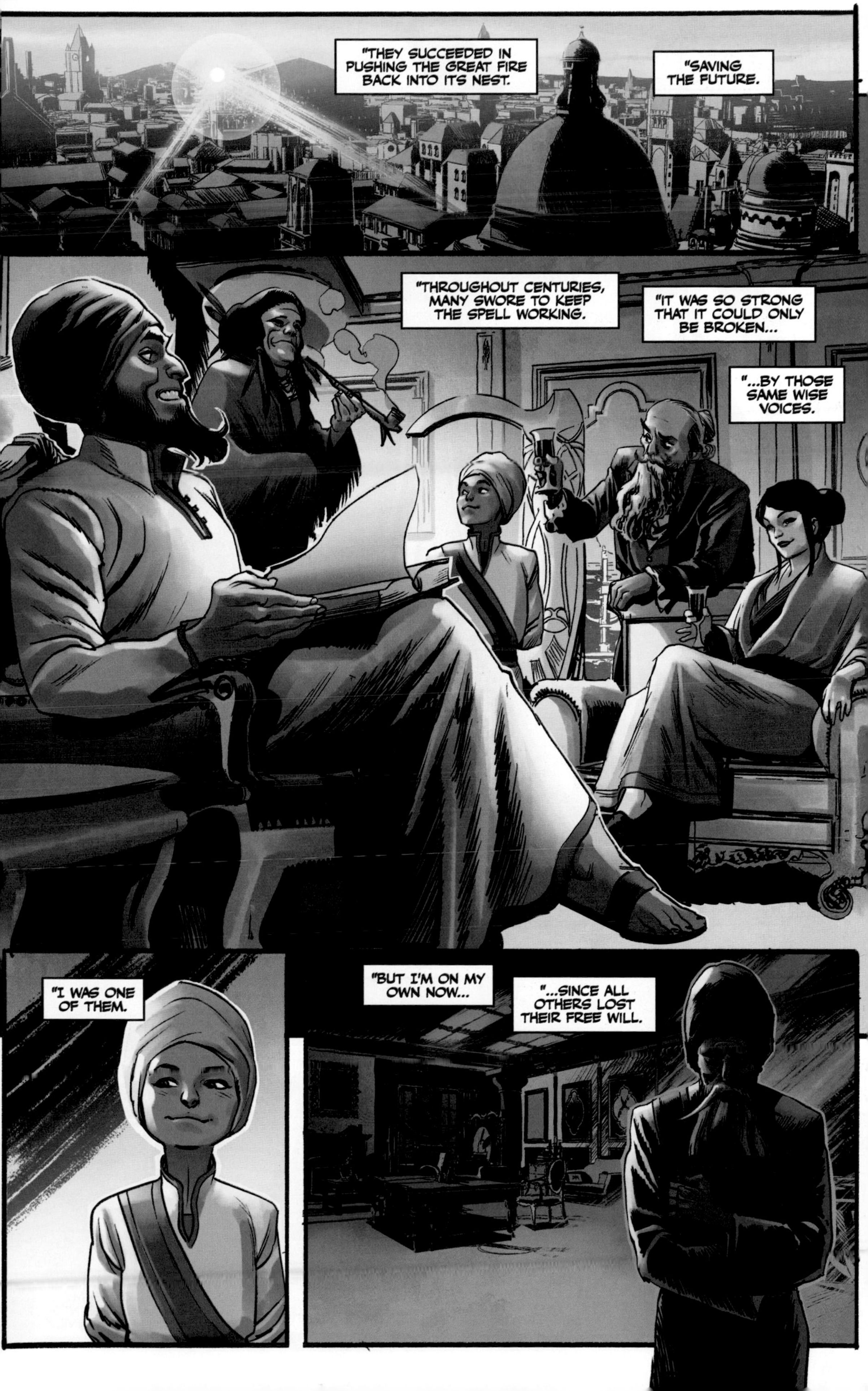
"THEY SUCCEEDED IN PUSHING THE GREAT FIRE BACK INTO ITS NEST.
"SAVING THE FUTURE.
"THROUGHOUT CENTURIES, MANY SWORE TO KEEP THE SPELL WORKING.
"IT WAS SO STRONG THAT IT COULD ONLY BE BROKEN...
"...BY THOSE SAME WISE VOICES.
"I WAS ONE OF THEM.
"BUT I'M ON MY OWN NOW...
"...SINCE ALL OTHERS LOST THEIR FREE WILL.

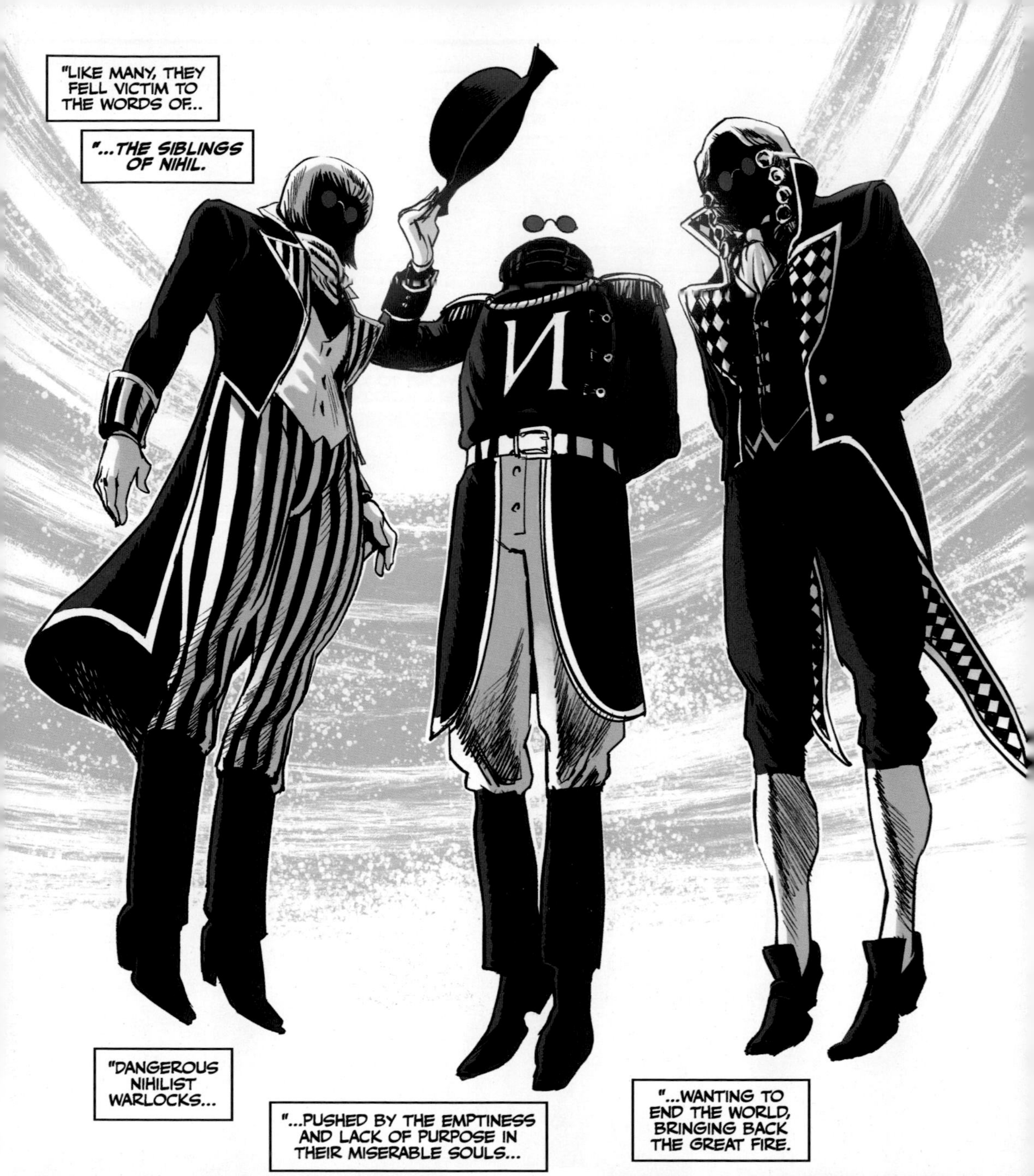
"LIKE MANY, THEY FELL VICTIM TO THE WORDS OF...
"...THE SIBLINGS OF NIHIL.
"DANGEROUS NIHILIST WARLOCKS...
"...PUSHED BY THE EMPTINESS AND LACK OF PURPOSE IN THEIR MISERABLE SOULS...
"...WANTING TO END THE WORLD, BRINGING BACK THE GREAT FIRE.

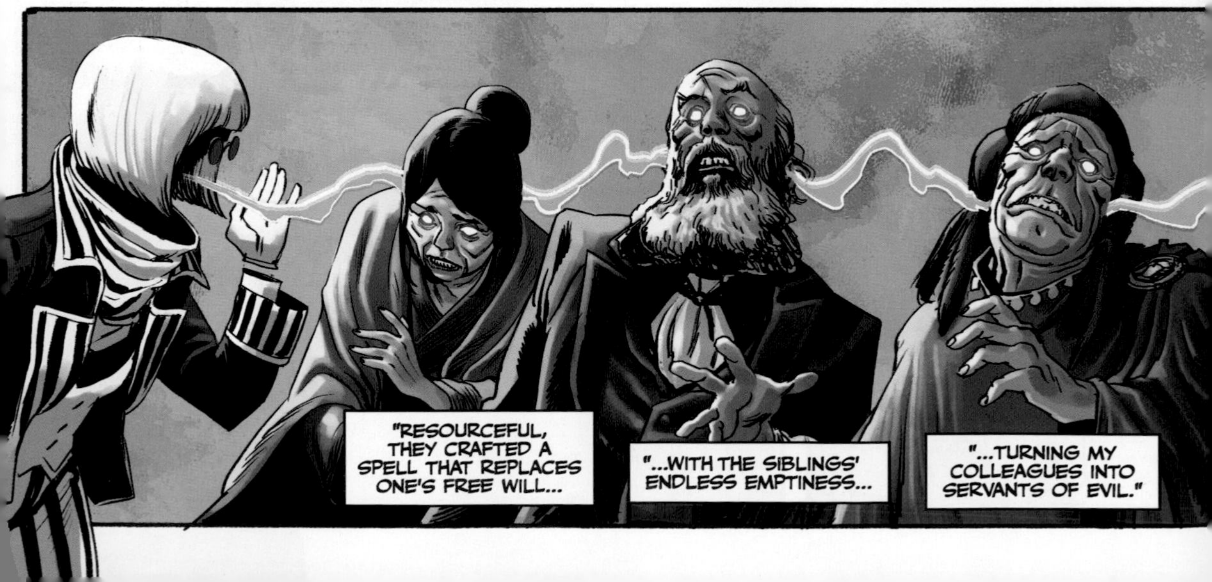
"RESOURCEFUL, THEY CRAFTED A SPELL THAT REPLACES ONE'S FREE WILL...
"...WITH THE SIBLINGS' ENDLESS EMPTINESS...
"...TURNING MY COLLEAGUES INTO SERVANTS OF EVIL."

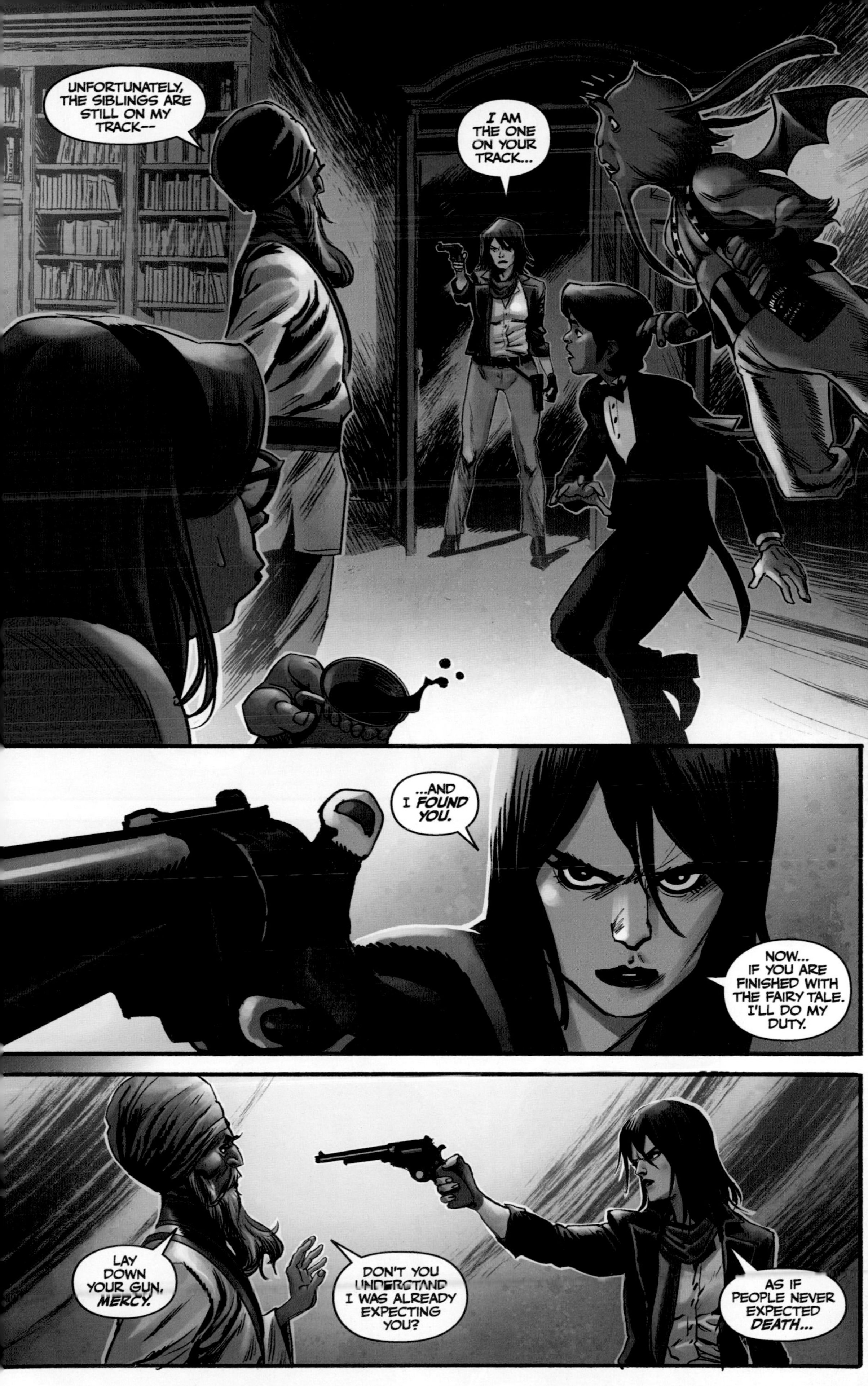
UNFORTUNATELY, THE SIBLINGS ARE STILL ON MY TRACK--
I AM THE ONE ON YOUR TRACK...
...AND I FOUND YOU.
NOW... IF YOU ARE FINISHED WITH THE FAIRY TALE. I'LL DO MY DUTY.
LAY DOWN YOUR GUN, MERCY.
DON'T YOU UNDERSTAND I WAS ALREADY EXPECTING YOU?
AS IF PEOPLE NEVER EXPECTED DEATH...

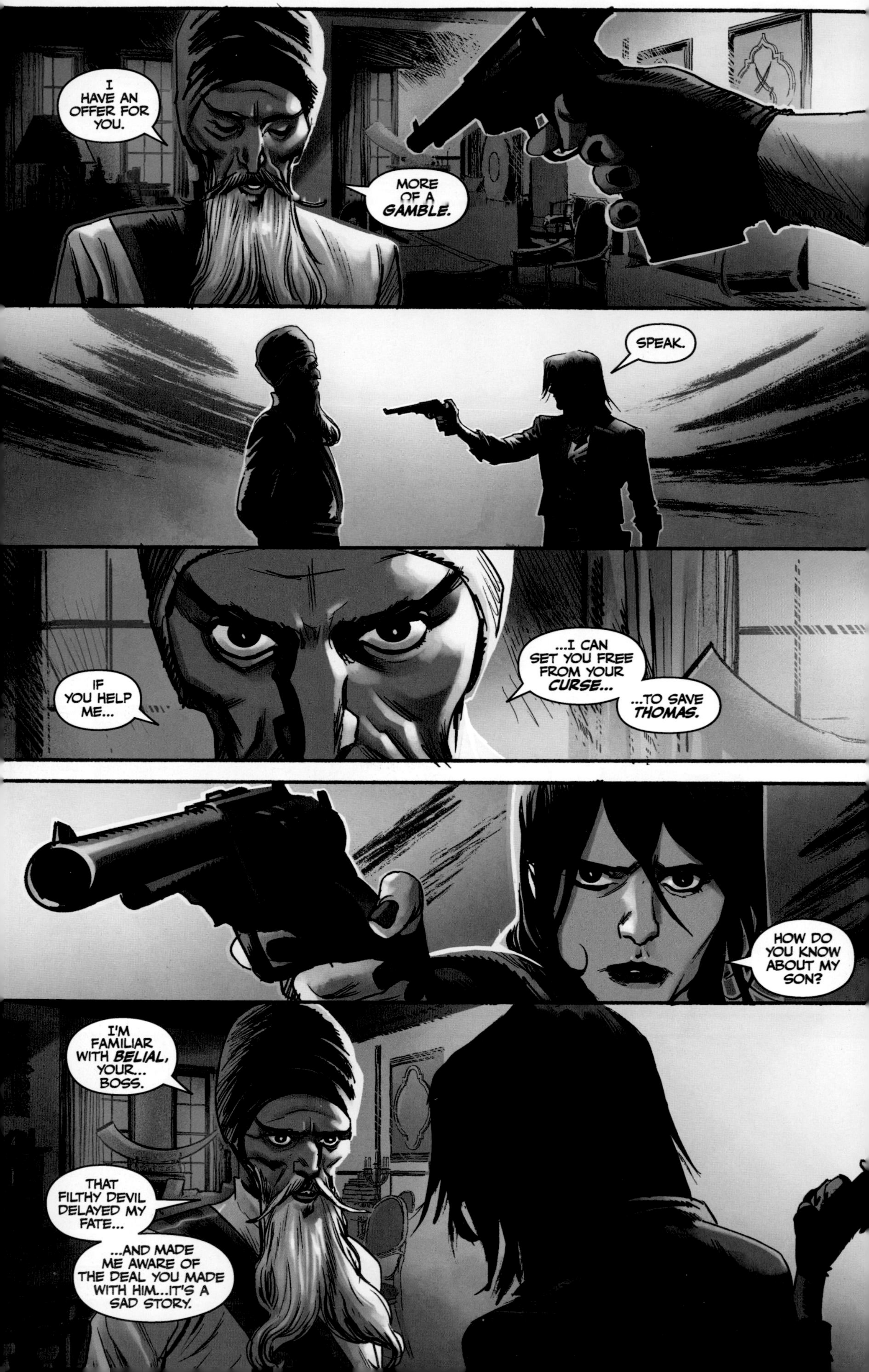
I HAVE AN OFFER FOR YOU.
MORE OF A GAMBLE.
SPEAK.
IF YOU HELP ME...
...I CAN SET YOU FREE FROM YOUR CURSE...
...TO SAVE THOMAS.
HOW DO YOU KNOW ABOUT MY SON?
I'M FAMILIAR WITH BELIAL, YOUR... BOSS.
THAT FILTHY DEVIL DELAYED MY FATE...
...AND MADE ME AWARE OF THE DEAL YOU MADE WITH HIM...IT'S A SAD STORY.

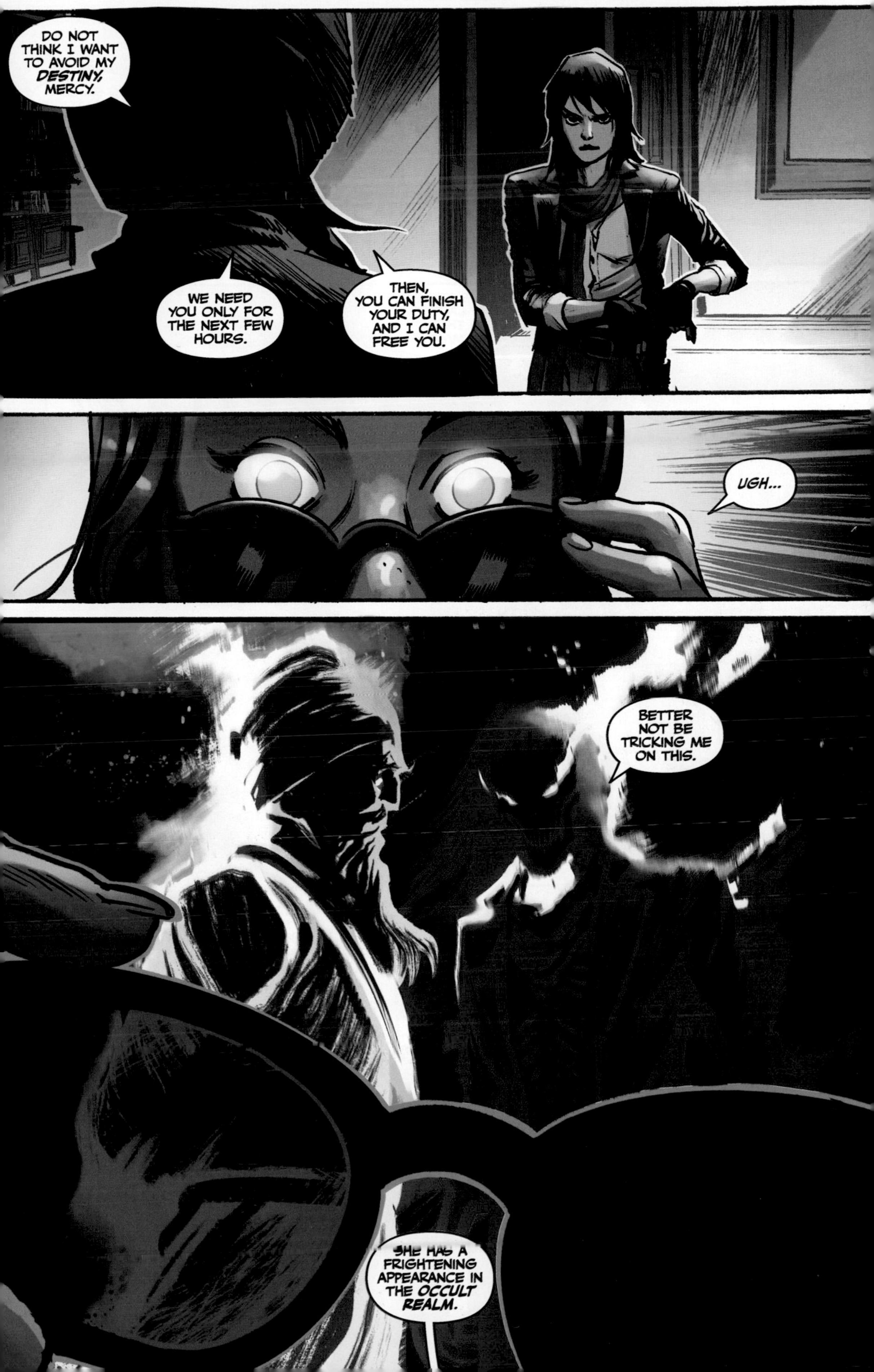
DO NOT THINK I WANT TO AVOID MY *DESTINY,* MERCY.
WE NEED YOU ONLY FOR THE NEXT FEW HOURS.
THEN, YOU CAN FINISH YOUR DUTY, AND I CAN FREE YOU.
UGH...
BETTER NOT BE TRICKING ME ON THIS.
SHE HAS A FRIGHTENING APPEARANCE IN THE *OCCULT* *REALM.*

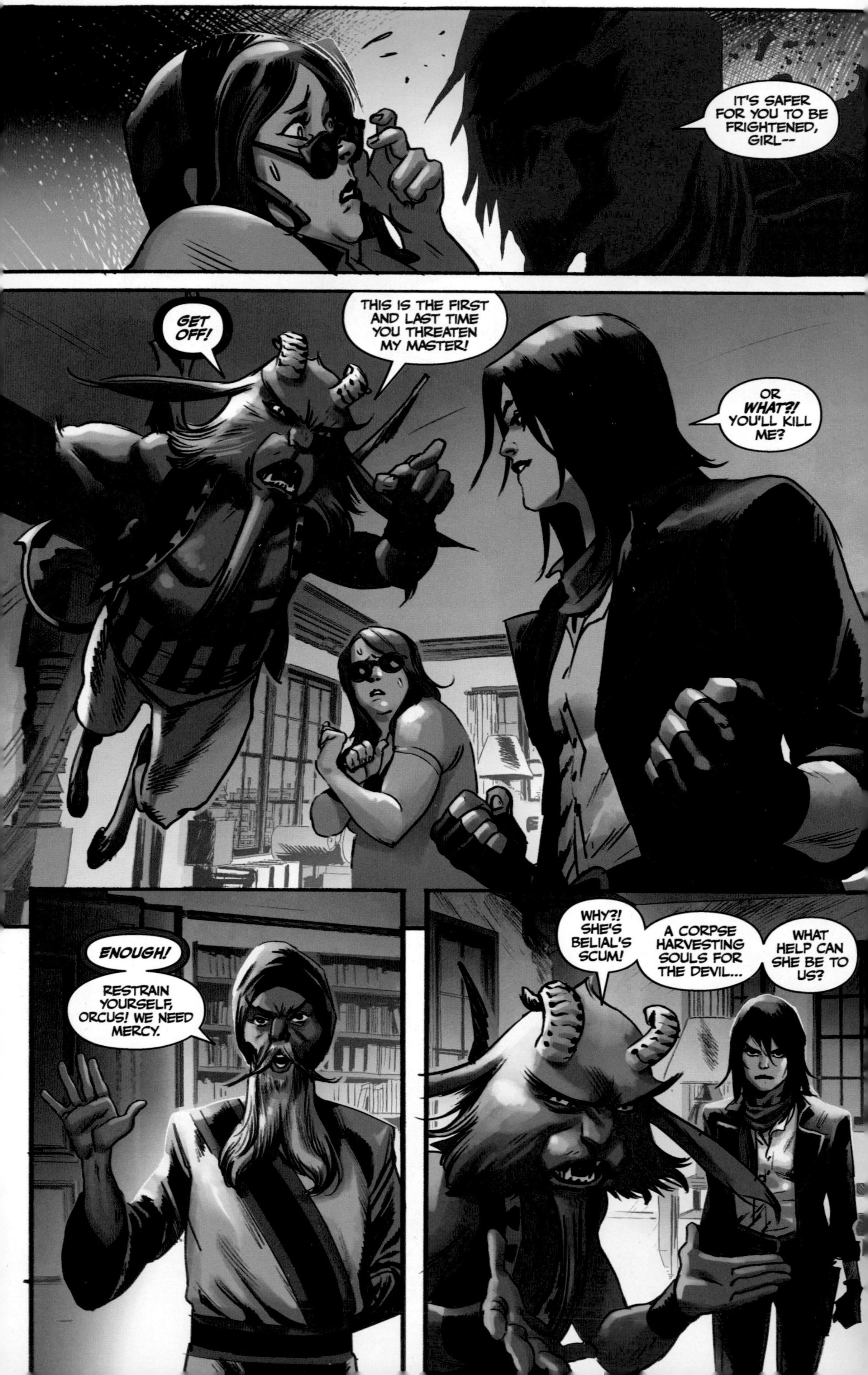
IT'S SAFER FOR YOU TO BE FRIGHTENED, GIRL--
GET OFF!
THIS IS THE FIRST AND LAST TIME YOU THREATEN MY MASTER!
OR WHAT?! YOU'LL KILL ME?
ENOUGH!
RESTRAIN YOURSELF, ORCUS! WE NEED MERCY.
WHY?! SHE'S BELIAL'S SCUM!
A CORPSE HARVESTING SOULS FOR THE DEVIL...
WHAT HELP CAN SHE BE TO US?

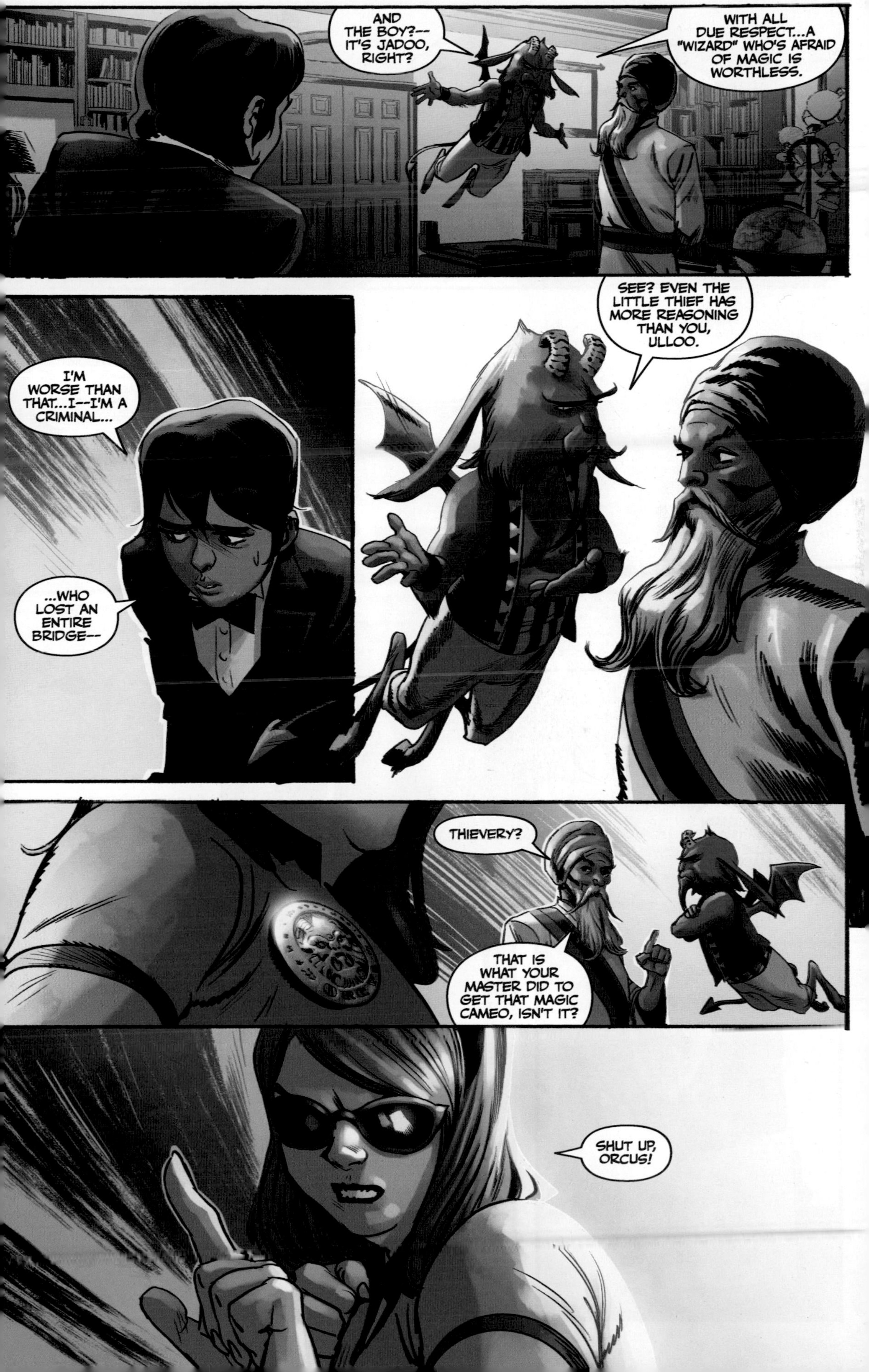
AND THE BOY?-- IT'S JADOO, RIGHT?
WITH ALL DUE RESPECT...A "WIZARD" WHO'S AFRAID OF MAGIC IS WORTHLESS.
I'M WORSE THAN THAT...I--I'M A CRIMINAL...
...WHO LOST AN ENTIRE BRIDGE--
SEE? EVEN THE LITTLE THIEF HAS MORE REASONING THAN YOU, ULLOO.
THIEVERY?
THAT IS WHAT YOUR MASTER DID TO GET THAT MAGIC CAMEO, ISN'T IT?
SHUT UP, ORCUS!

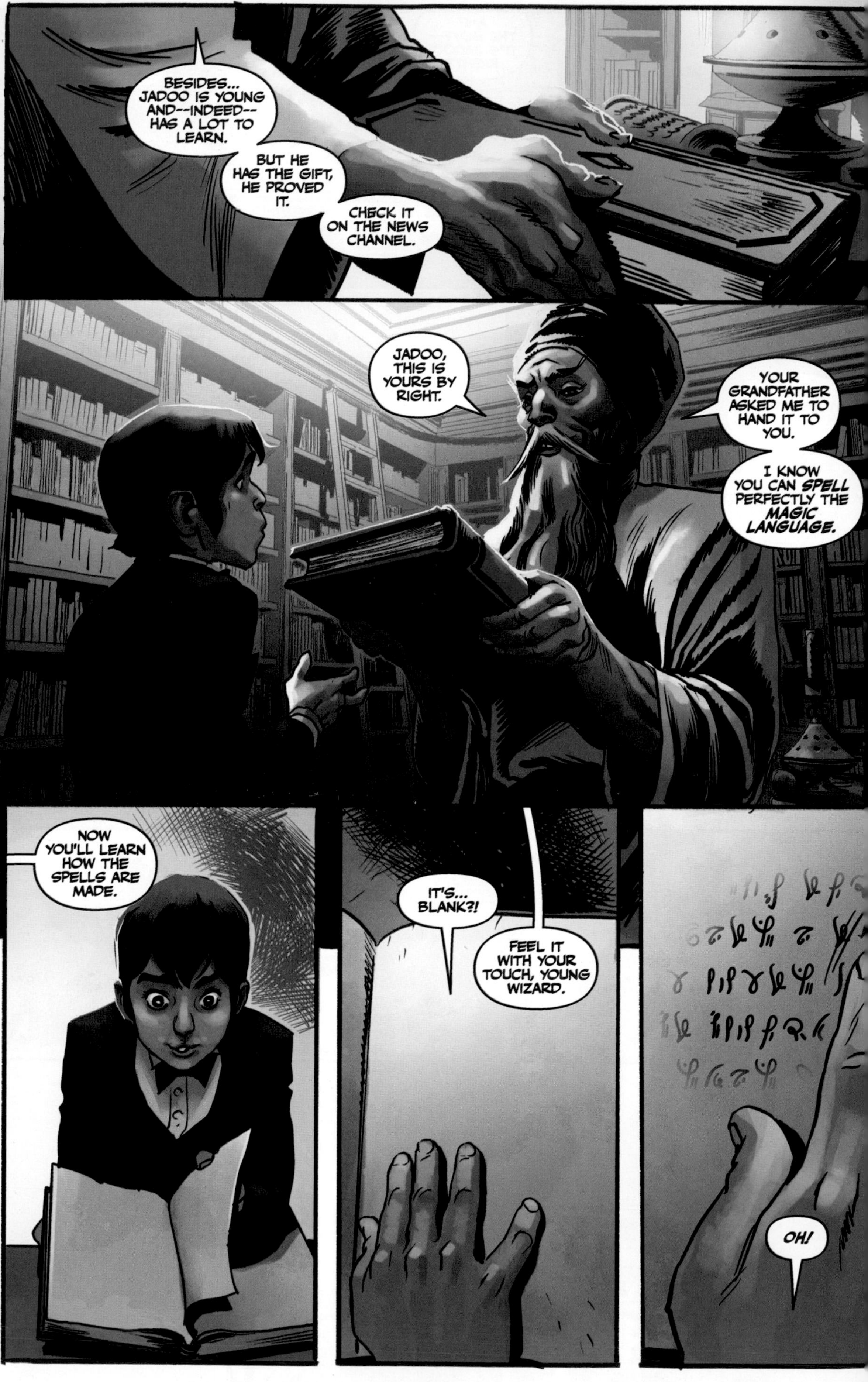
BESIDES... JADOO IS YOUNG AND--INDEED-- HAS A LOT TO LEARN.
BUT HE HAS THE GIFT, HE PROVED IT.
CHECK IT ON THE NEWS CHANNEL.
JADOO, THIS IS YOURS BY RIGHT.
YOUR GRANDFATHER ASKED ME TO HAND IT TO YOU.
I KNOW YOU CAN *SPELL* PERFECTLY THE *MAGIC LANGUAGE.*
NOW YOU'LL LEARN HOW THE SPELLS ARE MADE.
IT'S... BLANK?!
FEEL IT WITH YOUR TOUCH, YOUNG WIZARD.
OH!

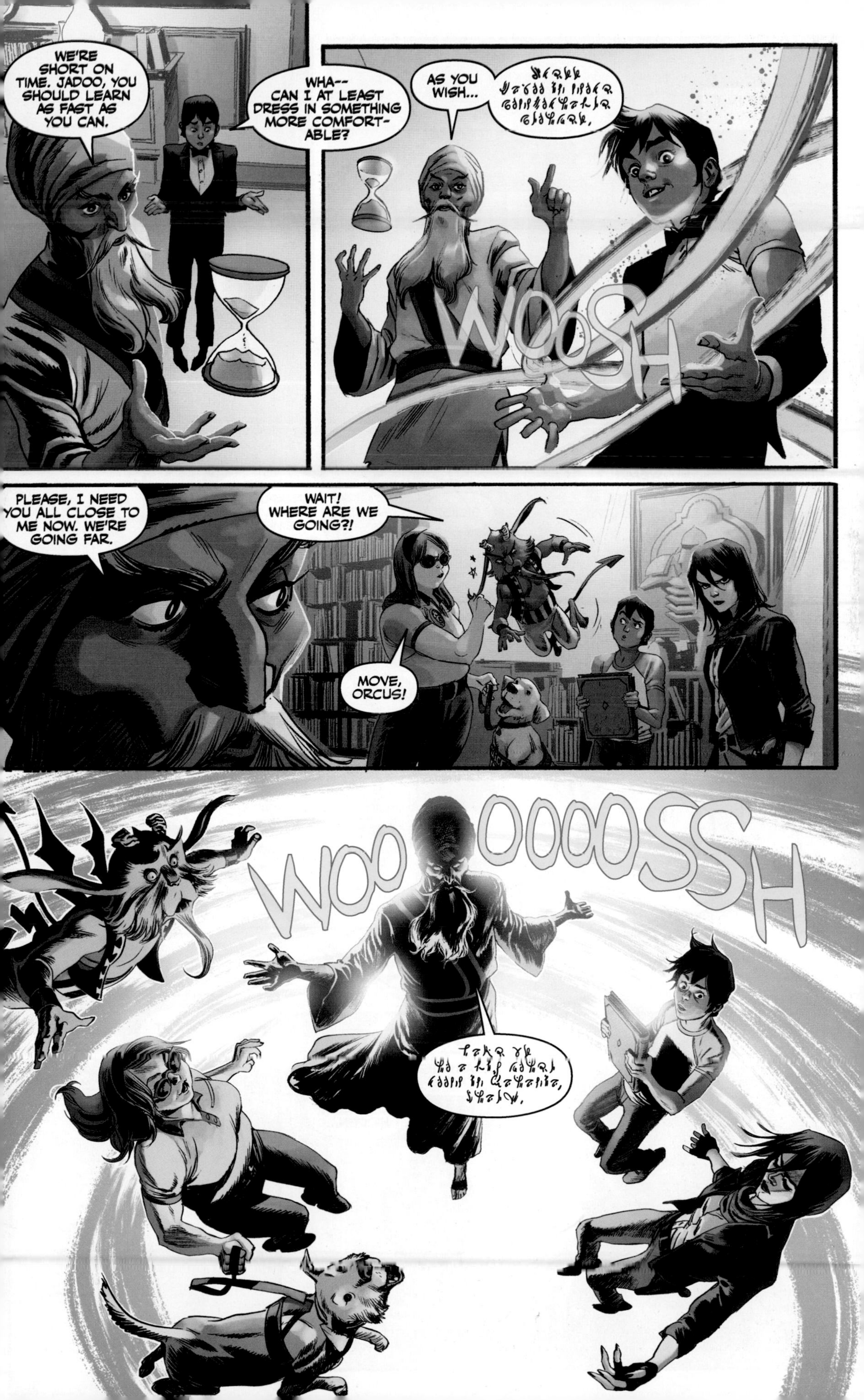
WE'RE SHORT ON TIME. JADOO, YOU SHOULD LEARN AS FAST AS YOU CAN.
WHA-- CAN I AT LEAST DRESS IN SOMETHING MORE COMFORT-ABLE?
AS YOU WISH...
WOOSH
PLEASE, I NEED YOU ALL CLOSE TO ME NOW. WE'RE GOING FAR.
WAIT! WHERE ARE WE GOING?!
MOVE, ORCUS!
WOOOOOOSSH

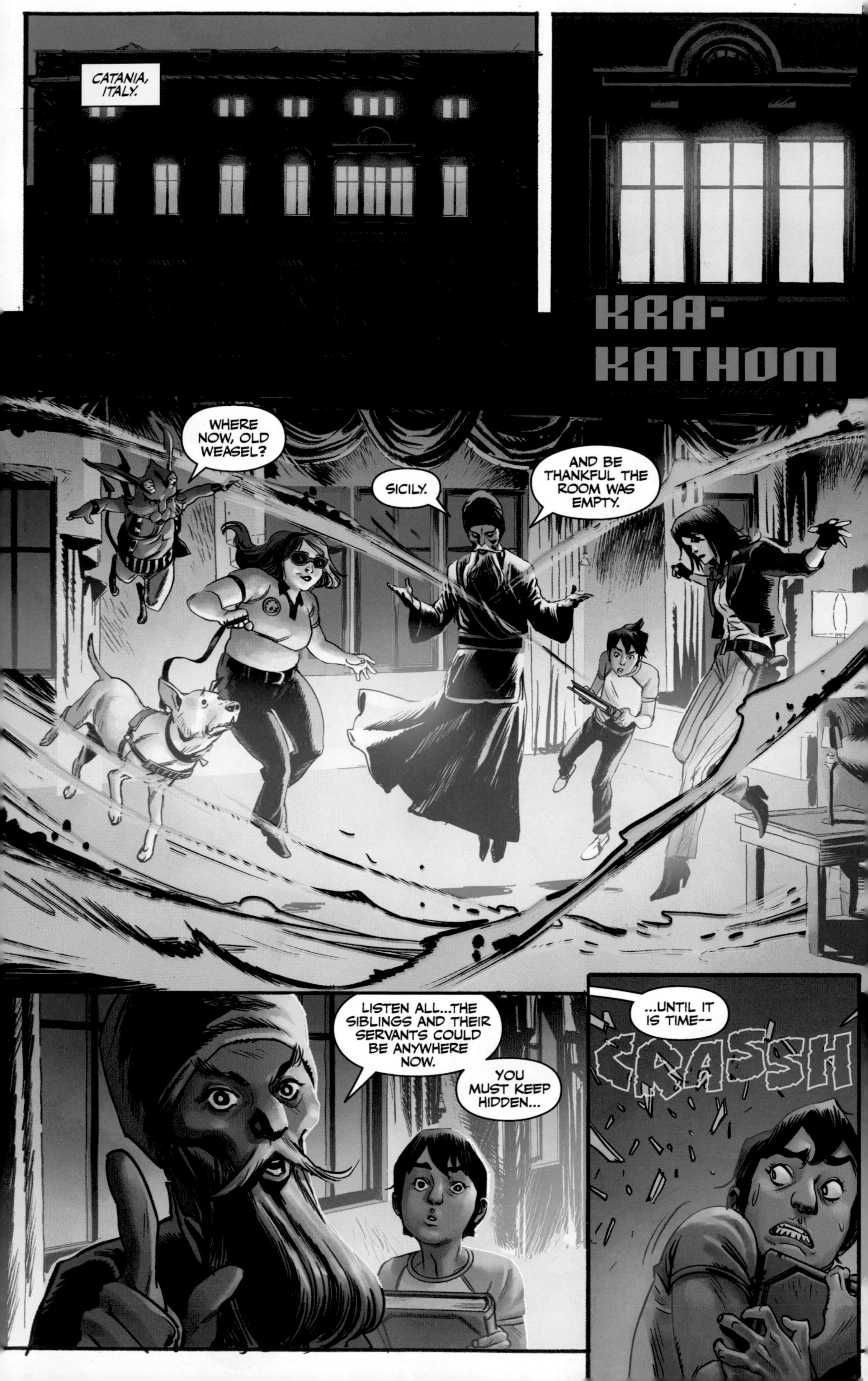
CATANIA, ITALY.
KRA-KATHOM
WHERE NOW, OLD WEASEL?
SICILY.
AND BE THANKFUL THE ROOM WAS EMPTY.
LISTEN ALL...THE SIBLINGS AND THEIR SERVANTS COULD BE ANYWHERE NOW.
YOU MUST KEEP HIDDEN...
...UNTIL IT IS TIME--
CRASSH

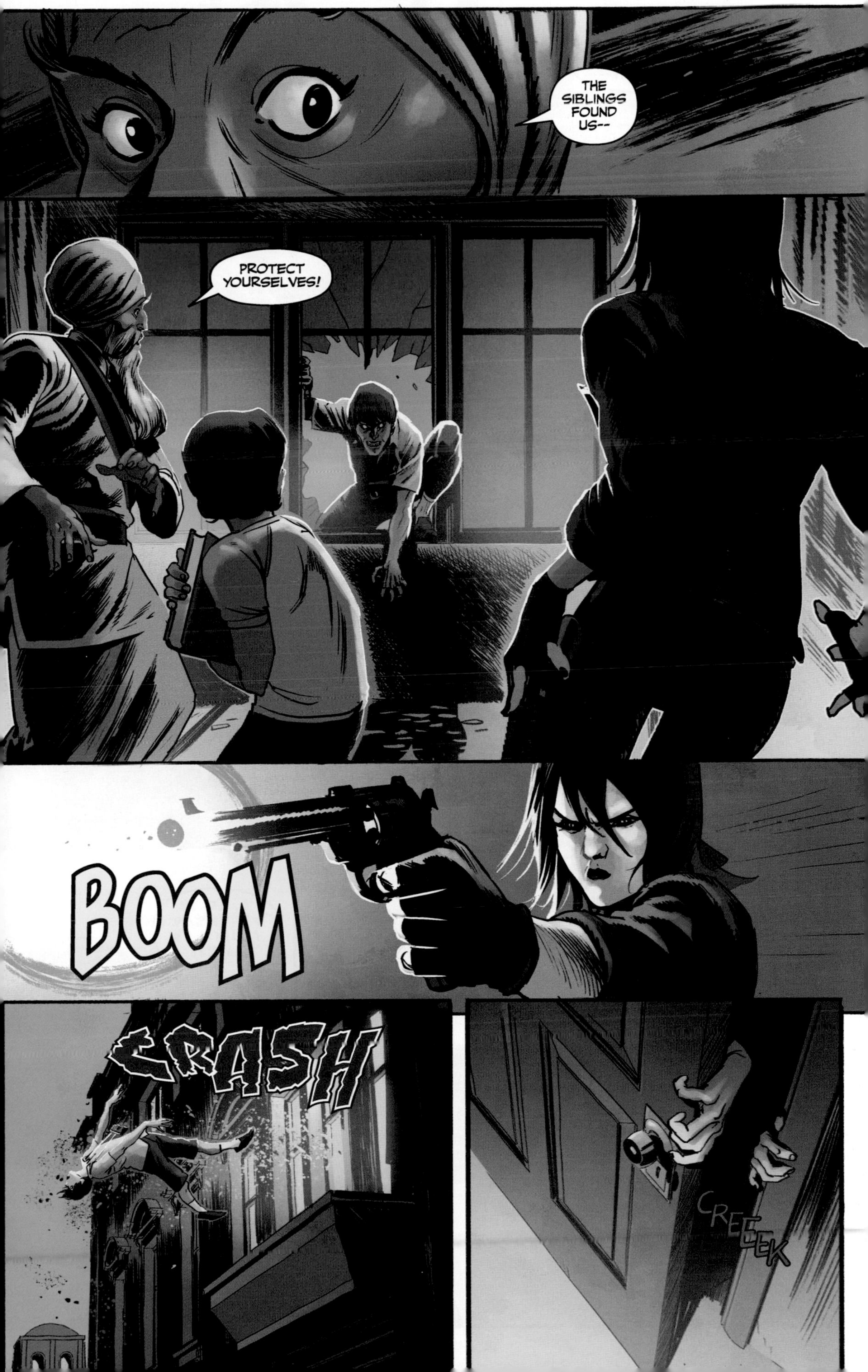
THE SIBLINGS FOUND US--
PROTECT YOURSELVES!
BOOM
CRASH
CREEEEK

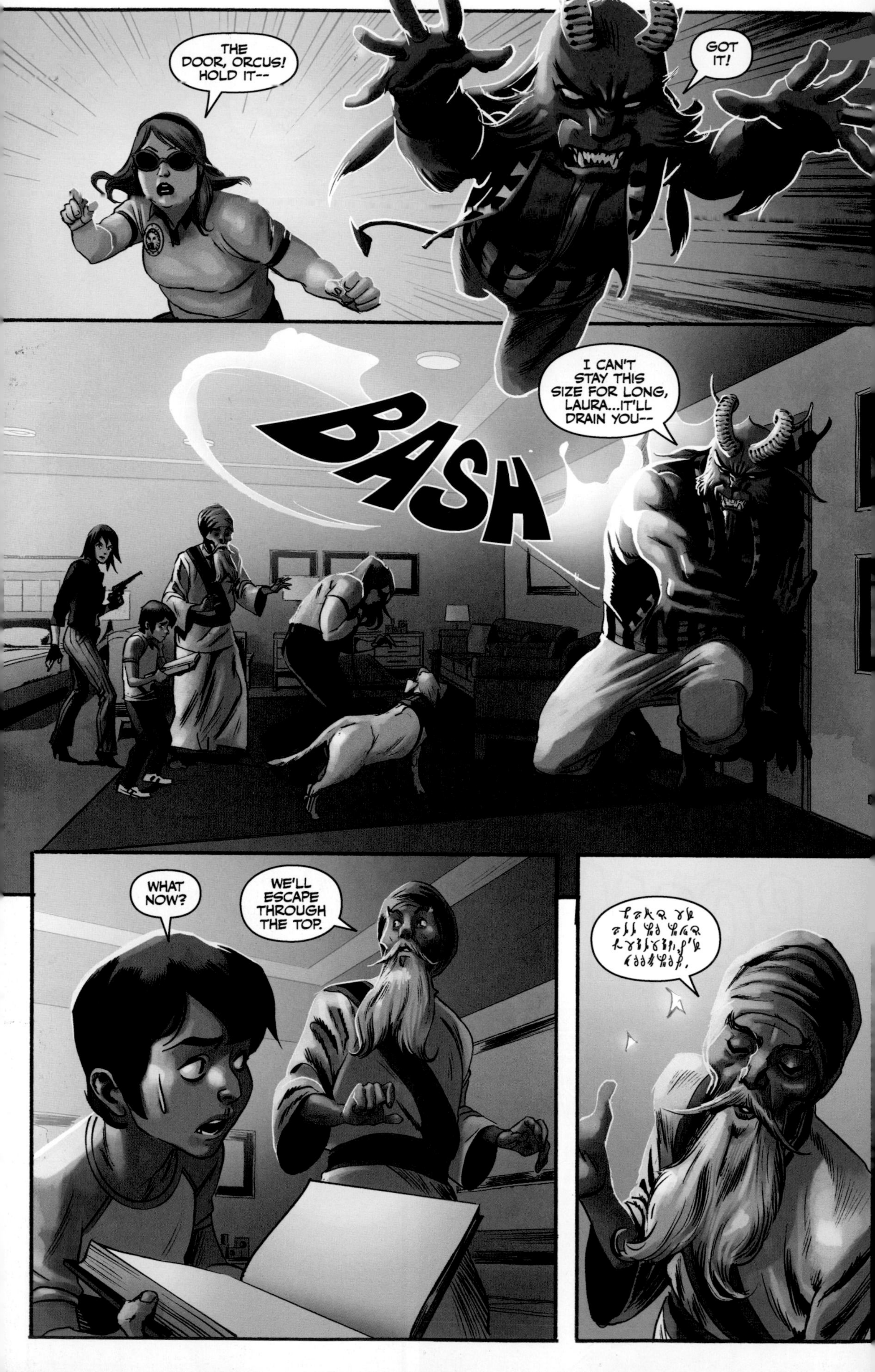
THE DOOR, ORCUS! HOLD IT--
GOT IT!
BASH
I CAN'T STAY THIS SIZE FOR LONG, LAURA...IT'LL DRAIN YOU--
WHAT NOW?
WE'LL ESCAPE THROUGH THE TOP.

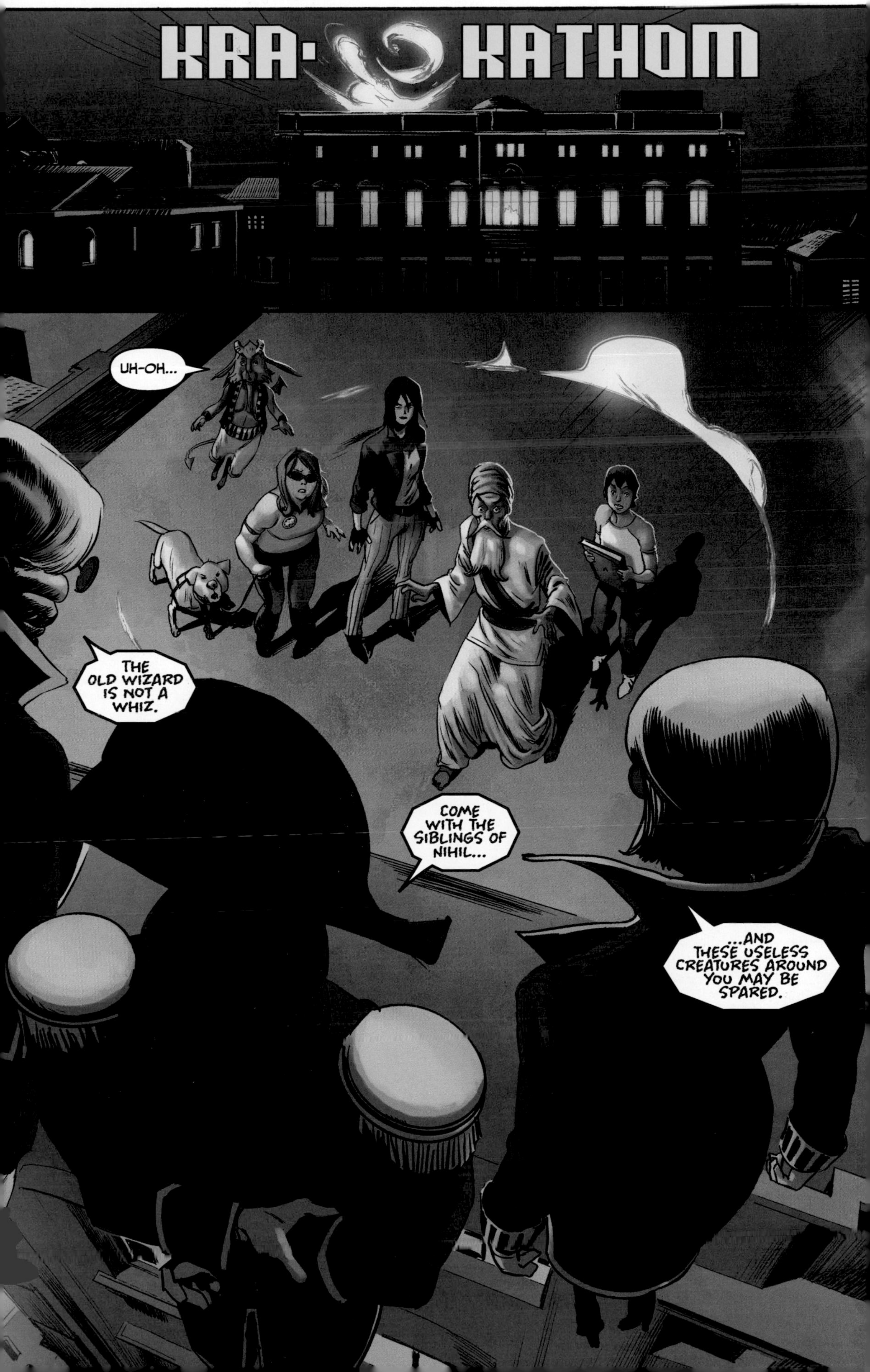
KRA-KATHOM
UH-OH...
THE OLD WIZARD IS NOT A WHIZ.
COME WITH THE SIBLINGS OF NIHIL...
...AND THESE USELESS CREATURES AROUND YOU MAY BE SPARED.

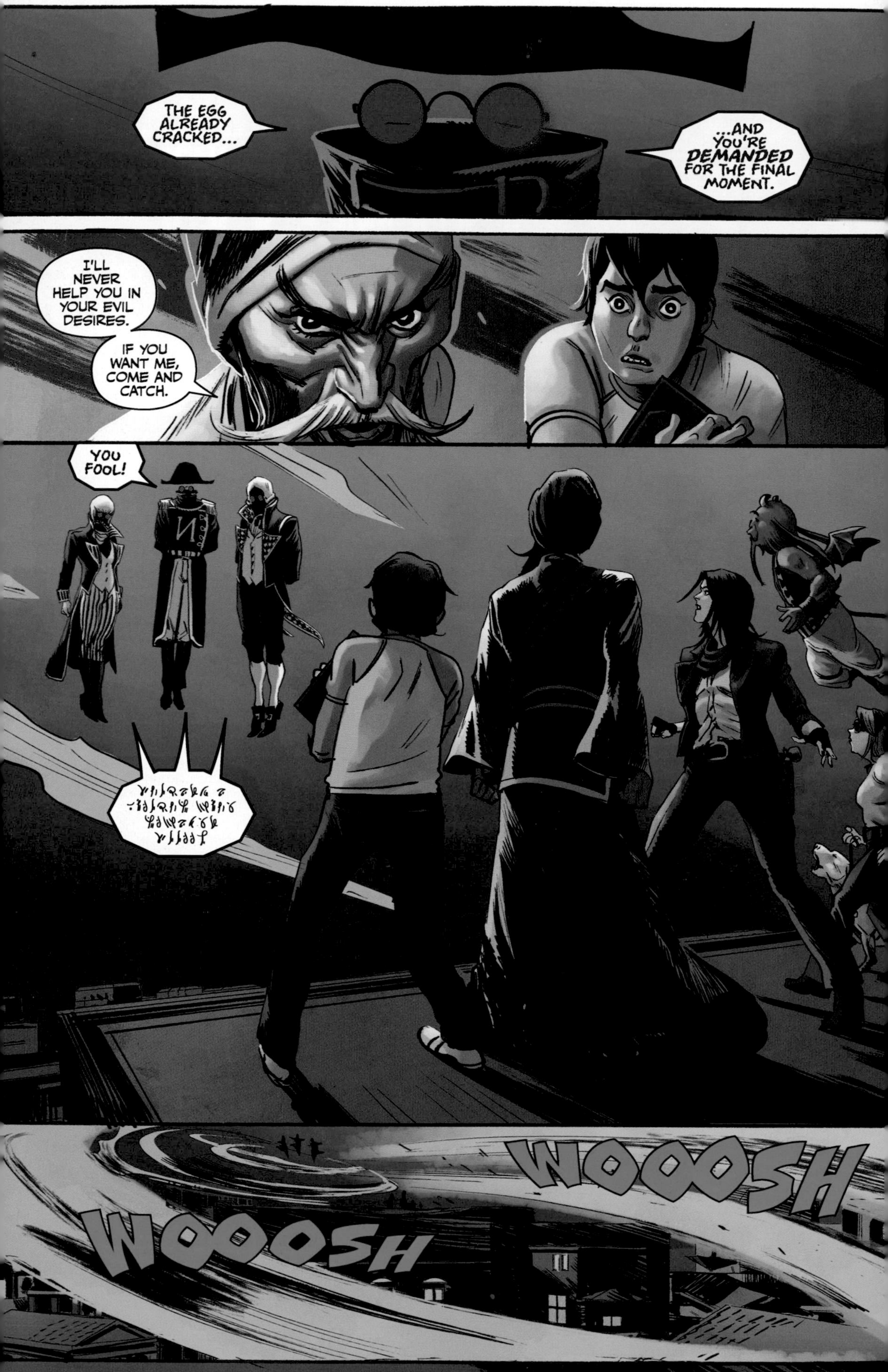
THE EGG ALREADY CRACKED...
...AND YOU'RE DEMANDED FOR THE FINAL MOMENT.
I'LL NEVER HELP YOU IN YOUR EVIL DESIRES.
IF YOU WANT ME, COME AND CATCH.
YOU FOOL!
WOOOSH
WOOOSH

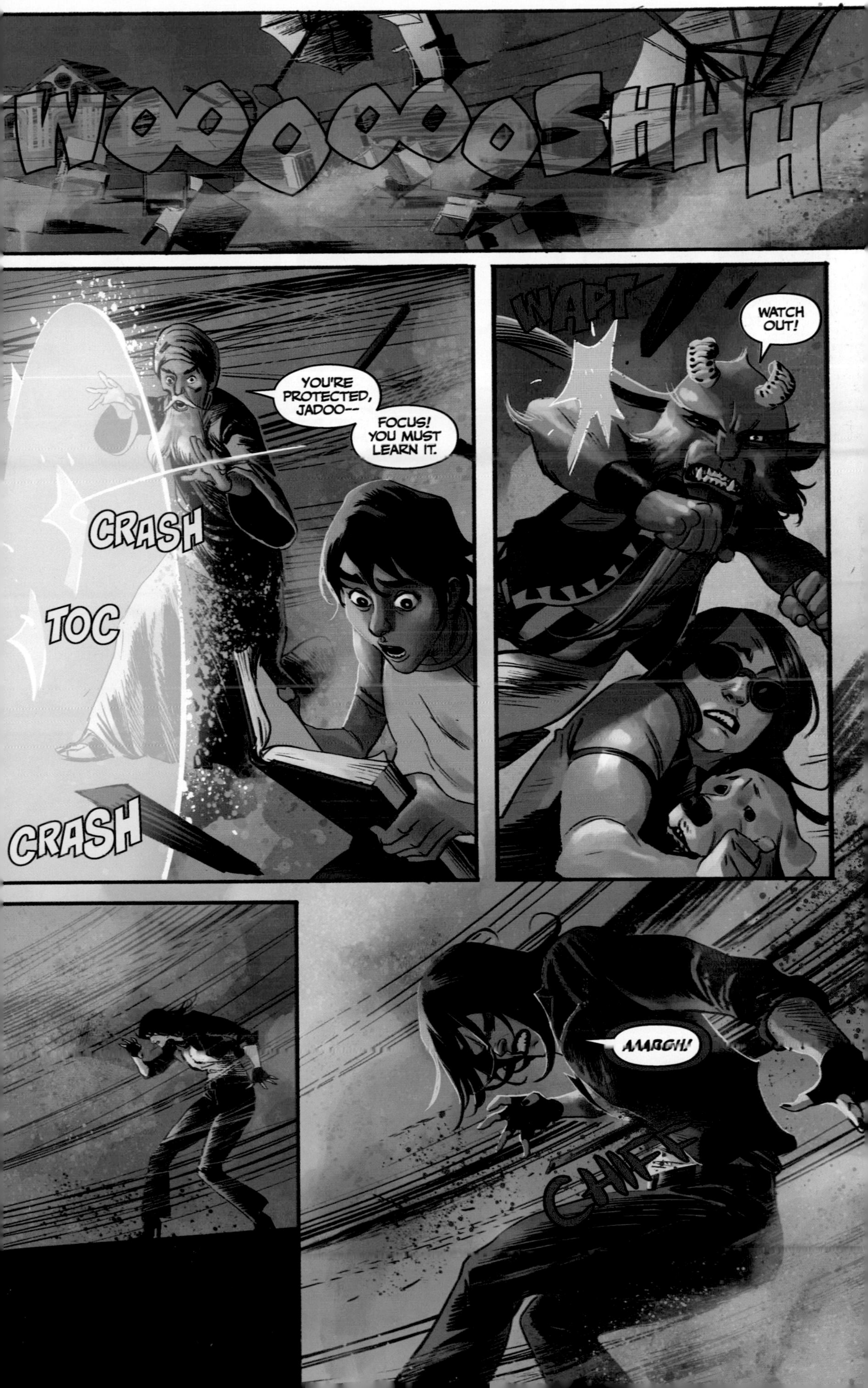
WOOOOOOSHHH
YOU'RE PROTECTED, JADOO--
FOCUS! YOU MUST LEARN IT.
CRASH
TOC
CRASH
WAPT
WATCH OUT!
AAARGH!

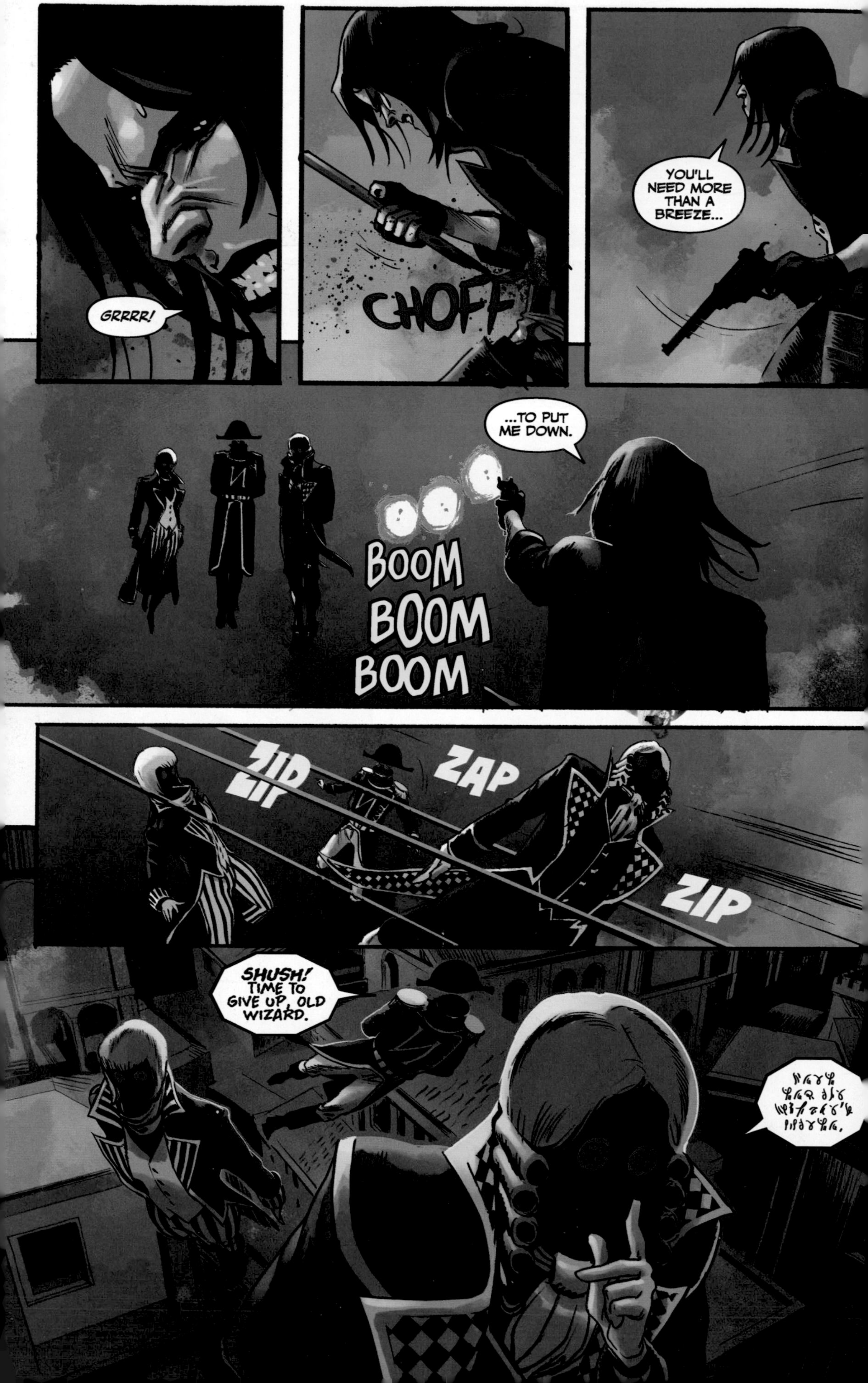
GRRRR!
CHOFF
YOU'LL NEED MORE THAN A BREEZE...
...TO PUT ME DOWN.
BOOM
BOOM
BOOM
ZIP
ZAP
ZIP
SHUSH! TIME TO GIVE UP, OLD WIZARD.

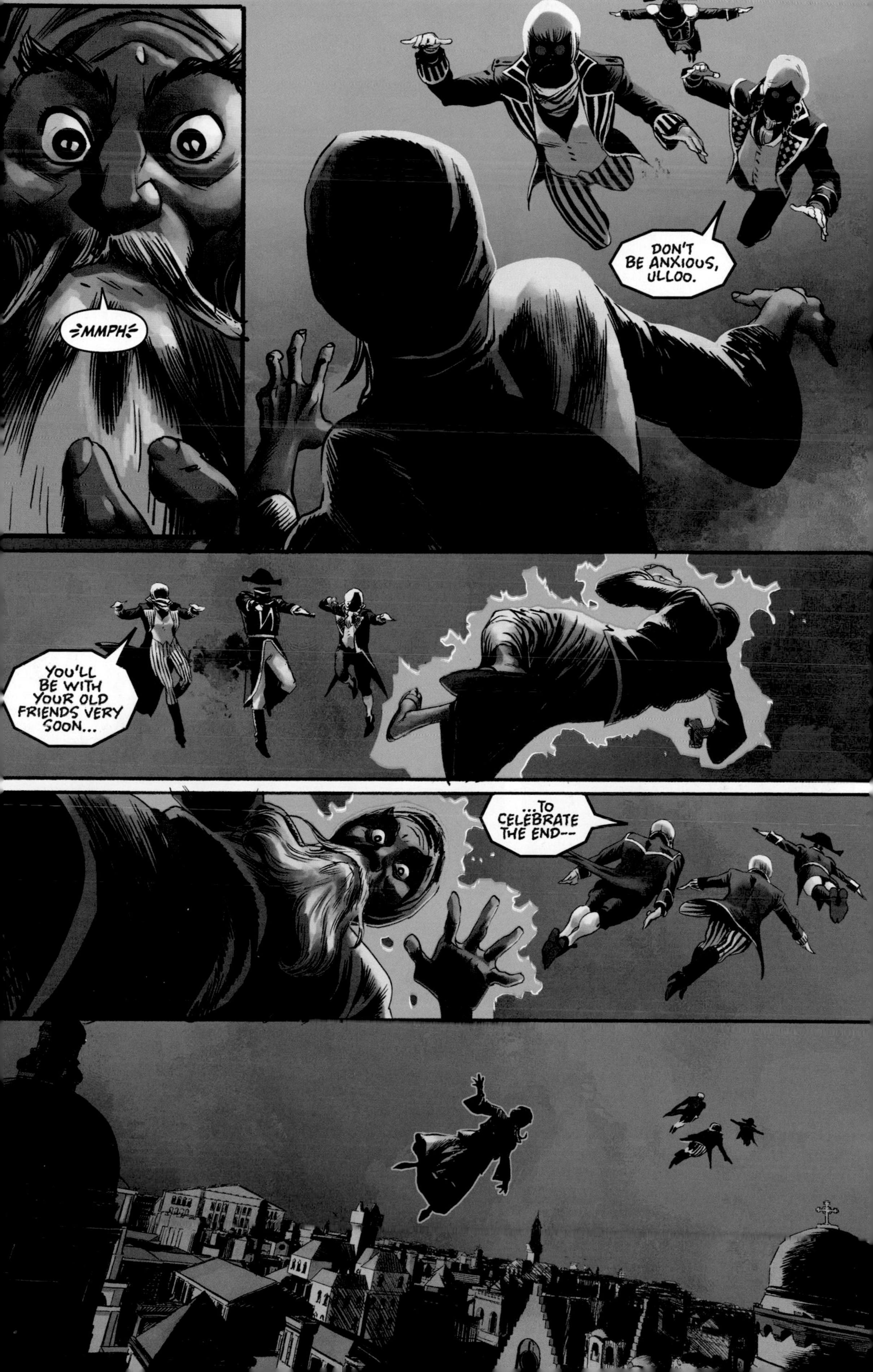
=MMPH=
DON'T BE ANXIOUS, ULLOO.
YOU'LL BE WITH YOUR OLD FRIENDS VERY SOON...
...TO CELEBRATE THE END--

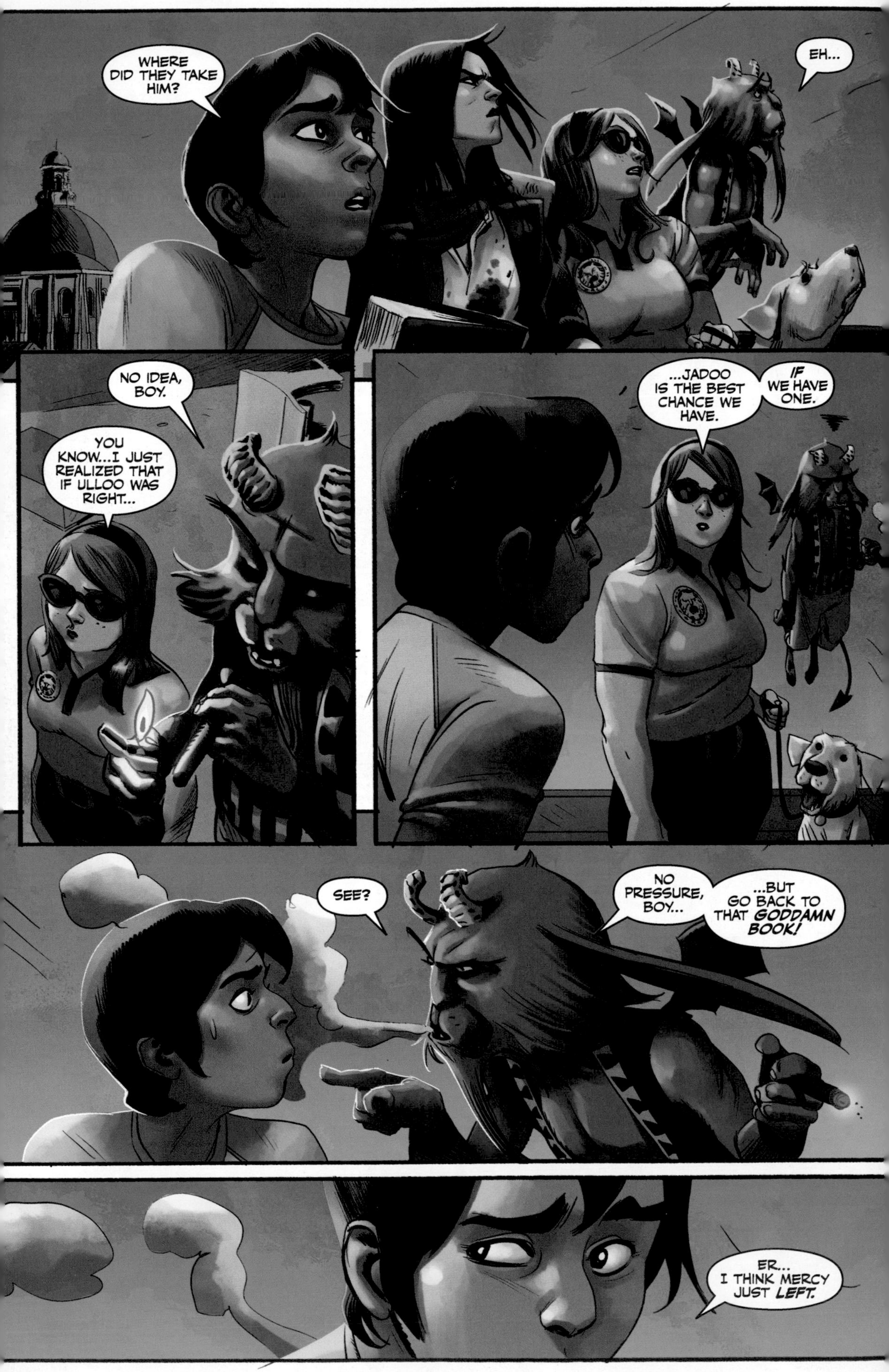
WHERE DID THEY TAKE HIM?
EH...
NO IDEA, BOY.
YOU KNOW...I JUST REALIZED THAT IF ULLOO WAS RIGHT...
...JADOO IS THE BEST CHANCE WE HAVE.
IF WE HAVE ONE.
SEE?
NO PRESSURE, BOY...
...BUT GO BACK TO THAT GODDAMN BOOK!
ER... I THINK MERCY JUST LEFT.

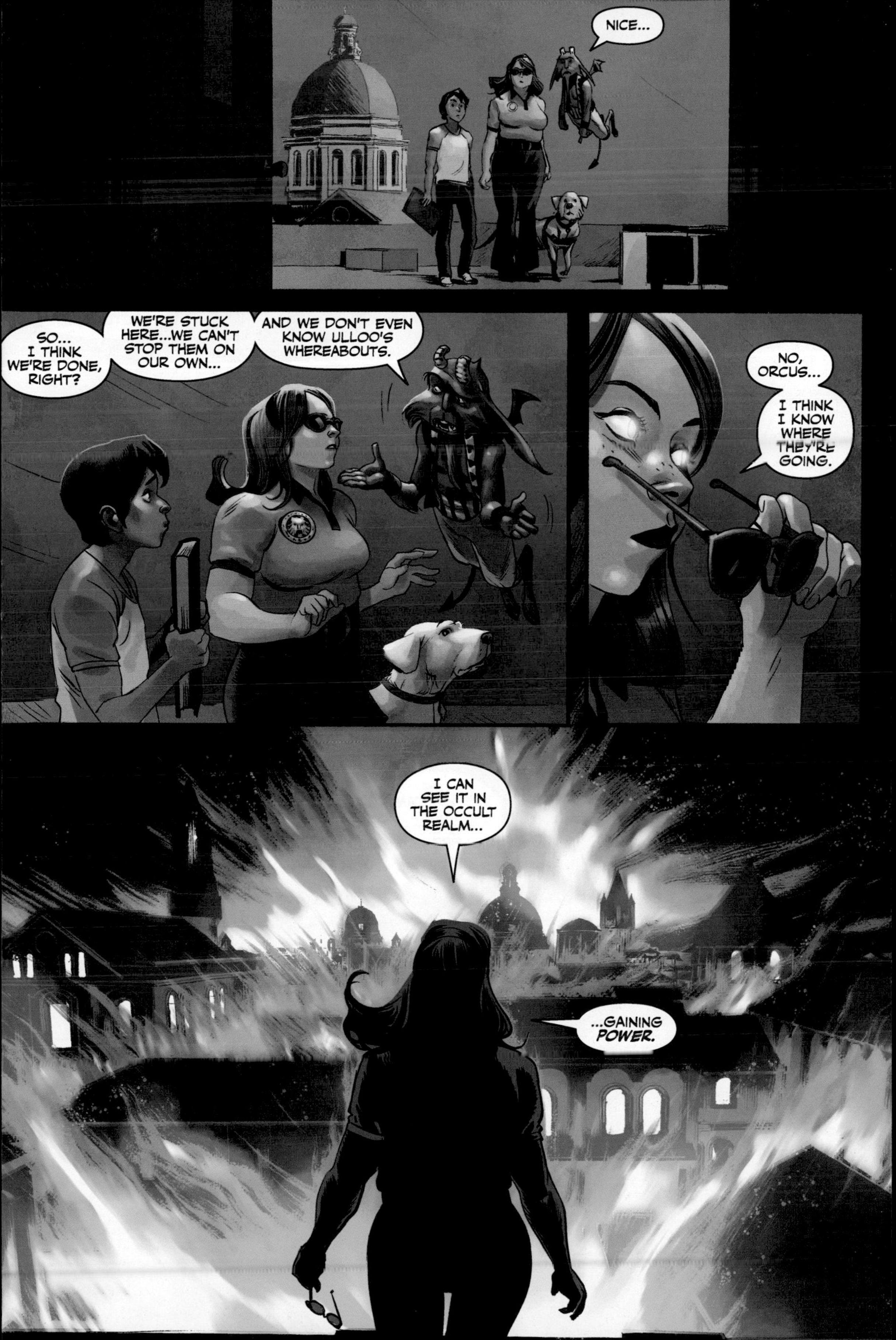

NICE...
SO... I THINK WE'RE DONE, RIGHT?
WE'RE STUCK HERE...WE CAN'T STOP THEM ON OUR OWN...
AND WE DON'T EVEN KNOW ULLOO'S WHEREABOUTS.
NO, ORCUS...
I THINK I KNOW WHERE THEY'RE GOING.
I CAN SEE IT IN THE OCCULT REALM...
...GAINING POWER.

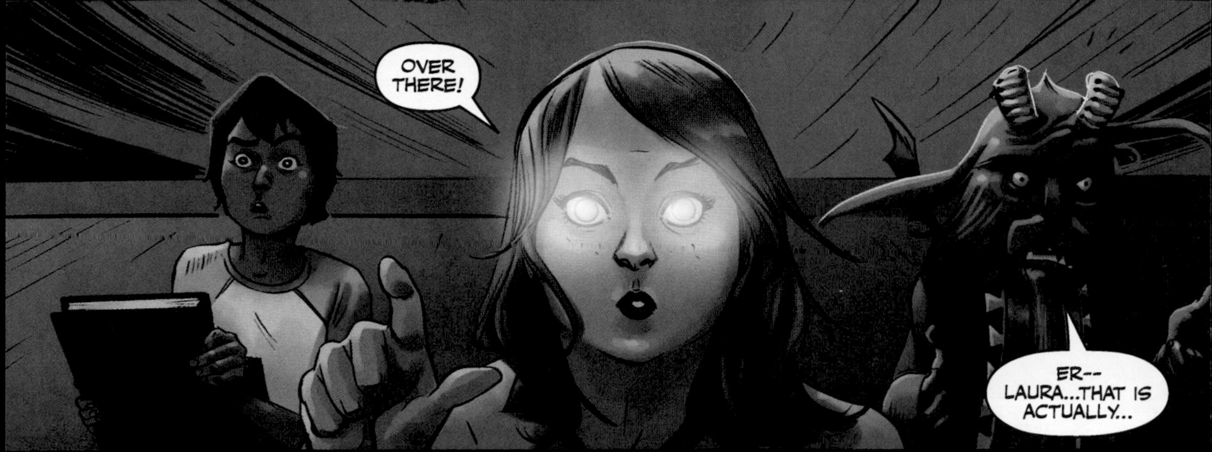
OVER THERE!
ER-- LAURA...THAT IS ACTUALLY...
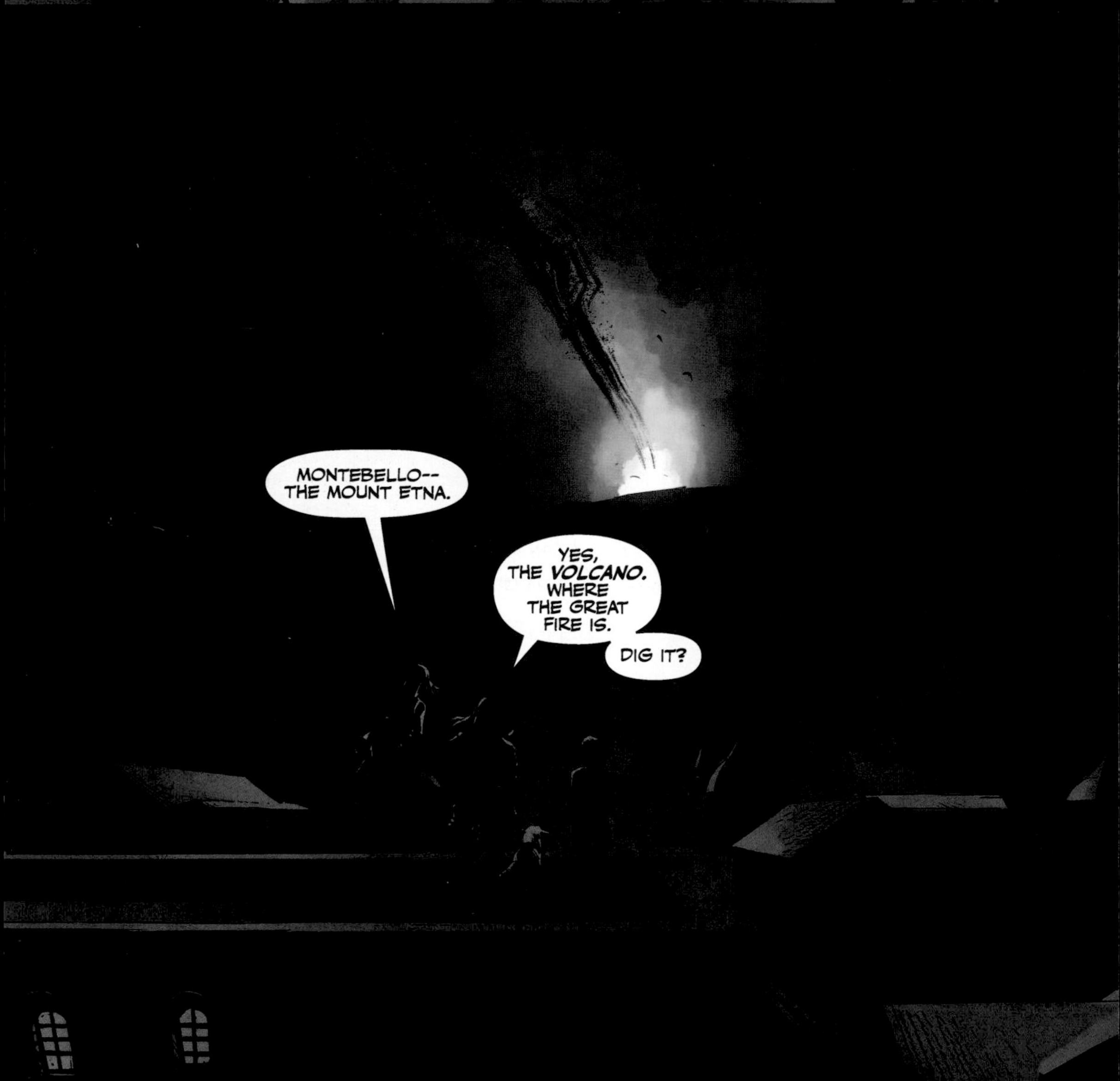
MONTEBELLO-- THE MOUNT ETNA.
YES, THE *VOLCANO.* WHERE THE GREAT FIRE IS.
DIG IT?

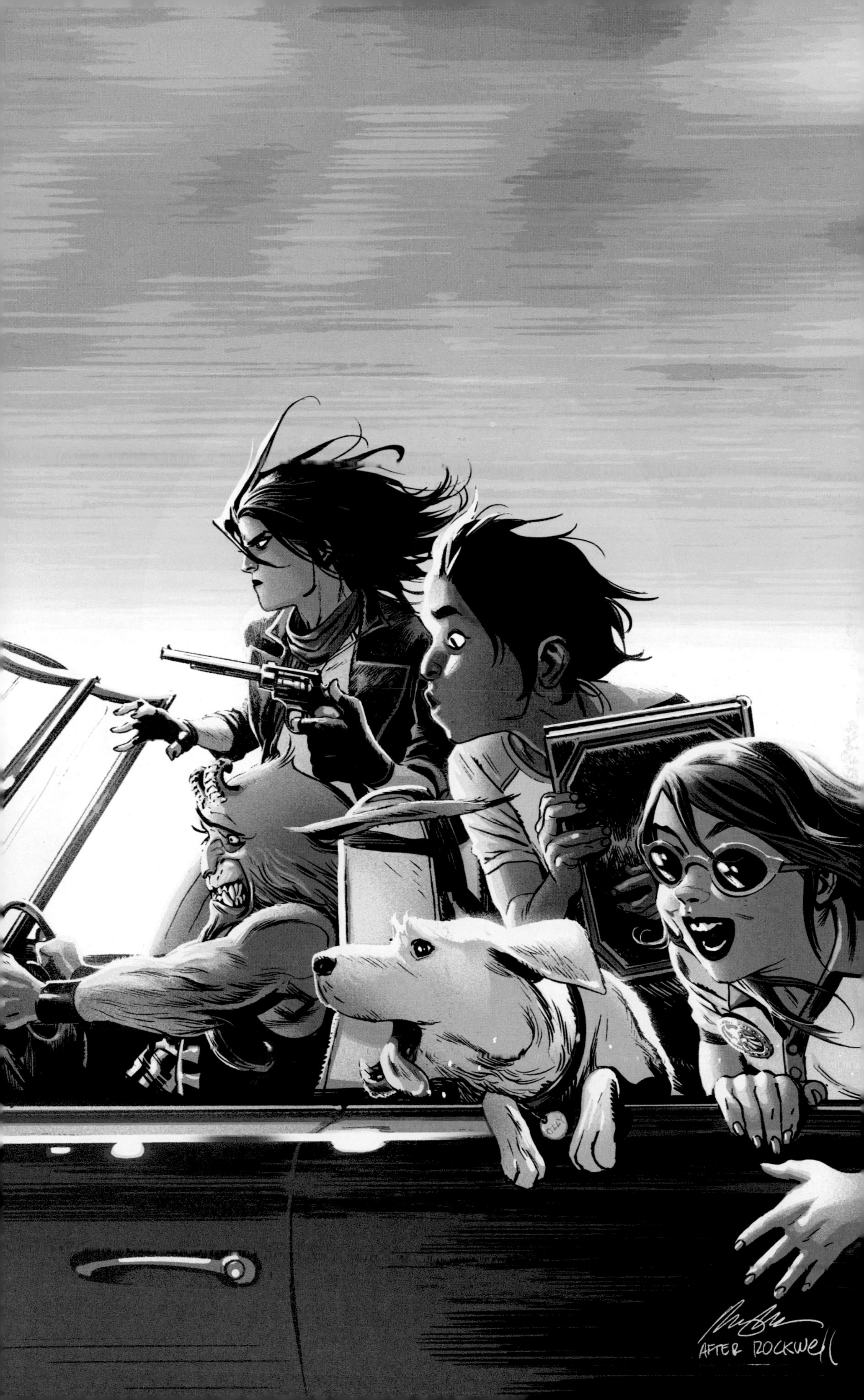
AFTER ROCKWELL

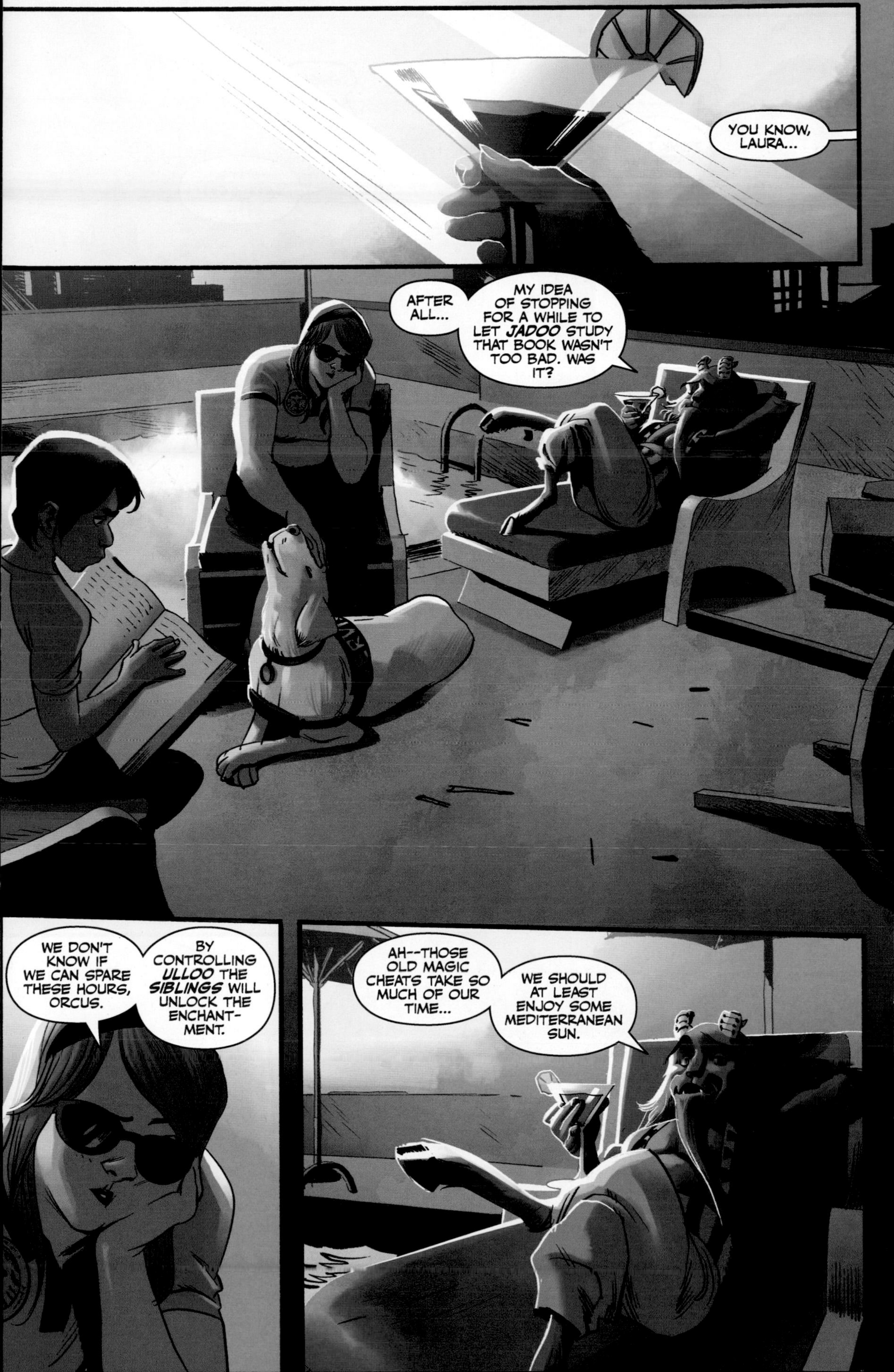
YOU KNOW, LAURA...
AFTER ALL...
MY IDEA OF STOPPING FOR A WHILE TO LET JADOO STUDY THAT BOOK WASN'T TOO BAD. WAS IT?
WE DON'T KNOW IF WE CAN SPARE THESE HOURS, ORCUS.
BY CONTROLLING ULLOO THE SIBLINGS WILL UNLOCK THE ENCHANT-MENT.
AH--THOSE OLD MAGIC CHEATS TAKE SO MUCH OF OUR TIME...
WE SHOULD AT LEAST ENJOY SOME MEDITERRANEAN SUN.

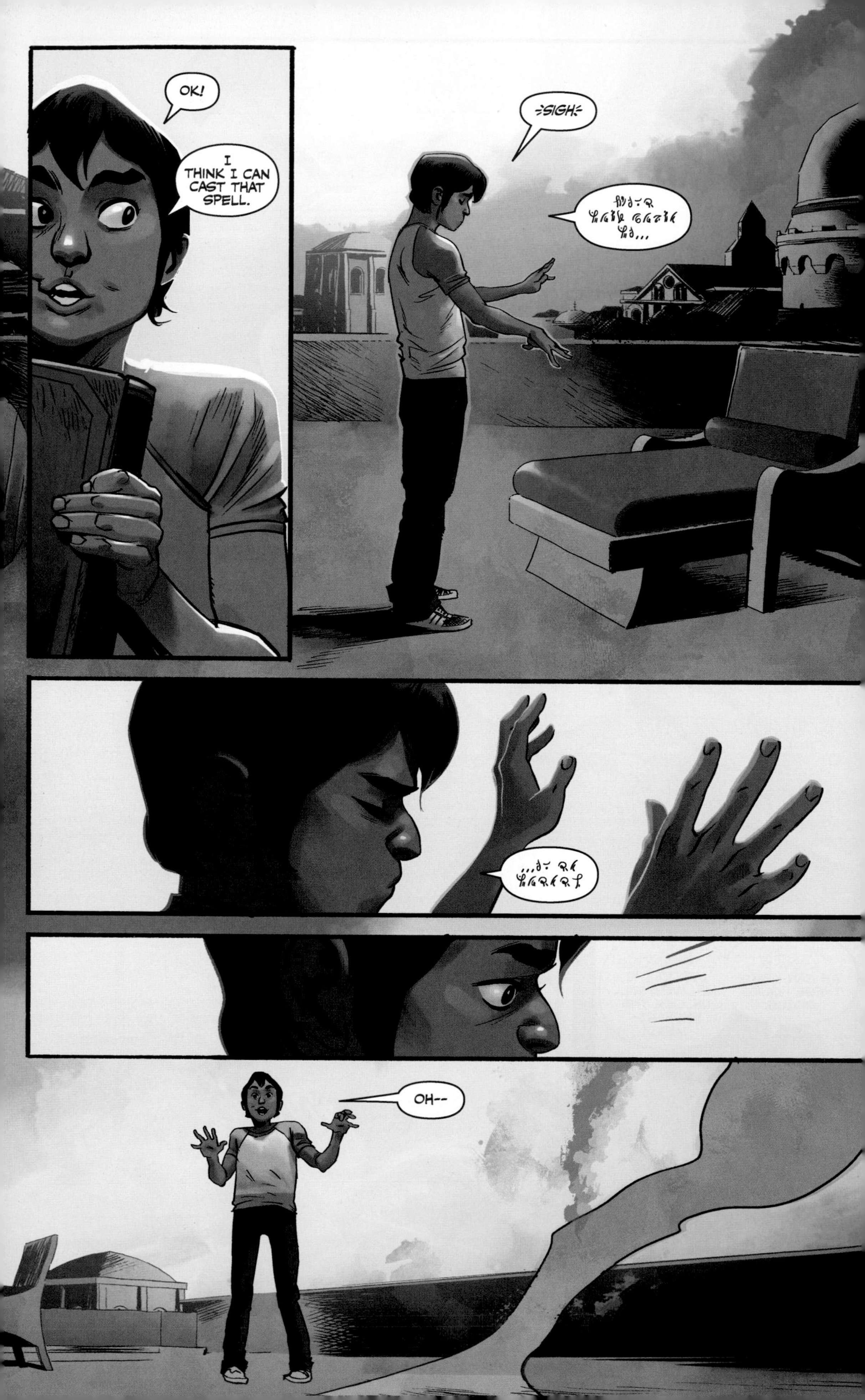
OK!
I THINK I CAN CAST THAT SPELL.
=SIGH=
OH--

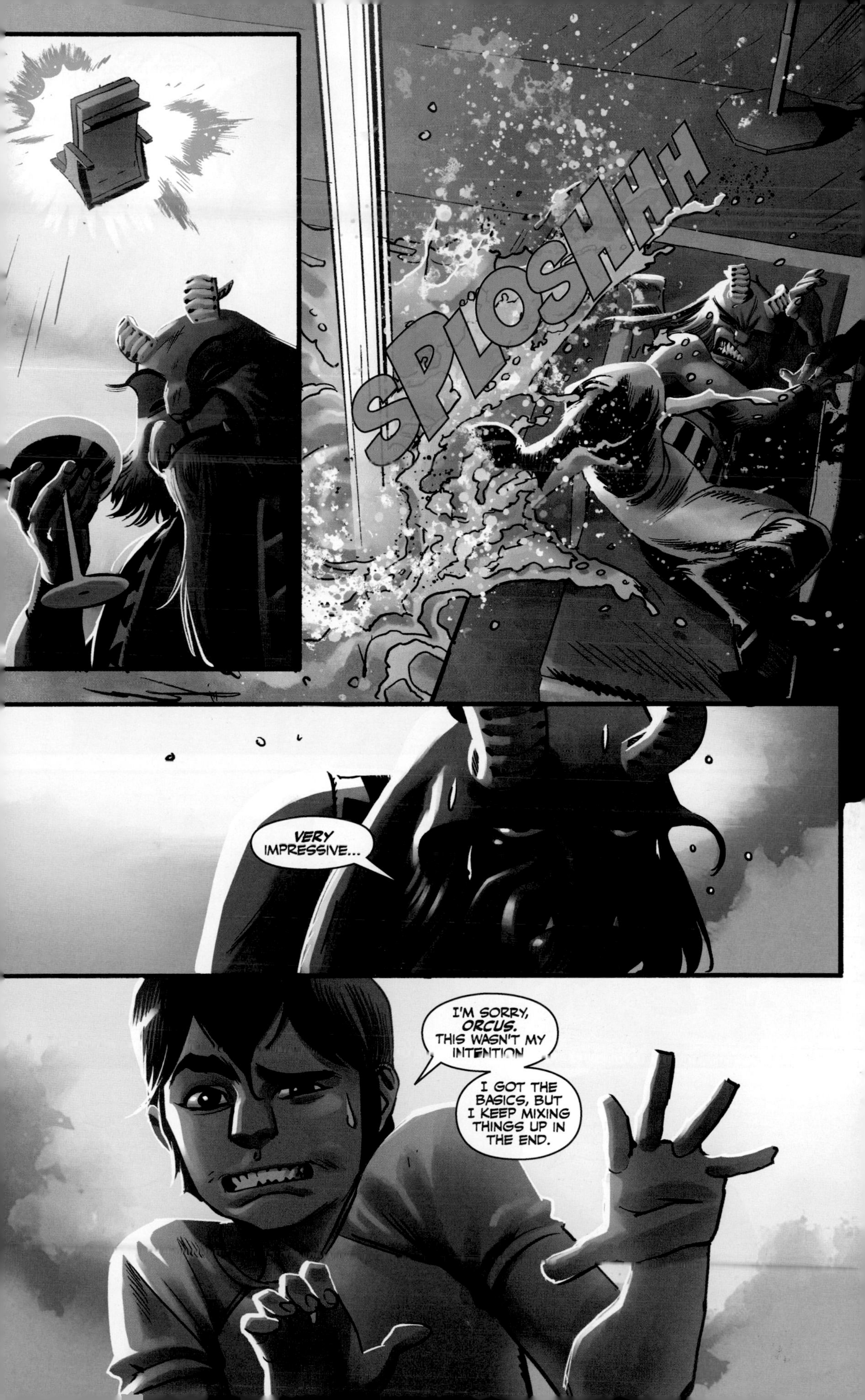
SPLOSHHH
VERY IMPRESSIVE...
I'M SORRY, ORCUS. THIS WASN'T MY INTENTION
I GOT THE BASICS, BUT I KEEP MIXING THINGS UP IN THE END.

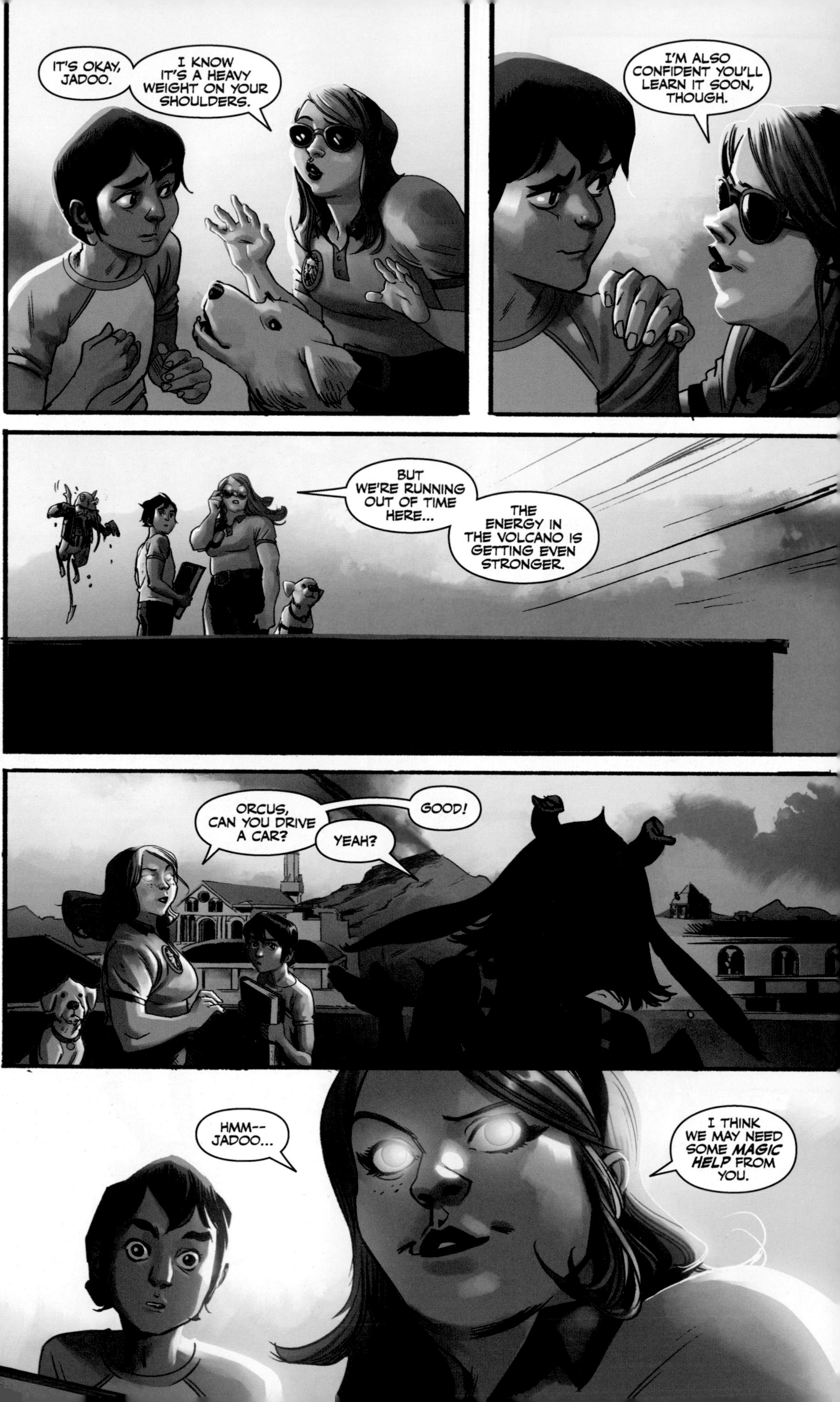
IT'S OKAY, JADOO.
I KNOW IT'S A HEAVY WEIGHT ON YOUR SHOULDERS.
I'M ALSO CONFIDENT YOU'LL LEARN IT SOON, THOUGH.
BUT WE'RE RUNNING OUT OF TIME HERE...
THE ENERGY IN THE VOLCANO IS GETTING EVEN STRONGER.
ORCUS, CAN YOU DRIVE A CAR?
YEAH?
GOOD!
HMM-- JADOO...
I THINK WE MAY NEED SOME *MAGIC HELP* FROM YOU.

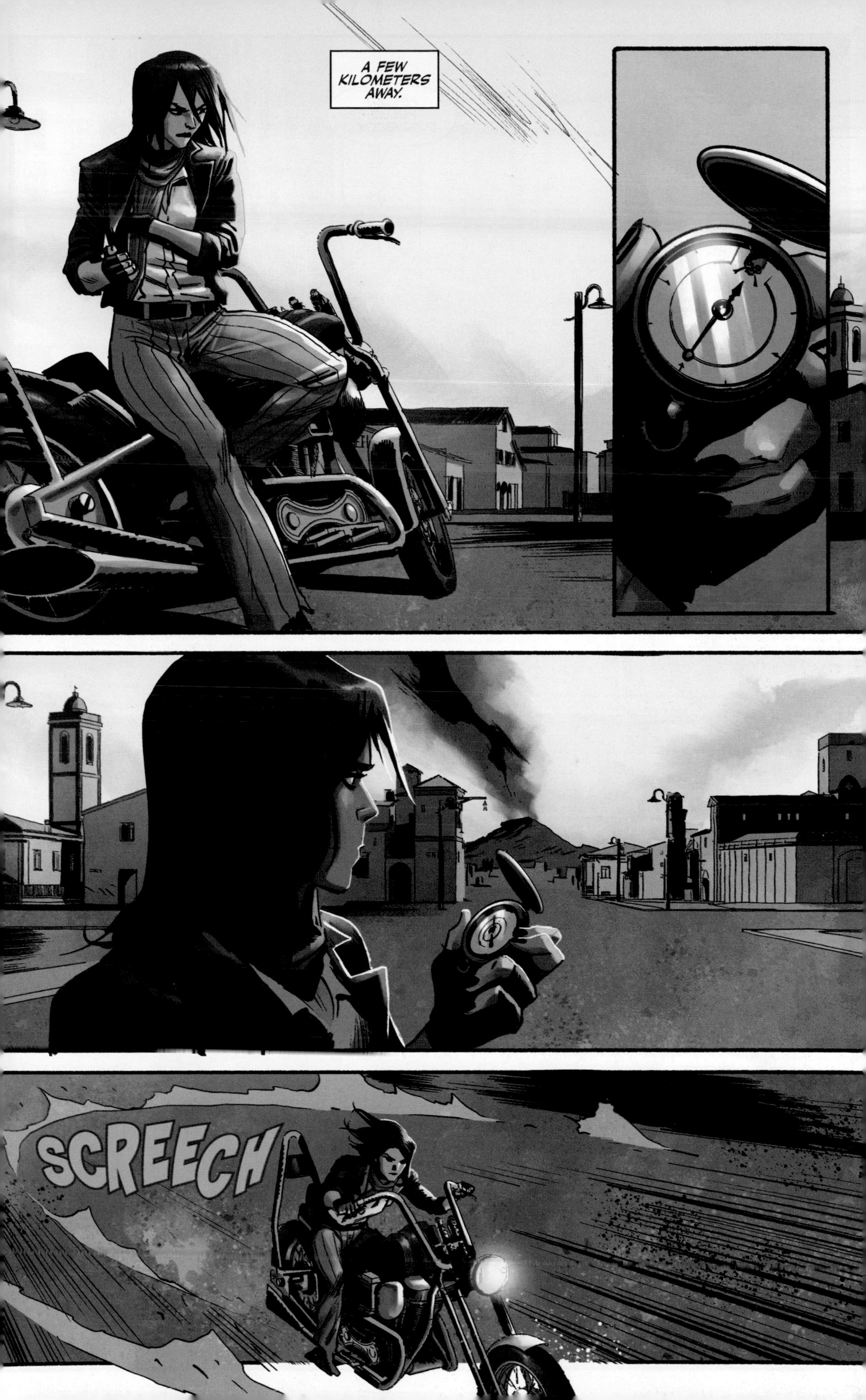
A FEW KILOMETERS AWAY.
SCREECH

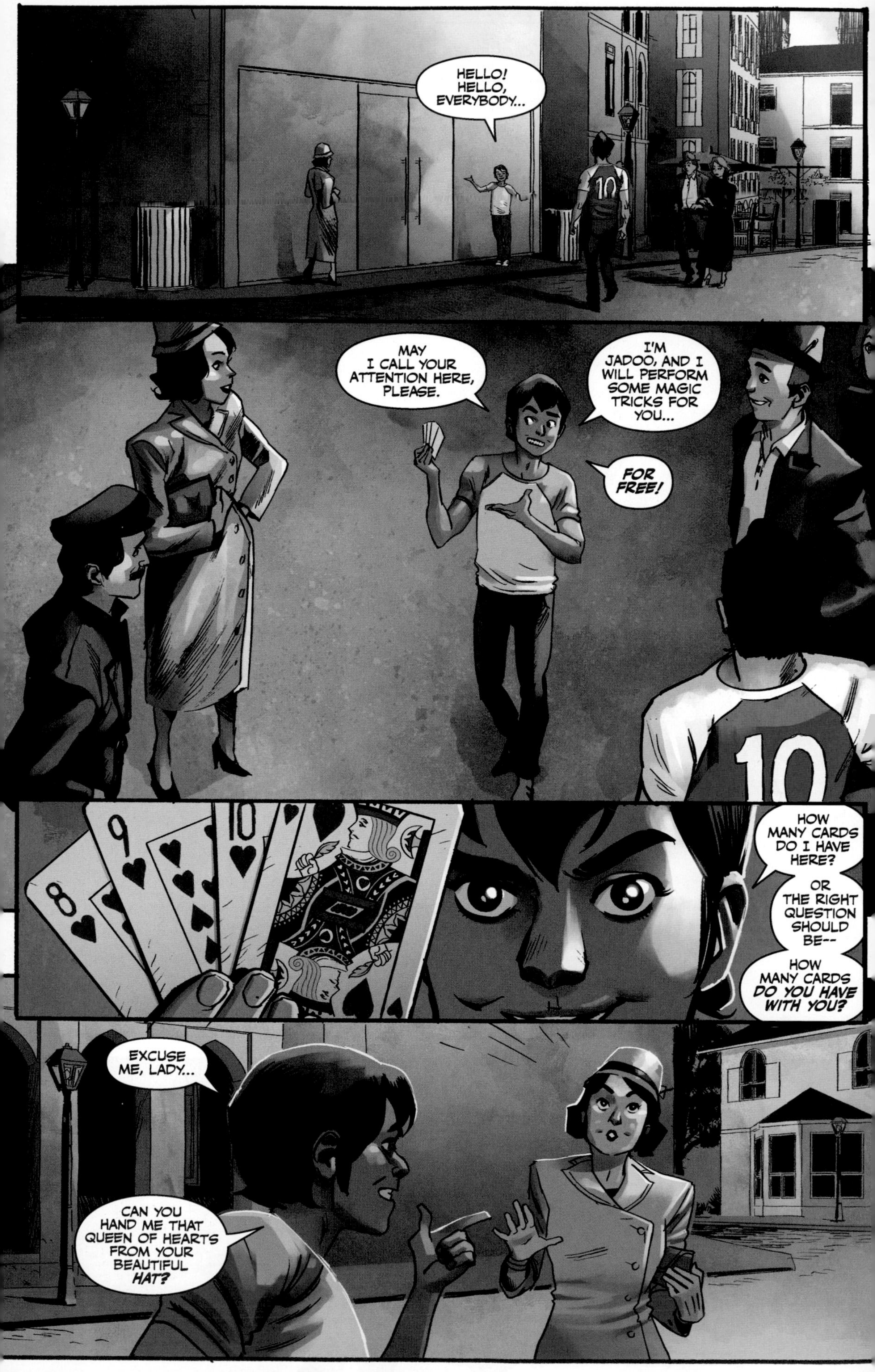
HELLO! HELLO, EVERYBODY...
MAY I CALL YOUR ATTENTION HERE, PLEASE.
I'M JADOO, AND I WILL PERFORM SOME MAGIC TRICKS FOR YOU...
FOR FREE!
10
HOW MANY CARDS DO I HAVE HERE?
OR THE RIGHT QUESTION SHOULD BE--
HOW MANY CARDS DO YOU HAVE WITH YOU?
EXCUSE ME, LADY...
CAN YOU HAND ME THAT QUEEN OF HEARTS FROM YOUR BEAUTIFUL HAT?

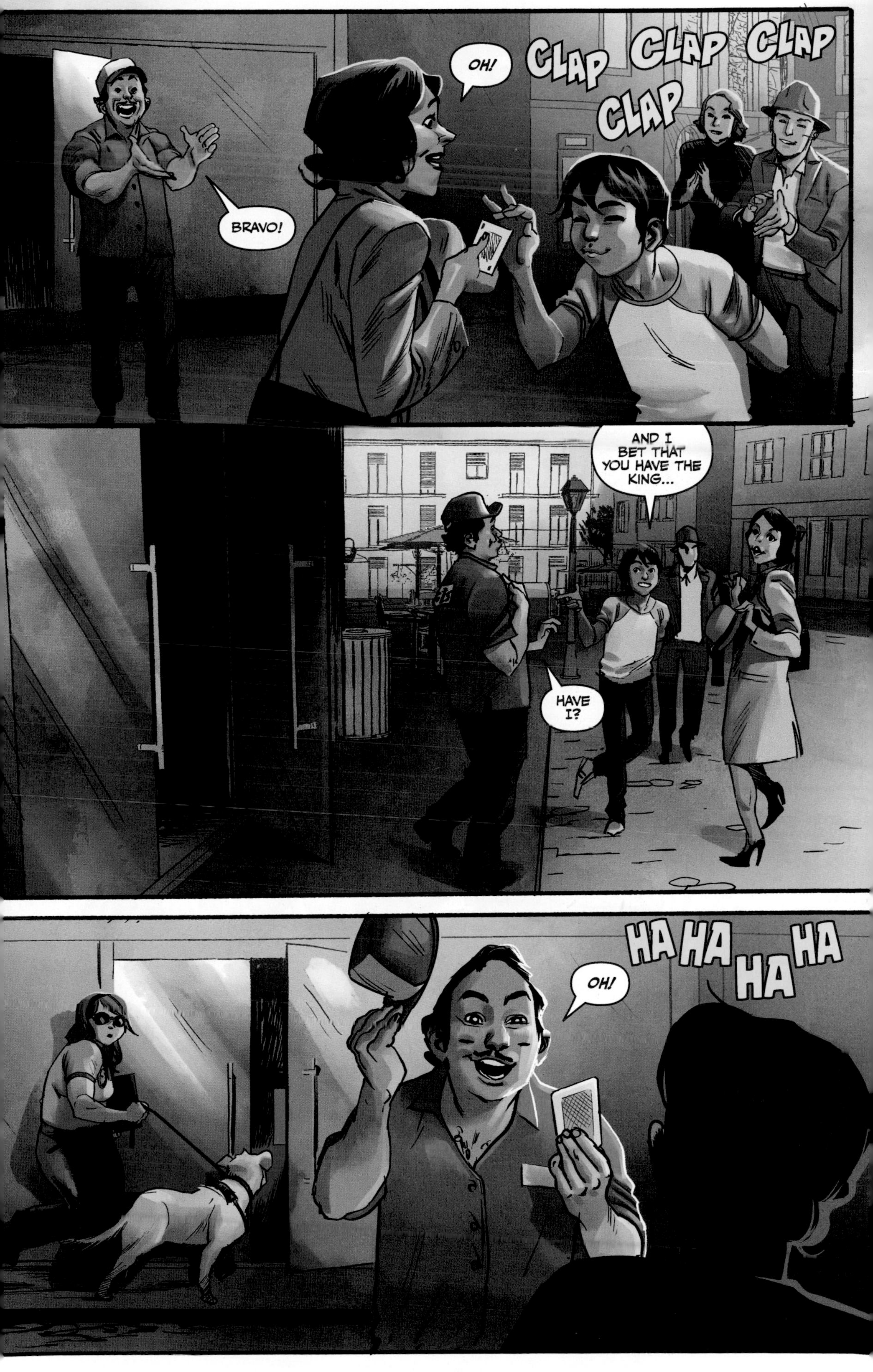
OH!
CLAP CLAP CLAP
CLAP
BRAVO!
AND I BET THAT YOU HAVE THE KING...
HAVE I?
OH!
HA HA HA HA HA

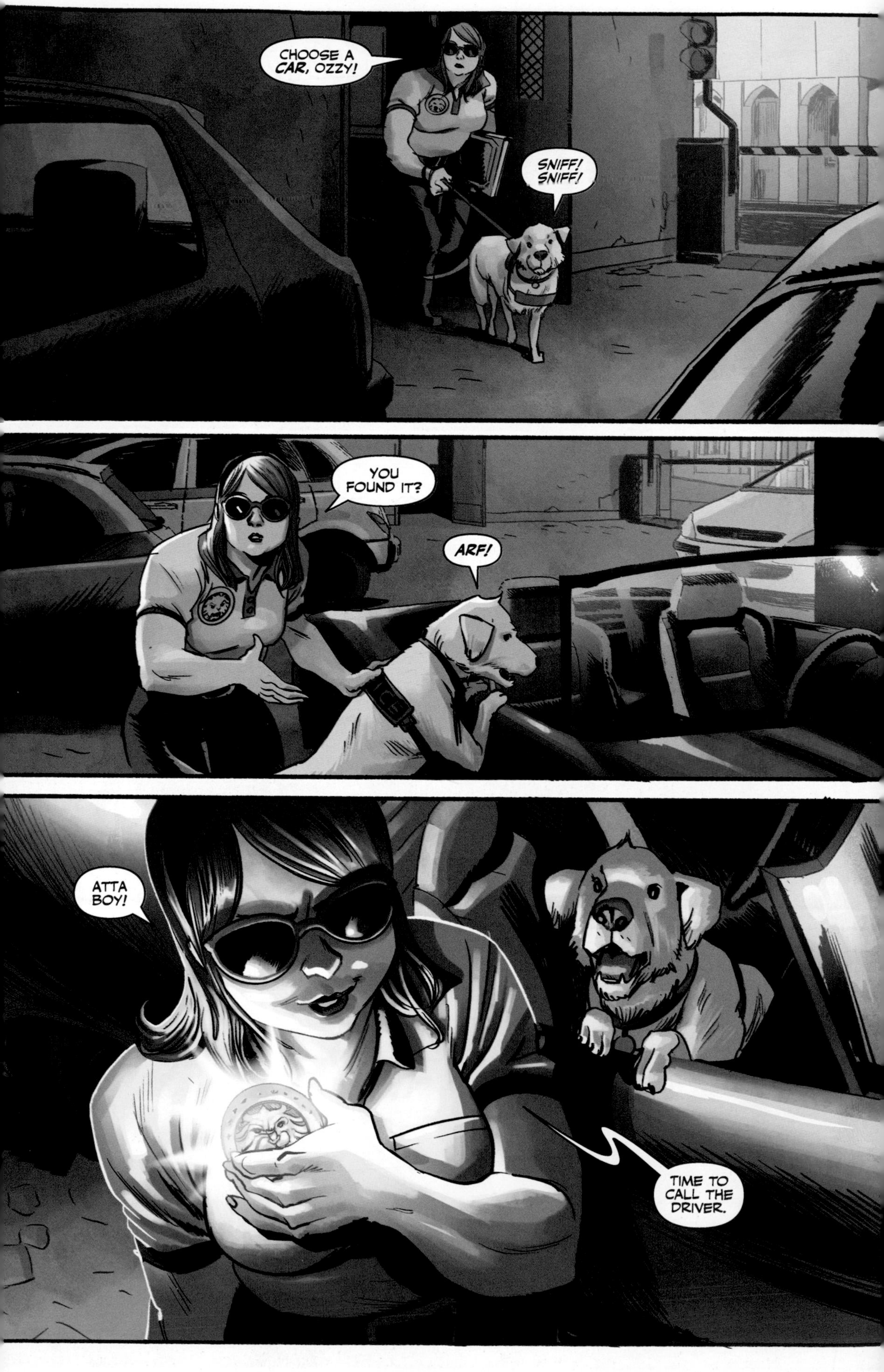

CHOOSE A CAR, OZZY!
SNIFF! SNIFF!
YOU FOUND IT?
ARF!
ATTA BOY!
TIME TO CALL THE DRIVER.

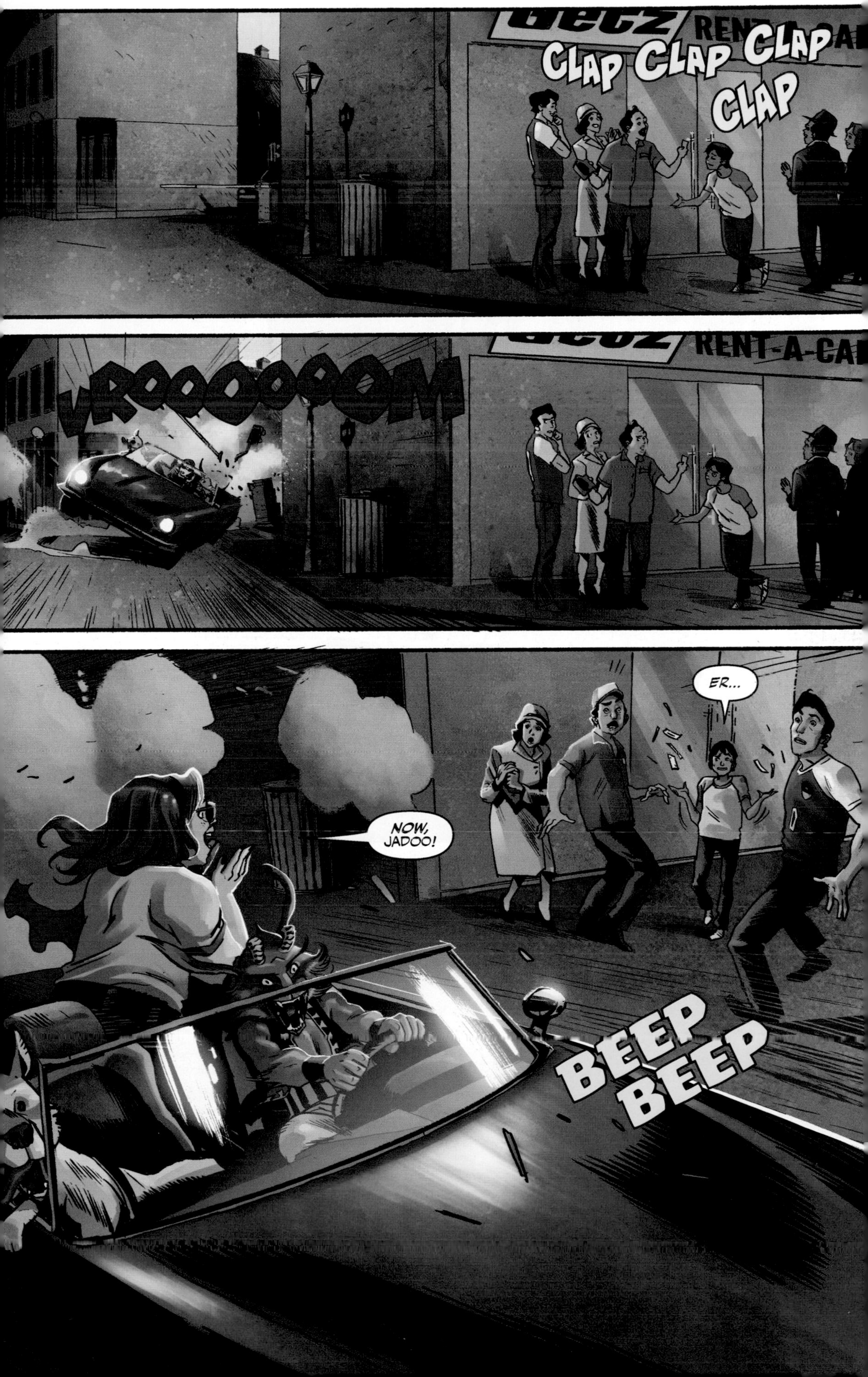
GETZ RENT-A-CAR
CLAP CLAP CLAP
CLAP
VROOOOOOM
GETZ RENT-A-CAR
ER...
NOW, JADOO!
BEEP BEEP

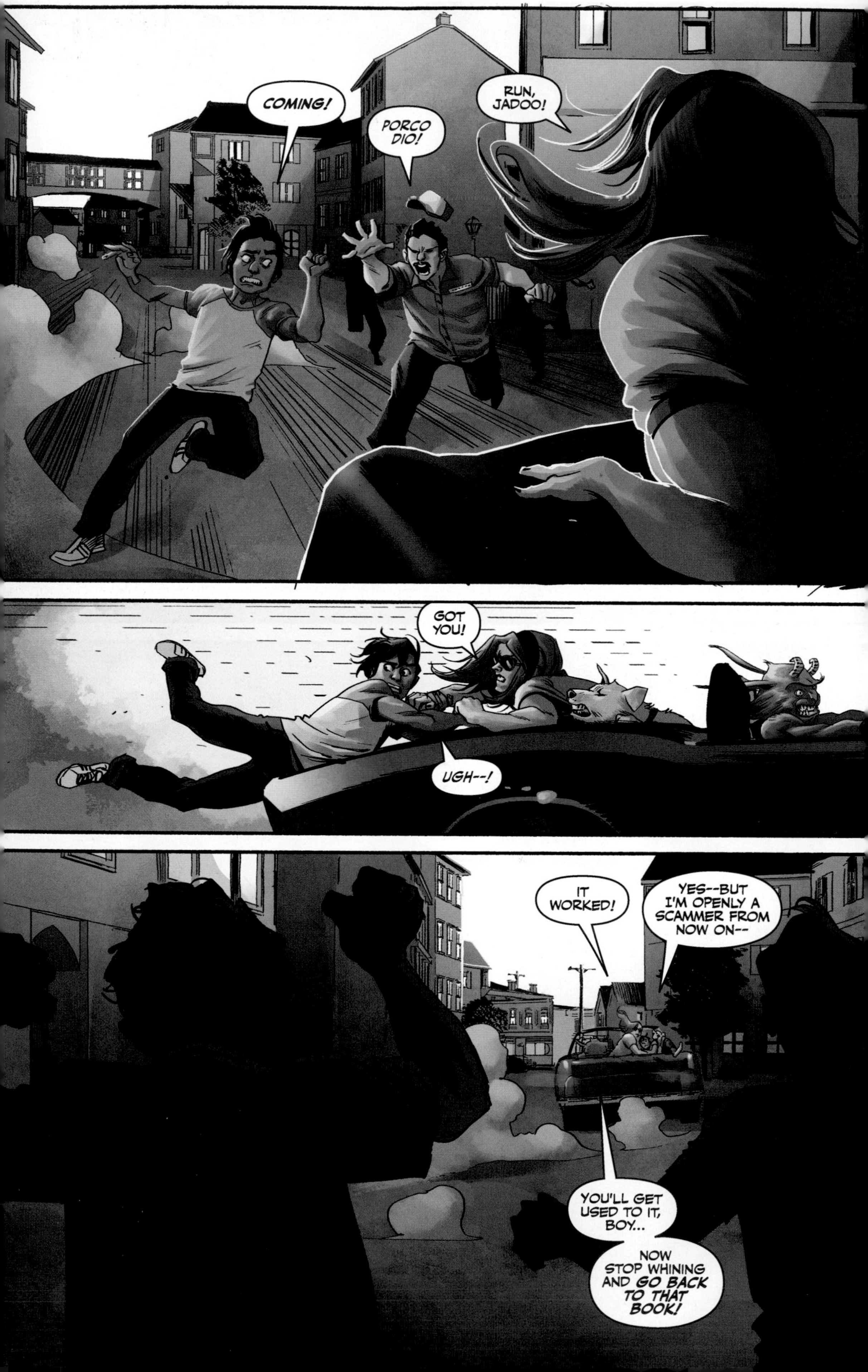
COMING!
PORCO DIO!
RUN, JADOO!
GOT YOU!
UGH--!
IT WORKED!
YES--BUT I'M OPENLY A SCAMMER FROM NOW ON--
YOU'LL GET USED TO IT, BOY...
NOW STOP WHINING AND GO BACK TO THAT BOOK!

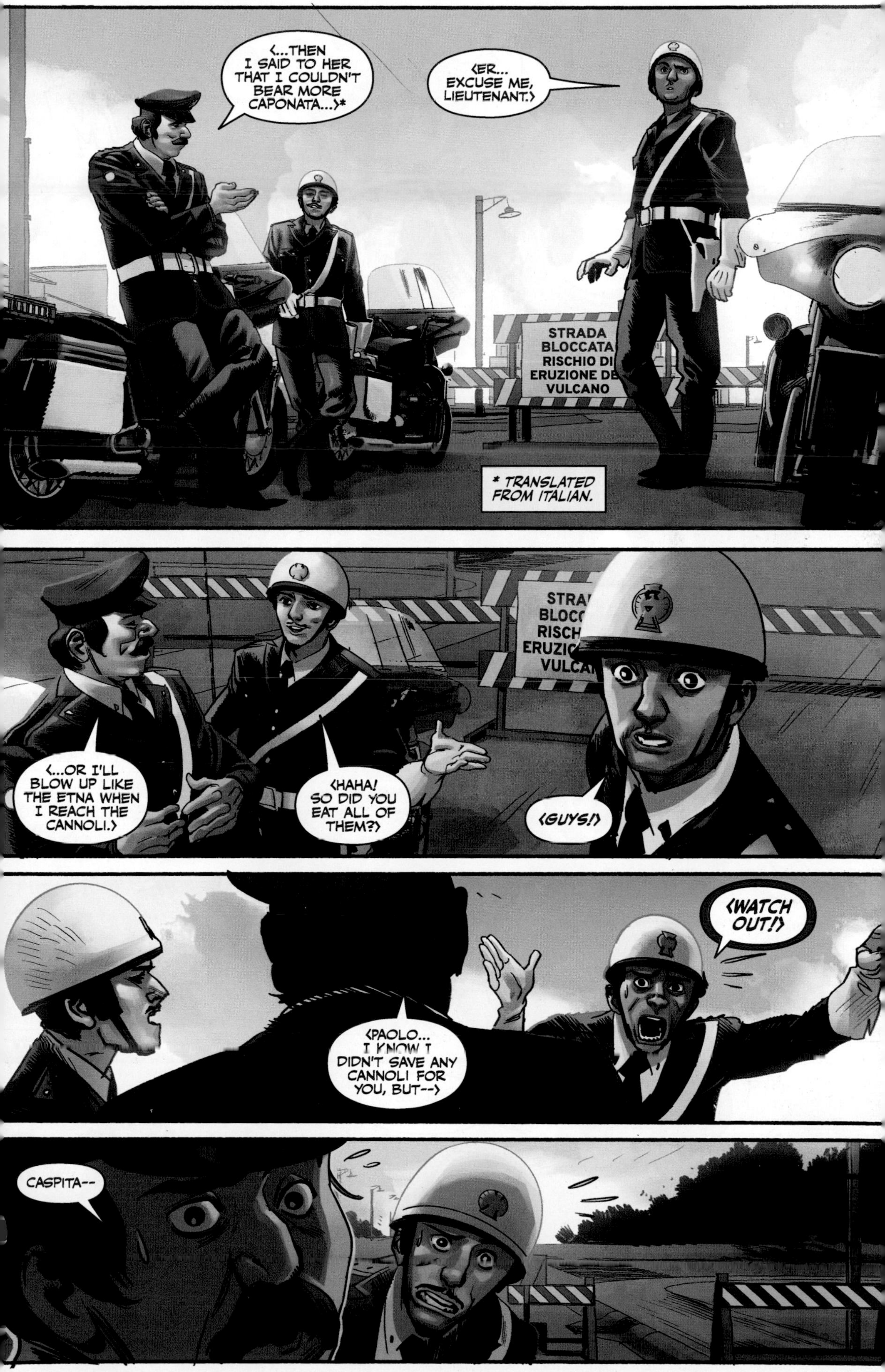
‹...THEN I SAID TO HER THAT I COULDN'T BEAR MORE CAPONATA...›*
‹ER... EXCUSE ME, LIEUTENANT.›
STRADA BLOCCATA RISCHIO DI ERUZIONE DE VULCANO
* TRANSLATED FROM ITALIAN.
‹...OR I'LL BLOW UP LIKE THE ETNA WHEN I REACH THE CANNOLI.›
‹HAHA! SO DID YOU EAT ALL OF THEM?›
‹GUYS!›
‹PAOLO... I KNOW I DIDN'T SAVE ANY CANNOLI FOR YOU, BUT--›
‹WATCH OUT!›
CASPITA--

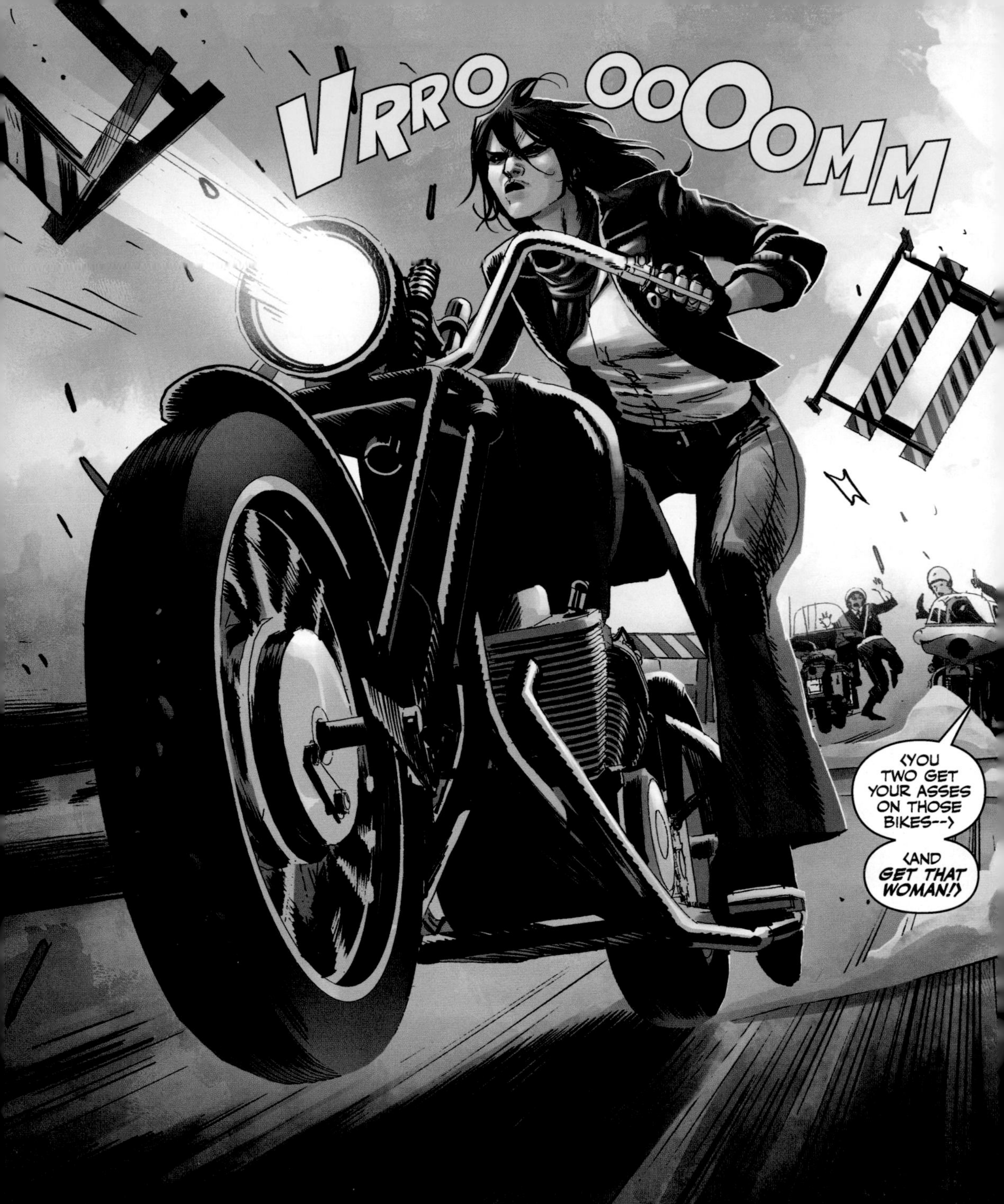
VRROOOOOOMM
‹YOU TWO GET YOUR ASSES ON THOSE BIKES--›
‹AND *GET THAT WOMAN!*›

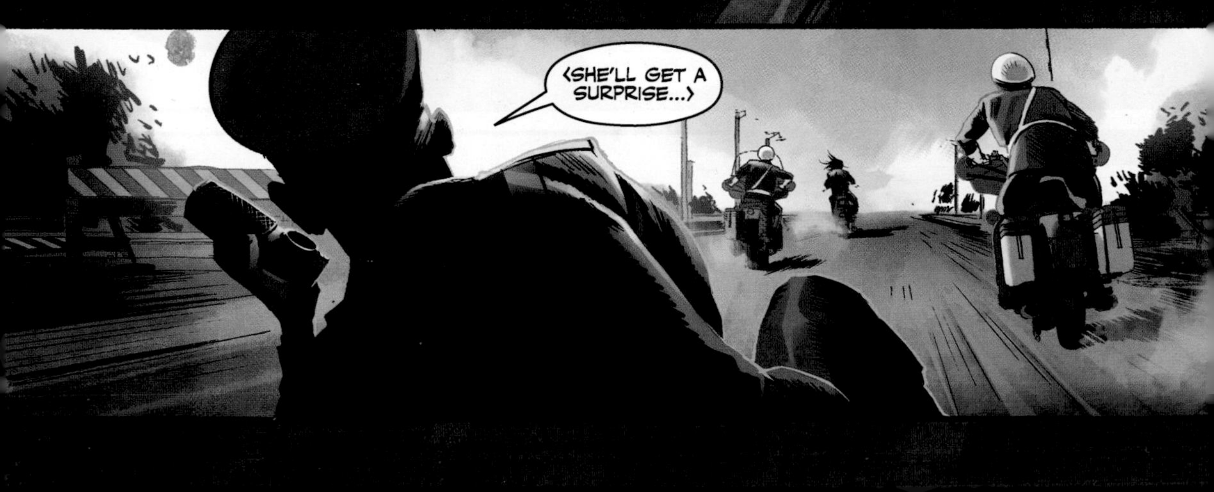
‹SHE'LL GET A SURPRISE...›

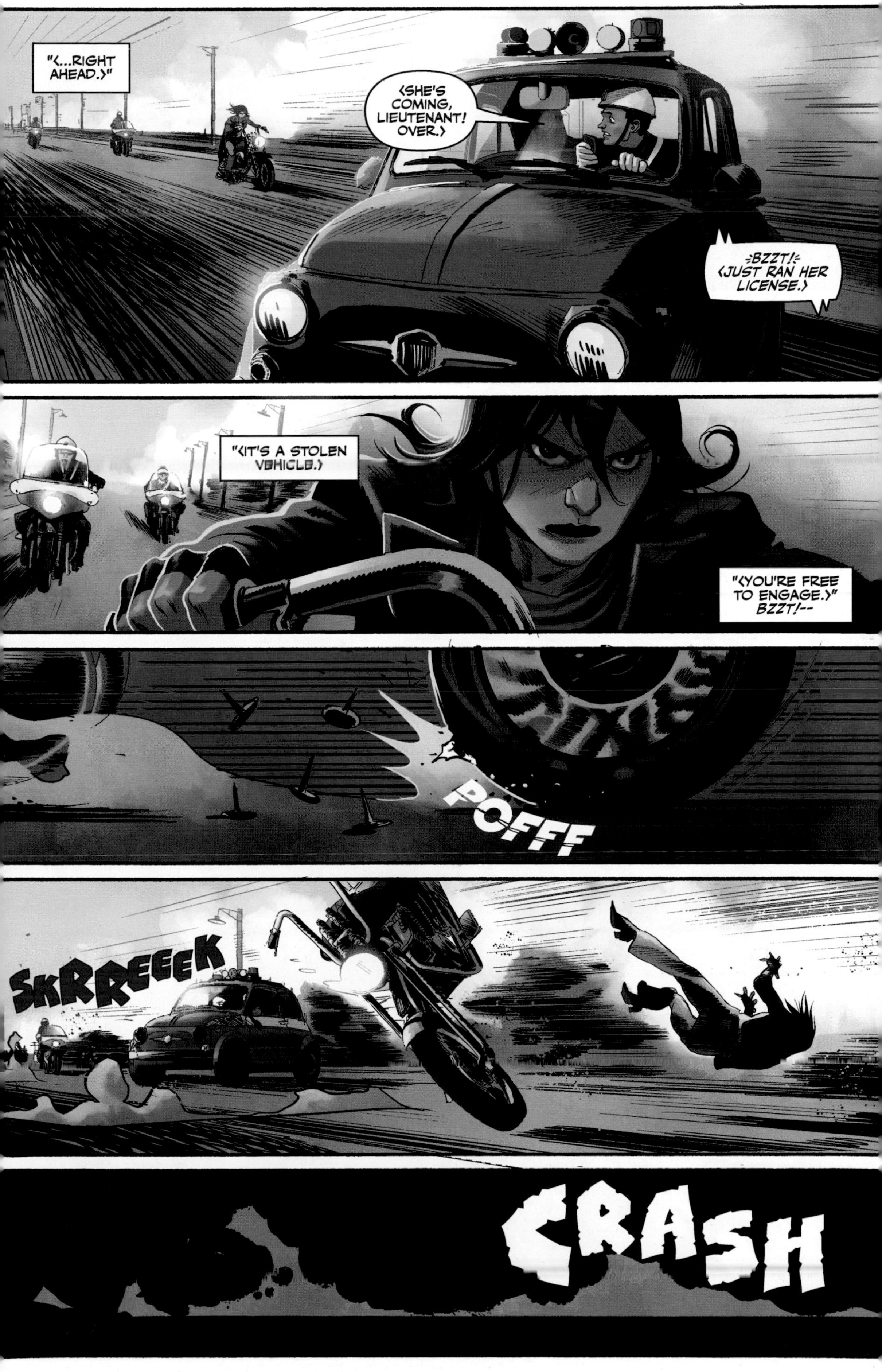
"‹...RIGHT AHEAD.›"
‹SHE'S COMING, LIEUTENANT! OVER.›
=BZZT!= ‹JUST RAN HER LICENSE.›
"‹IT'S A STOLEN VEHICLE.›
"‹YOU'RE FREE TO ENGAGE.›" BZZT!--
POFFF
SKRREEEK
CRASH

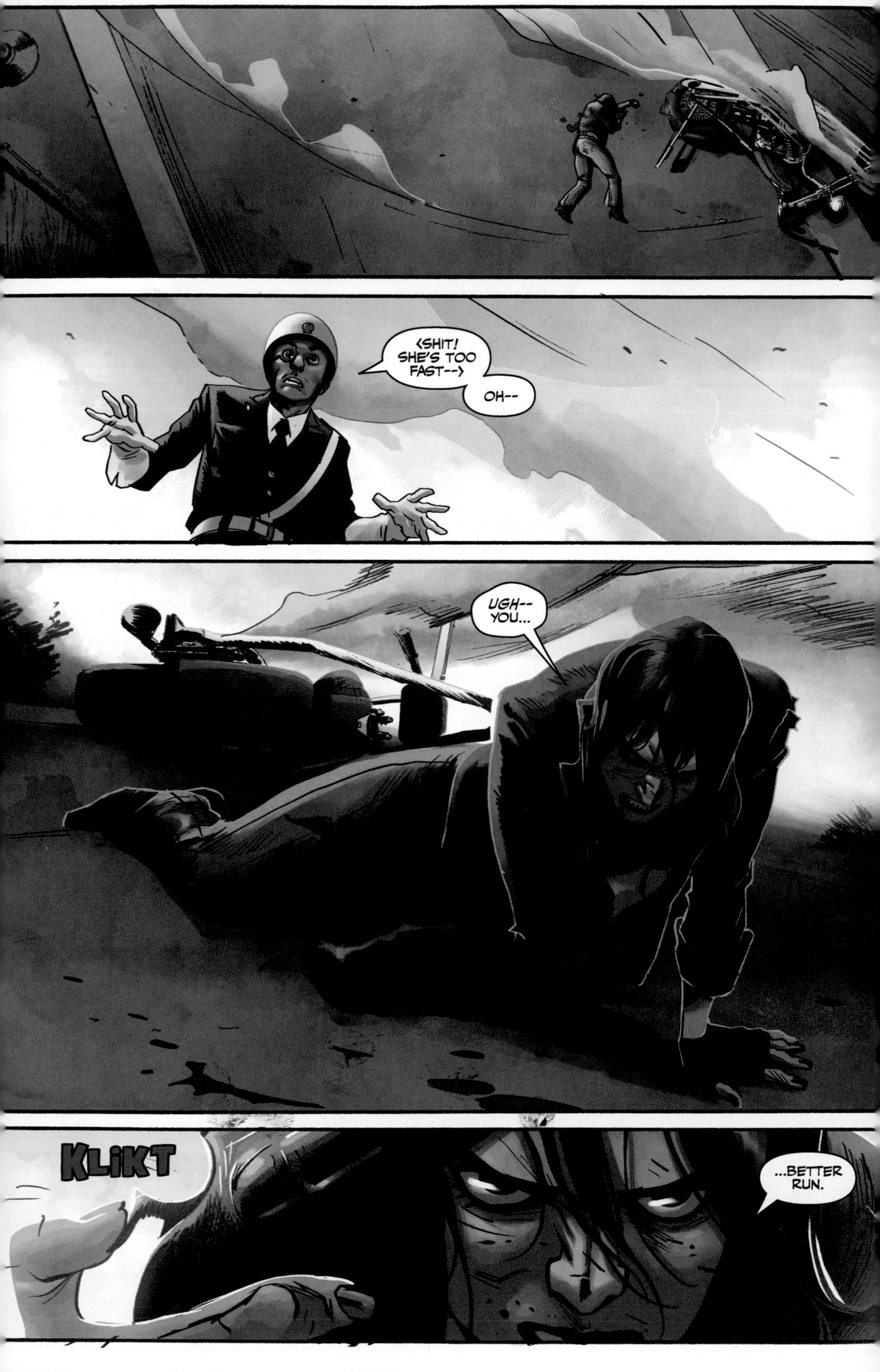
<SHIT! SHE'S TOO FAST-->
OH--
UGH-- YOU...
KLIKT
...BETTER RUN.

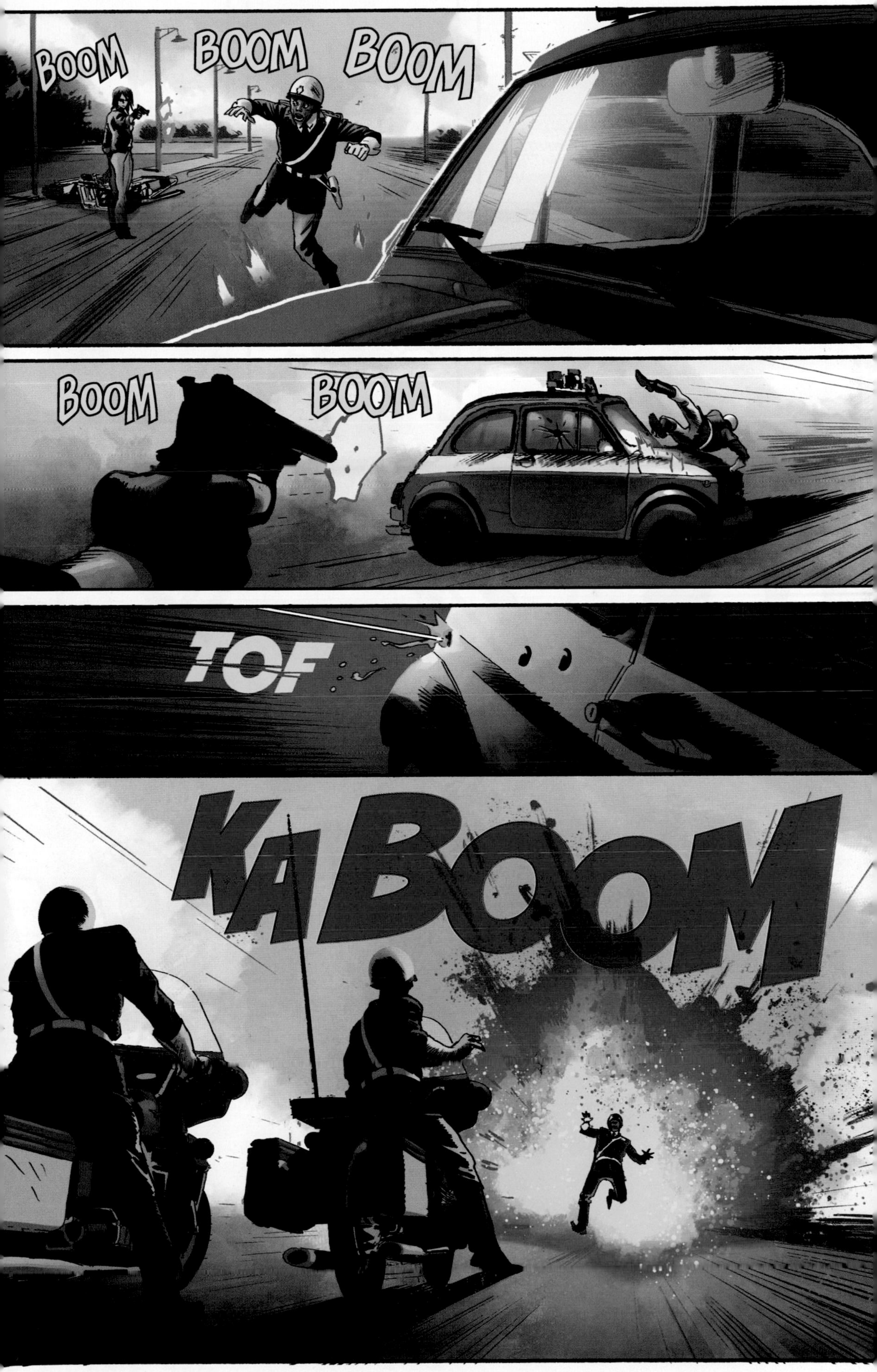
BOOM
BOOM
BOOM
BOOM
BOOM
TOF
KABOOM

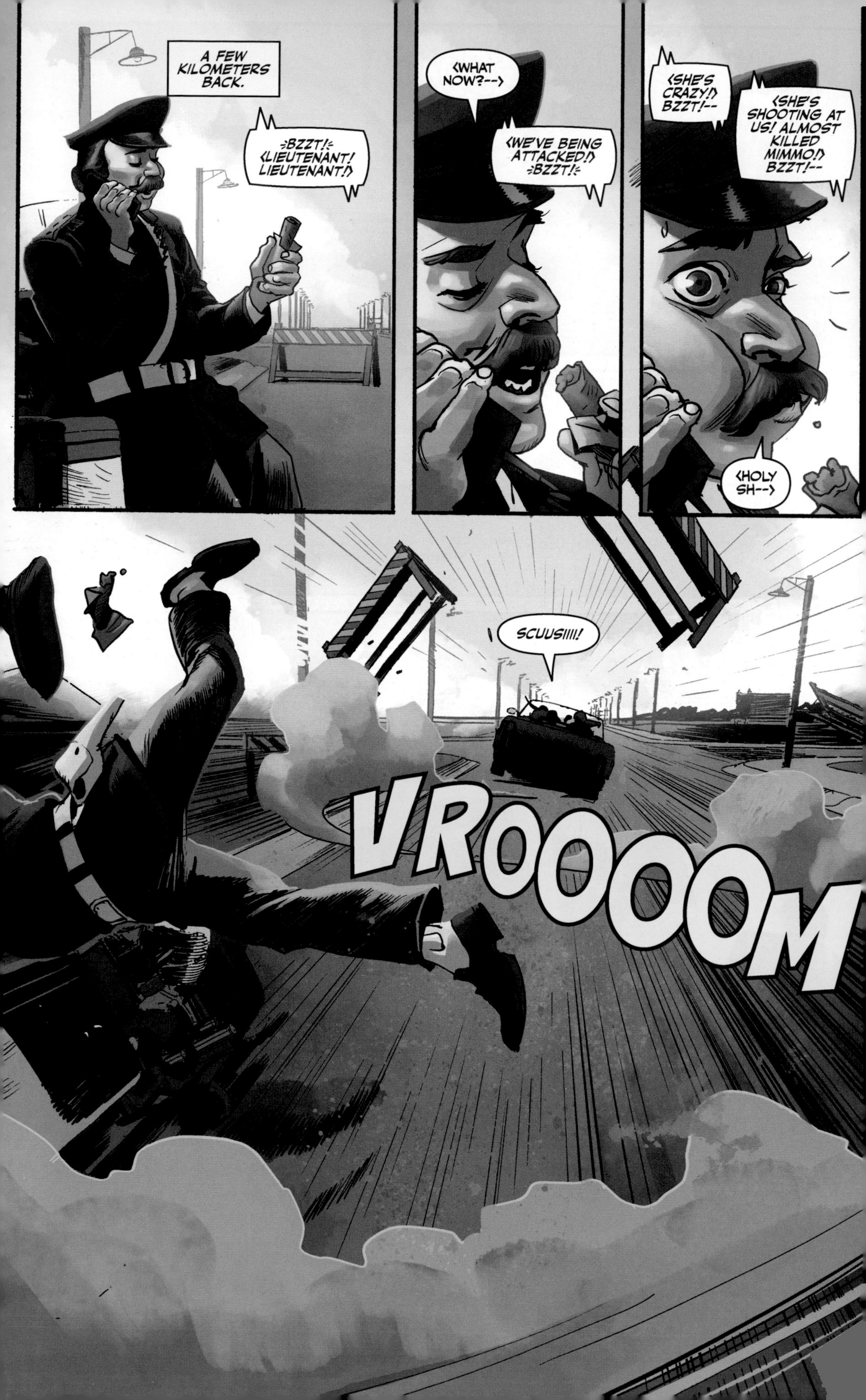
A FEW KILOMETERS BACK.
>BZZT!< <LIEUTENANT! LIEUTENANT!>
<WHAT NOW?-->
<WE'VE BEING ATTACKED!> >BZZT!<
<SHE'S CRAZY!> BZZT!--
<SHE'S SHOOTING AT US! ALMOST KILLED MIMMO!> BZZT!--
<HOLY SH-->
SCUUSIIII!
VROOOOOM

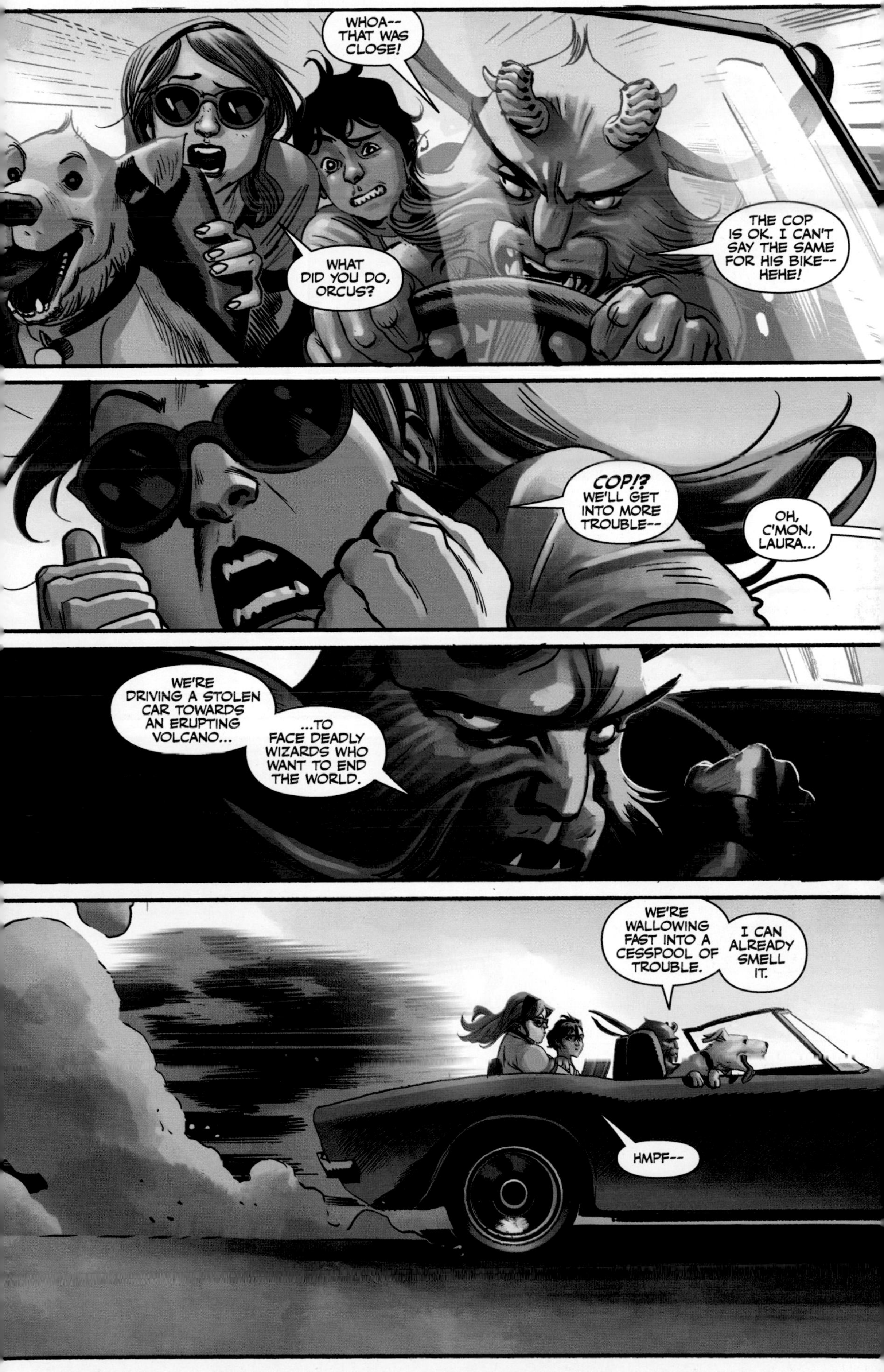
WHOA-- THAT WAS CLOSE!
WHAT DID YOU DO, ORCUS?
THE COP IS OK. I CAN'T SAY THE SAME FOR HIS BIKE-- HEHE!
COP!? WE'LL GET INTO MORE TROUBLE--
OH, C'MON, LAURA...
WE'RE DRIVING A STOLEN CAR TOWARDS AN ERUPTING VOLCANO...
...TO FACE DEADLY WIZARDS WHO WANT TO END THE WORLD.
WE'RE WALLOWING FAST INTO A CESSPOOL OF TROUBLE.
I CAN ALREADY SMELL IT.
HMPF--

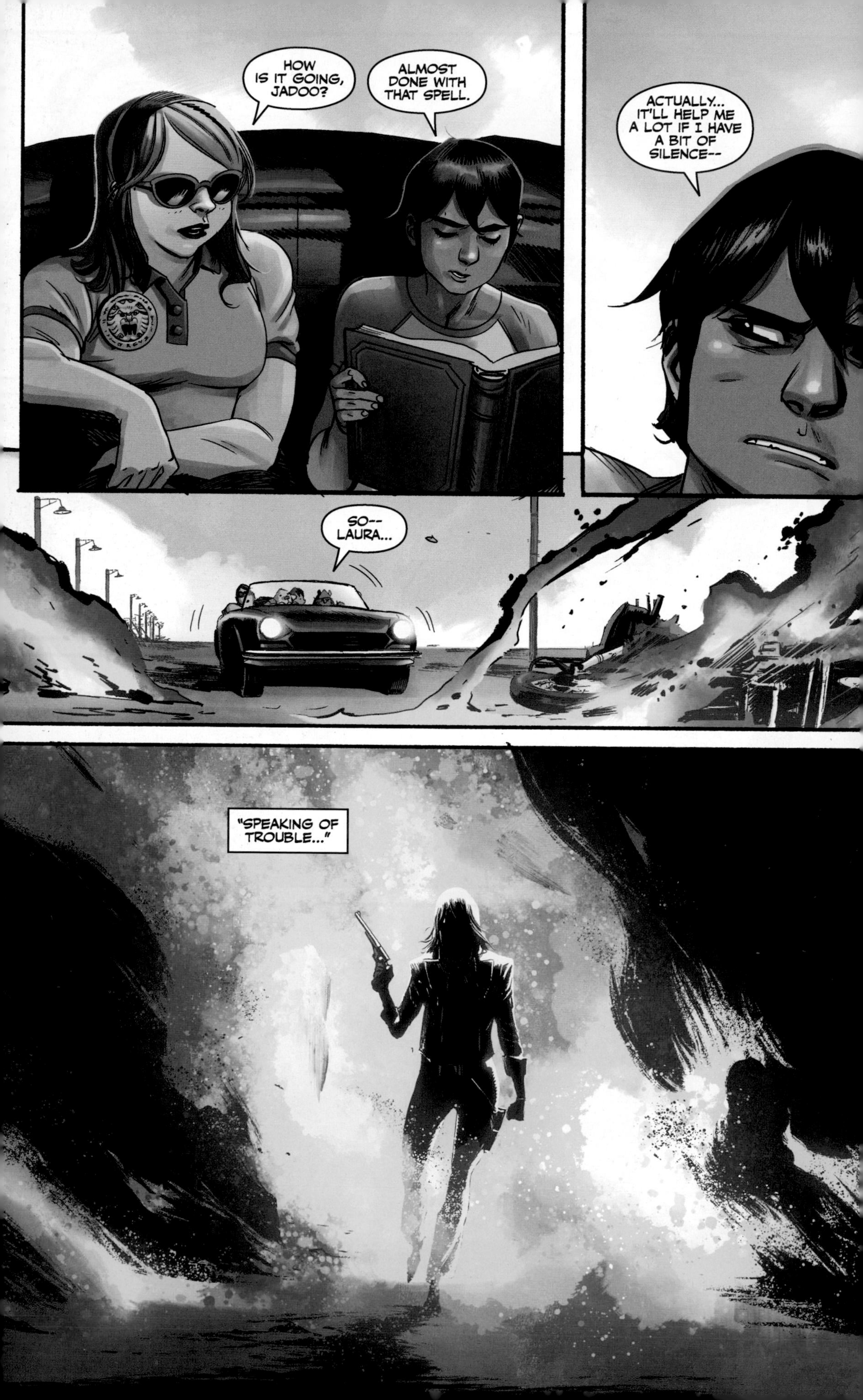
HOW IS IT GOING, JADOO?
ALMOST DONE WITH THAT SPELL.
ACTUALLY... IT'LL HELP ME A LOT IF I HAVE A BIT OF SILENCE--
SO-- LAURA...
"SPEAKING OF TROUBLE..."

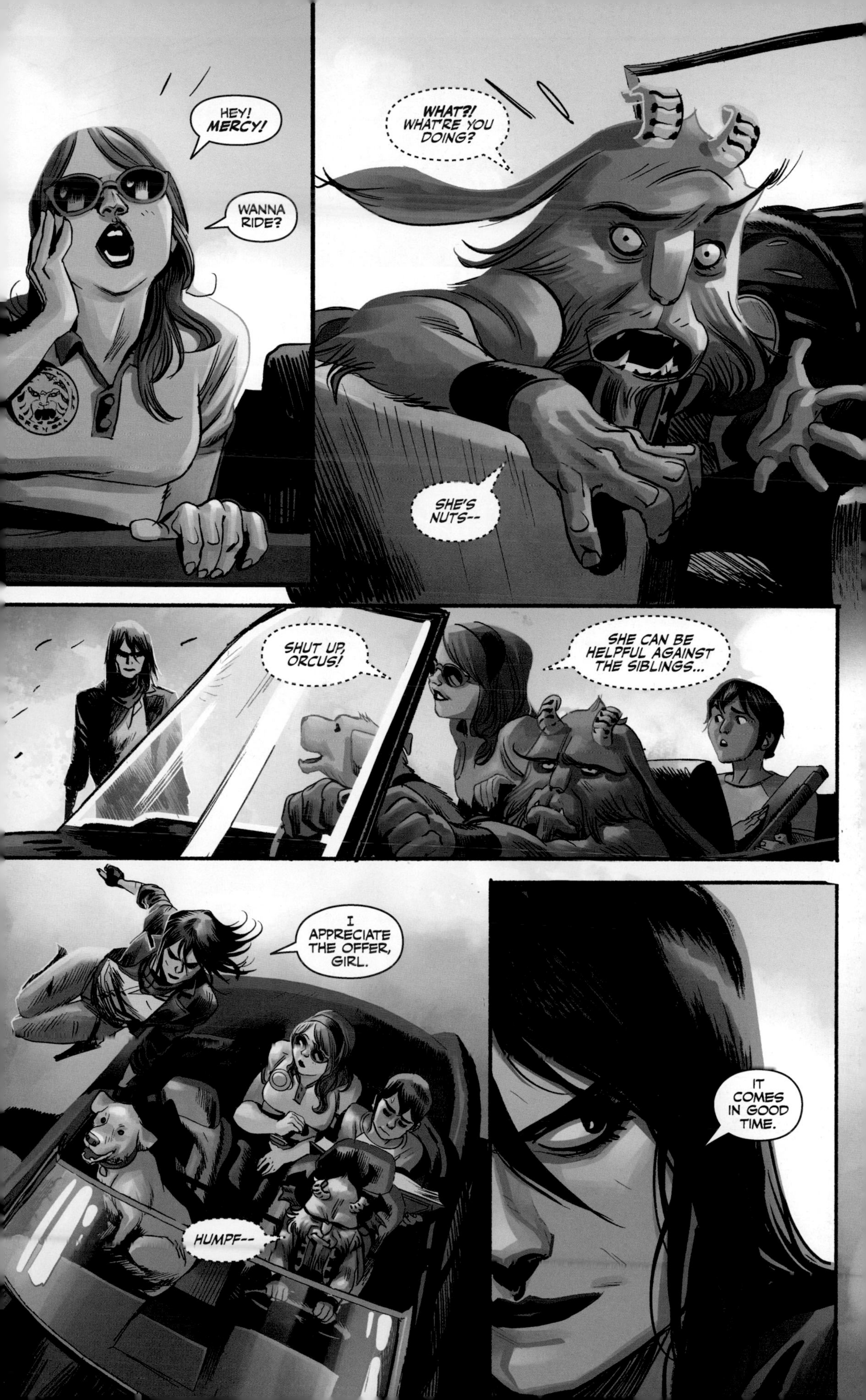
HEY! MERCY!
WANNA RIDE?
WHAT?! WHAT'RE YOU DOING?
SHE'S NUTS--
SHUT UP, ORCUS!
SHE CAN BE HELPFUL AGAINST THE SIBLINGS...
I APPRECIATE THE OFFER, GIRL.
HUMPF--
IT COMES IN GOOD TIME.

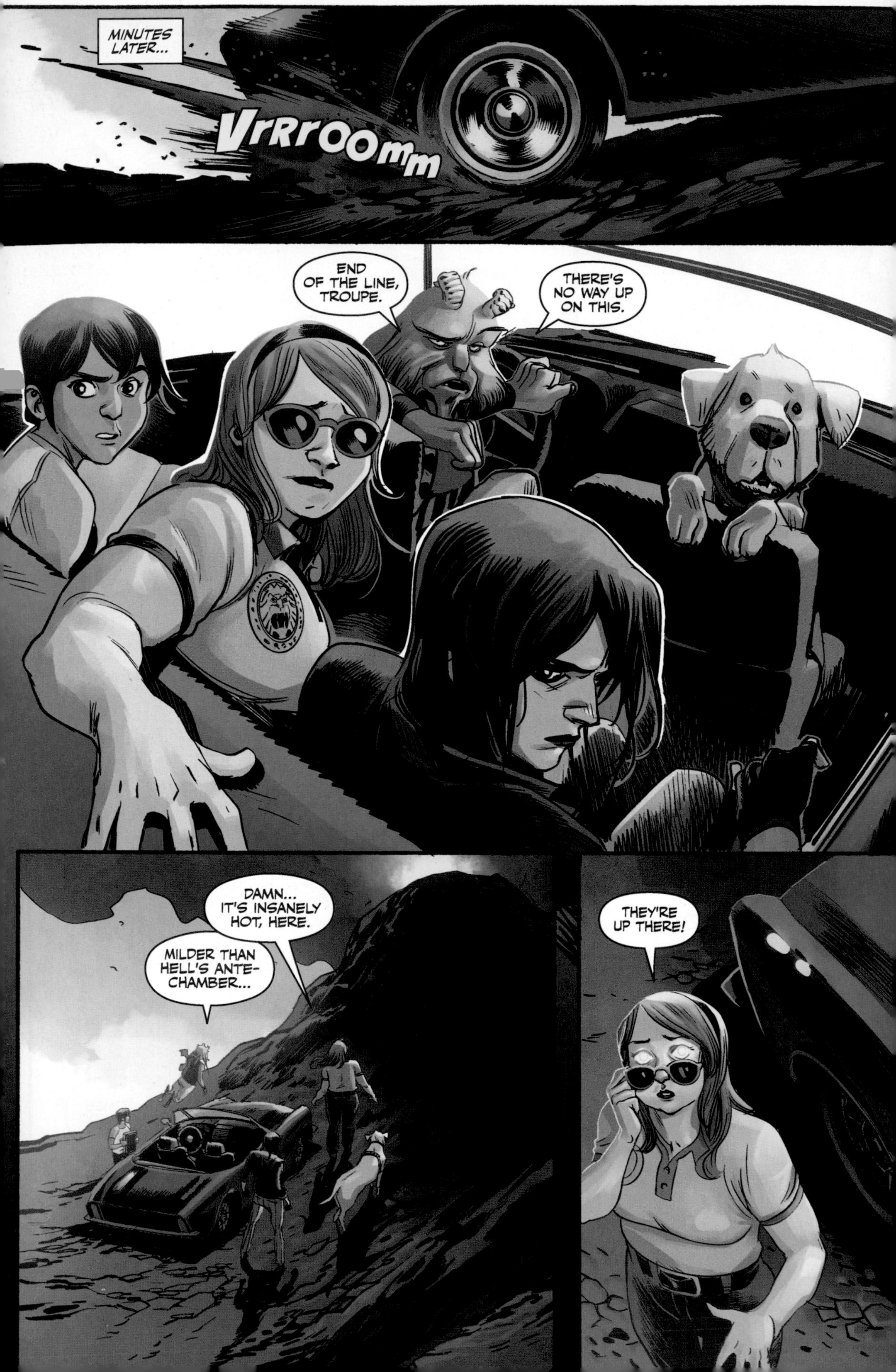
MINUTES LATER...
VRRROOMM
END OF THE LINE, TROUPE.
THERE'S NO WAY UP ON THIS.
DAMN... IT'S INSANELY HOT, HERE.
MILDER THAN HELL'S ANTE-CHAMBER...
THEY'RE UP THERE!

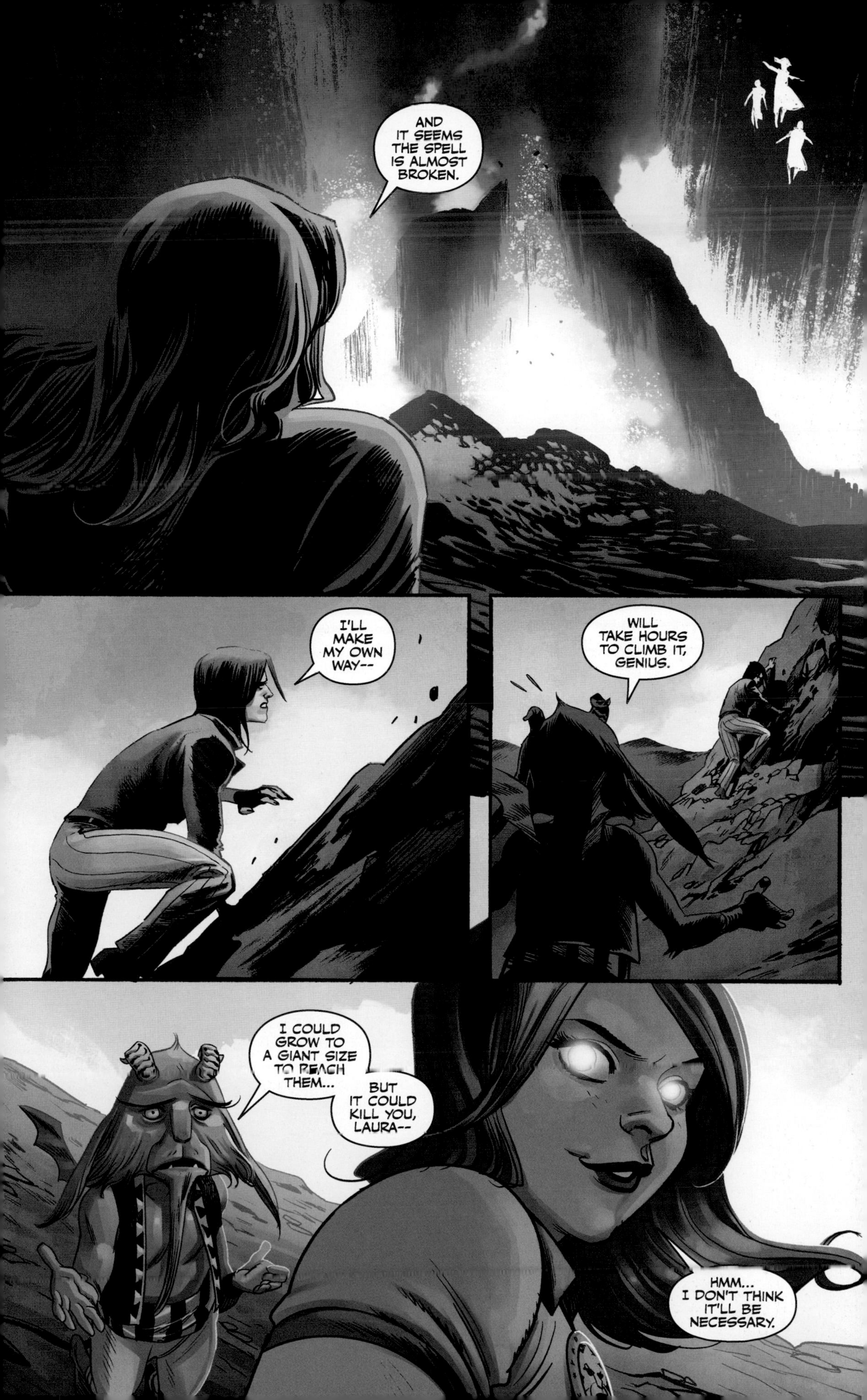
AND IT SEEMS THE SPELL IS ALMOST BROKEN.
I'LL MAKE MY OWN WAY--
WILL TAKE HOURS TO CLIMB IT, GENIUS.
I COULD GROW TO A GIANT SIZE TO REACH THEM...
BUT IT COULD KILL YOU, LAURA--
HMM... I DON'T THINK IT'LL BE NECESSARY.

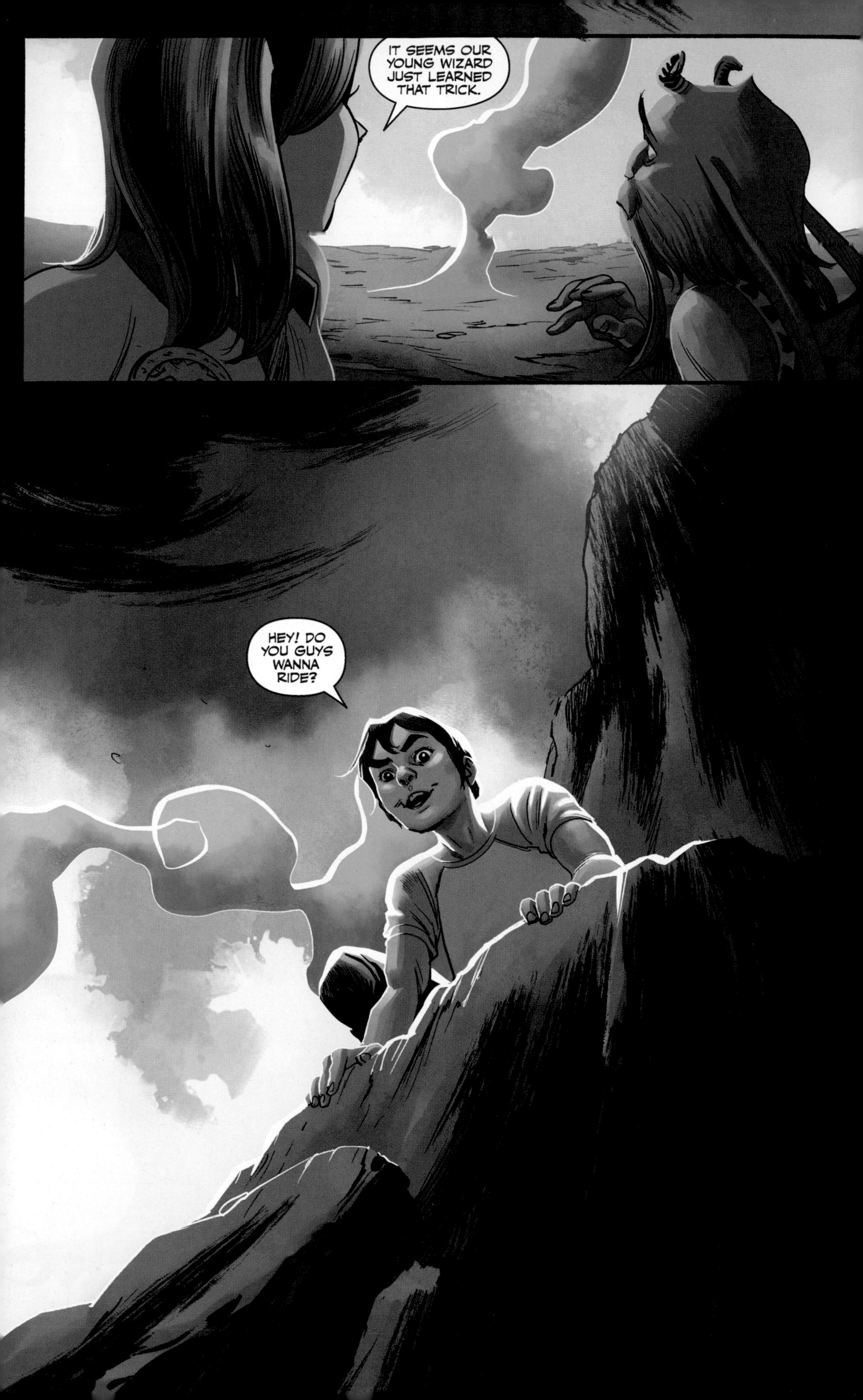
IT SEEMS OUR YOUNG WIZARD JUST LEARNED THAT TRICK.
HEY! DO YOU GUYS WANNA RIDE?

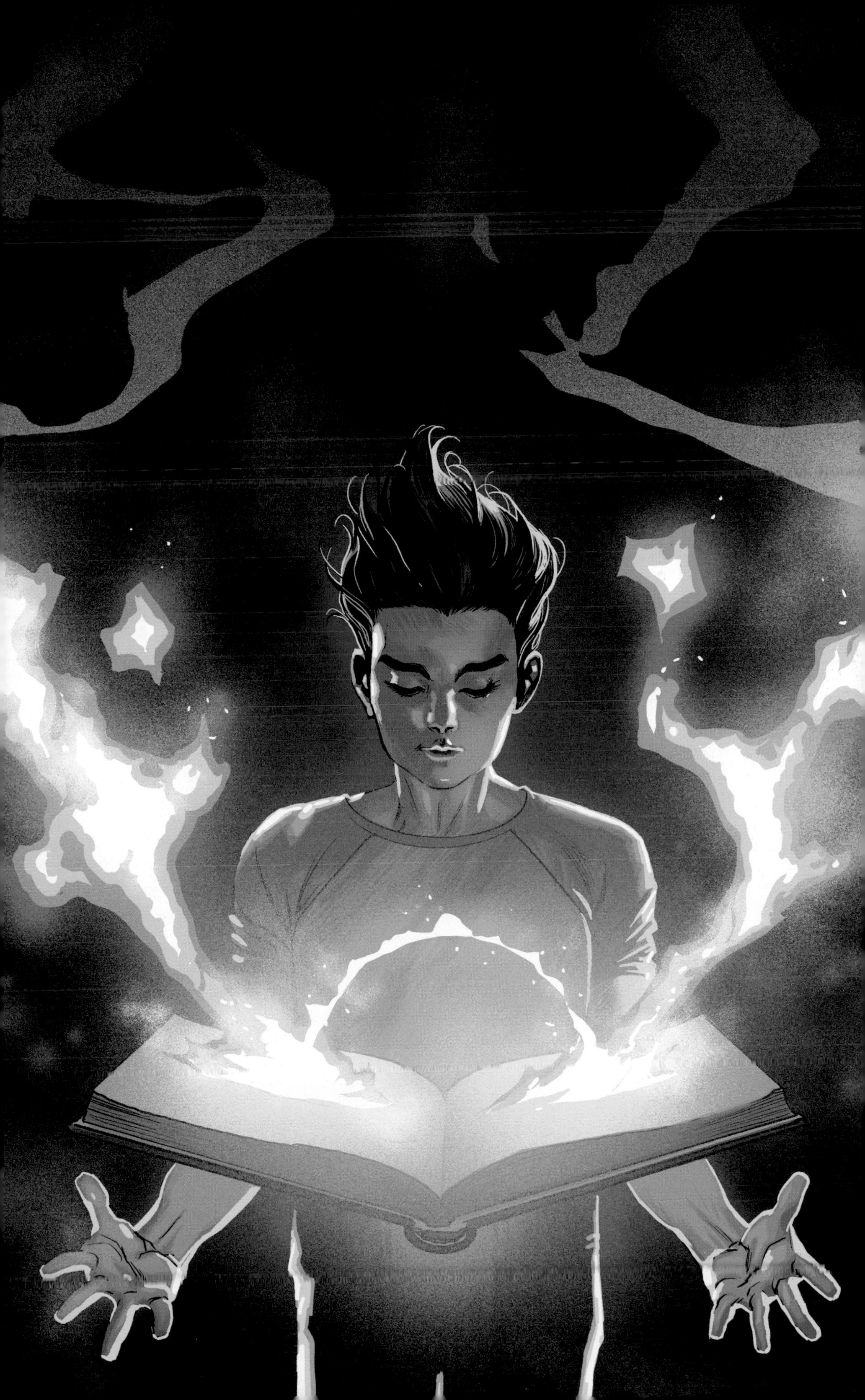

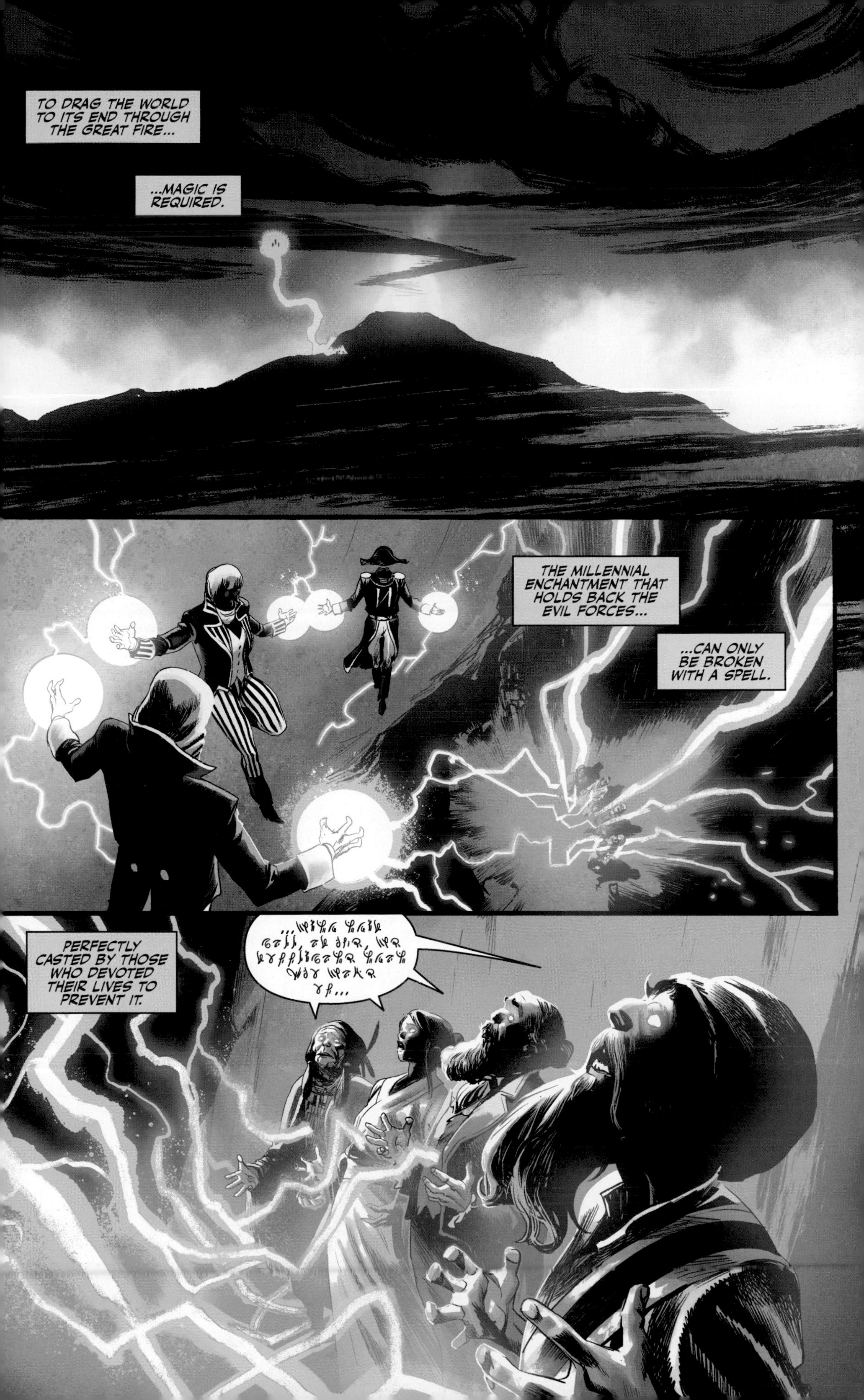
TO DRAG THE WORLD TO ITS END THROUGH THE GREAT FIRE...
...MAGIC IS REQUIRED.
THE MILLENNIAL ENCHANTMENT THAT HOLDS BACK THE EVIL FORCES...
...CAN ONLY BE BROKEN WITH A SPELL.
PERFECTLY CASTED BY THOSE WHO DEVOTED THEIR LIVES TO PREVENT IT.

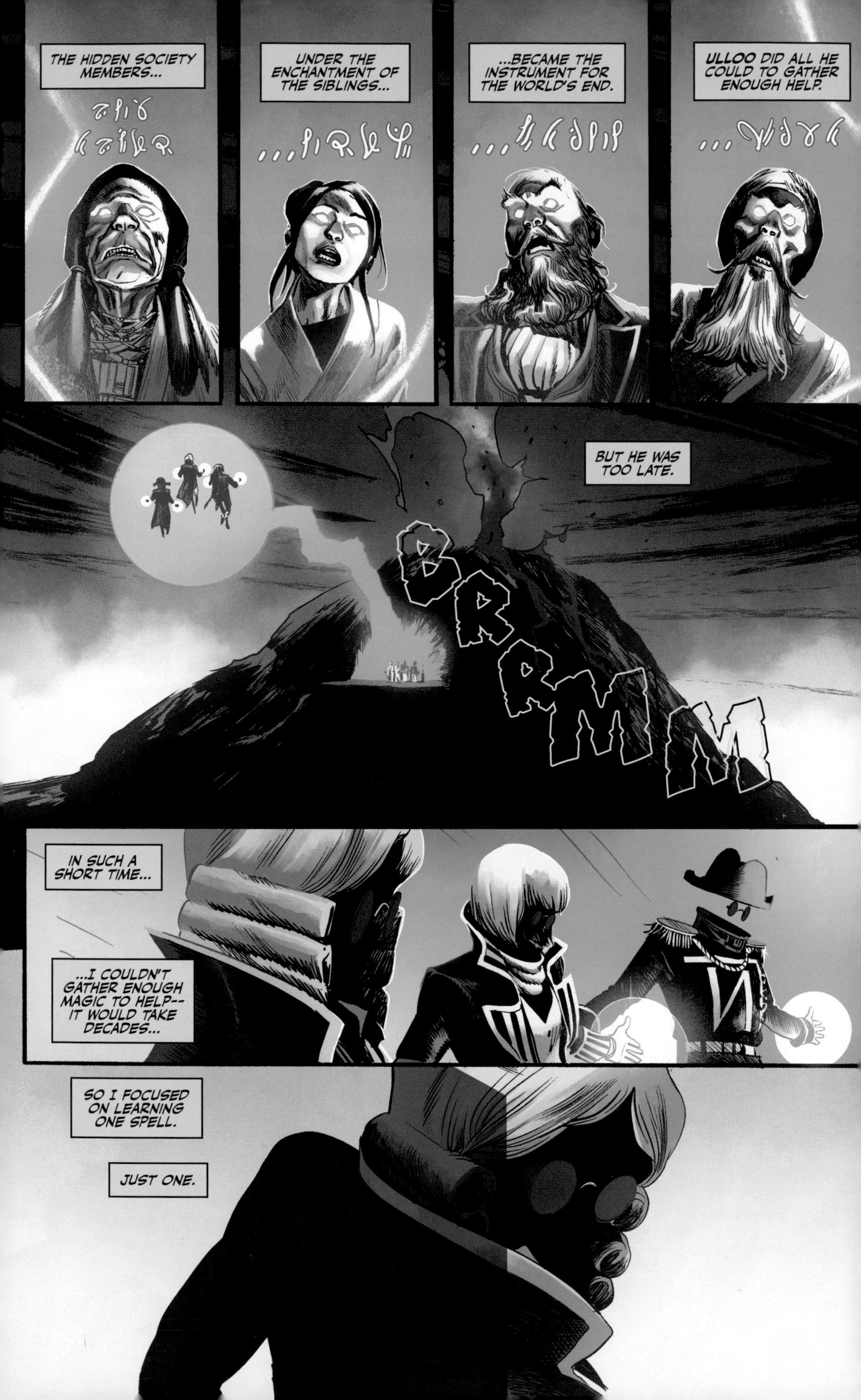
THE HIDDEN SOCIETY MEMBERS...
UNDER THE ENCHANTMENT OF THE SIBLINGS...
...BECAME THE INSTRUMENT FOR THE WORLD'S END.
ULLOO DID ALL HE COULD TO GATHER ENOUGH HELP.
BUT HE WAS TOO LATE.
BRRMM
IN SUCH A SHORT TIME...
...I COULDN'T GATHER ENOUGH MAGIC TO HELP-- IT WOULD TAKE DECADES...
SO I FOCUSED ON LEARNING ONE SPELL.
JUST ONE.

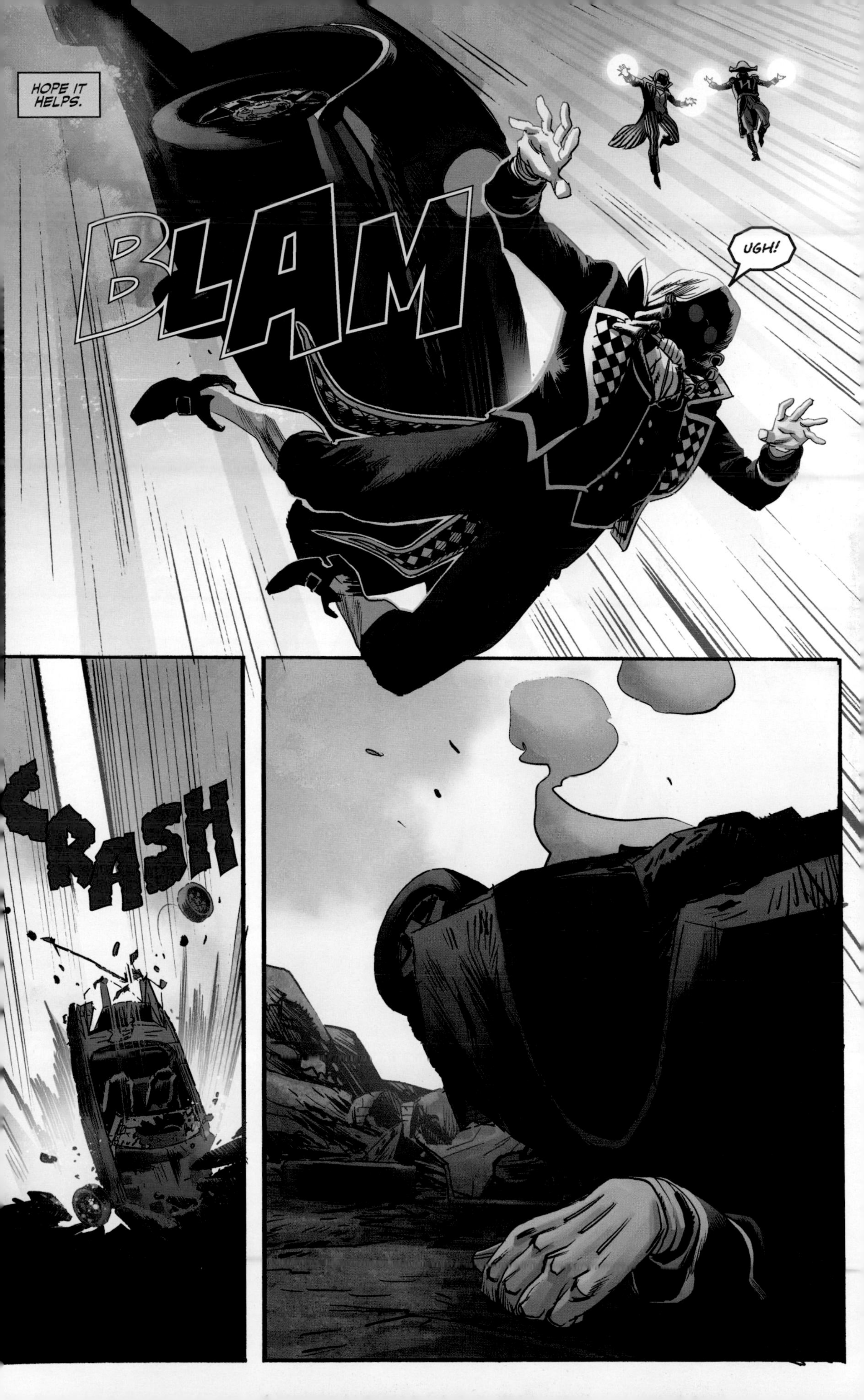
HOPE IT HELPS.
BLAM
UGH!
CRASH

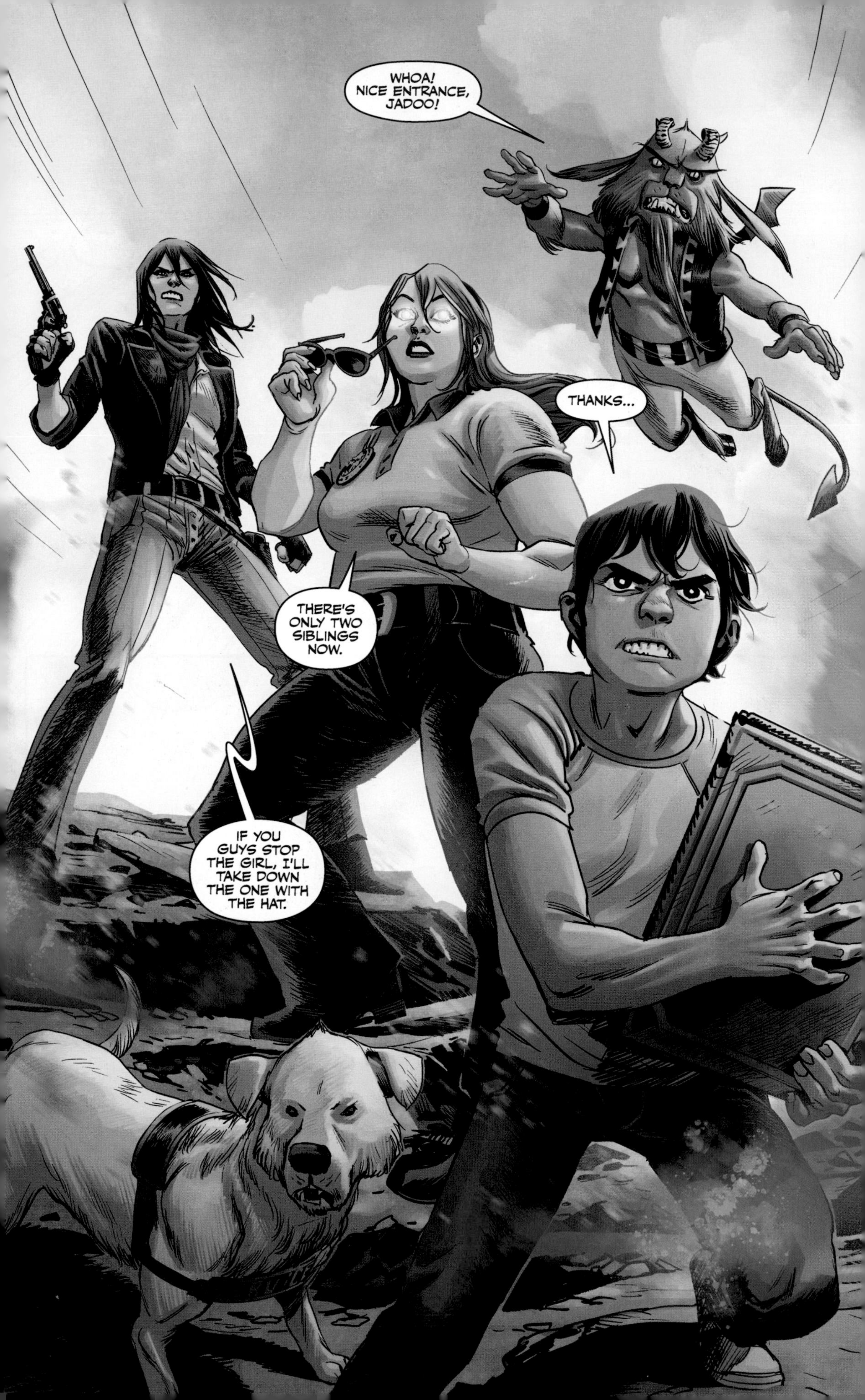
WHOA! NICE ENTRANCE, JADOO!
THANKS...
THERE'S ONLY TWO SIBLINGS NOW.
IF YOU GUYS STOP THE GIRL, I'LL TAKE DOWN THE ONE WITH THE HAT.

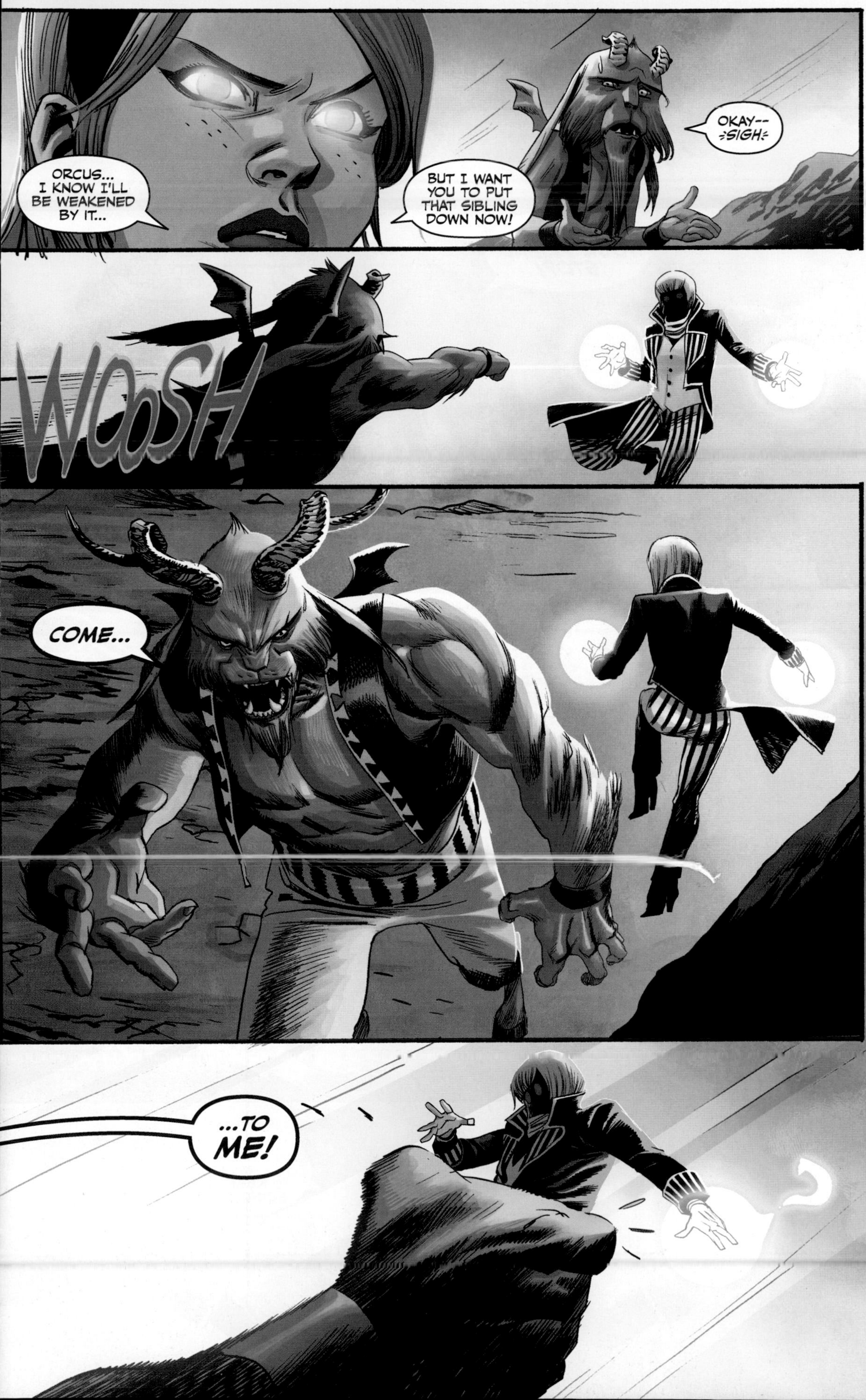
ORCUS... I KNOW I'LL BE WEAKENED BY IT...
BUT I WANT YOU TO PUT THAT SIBLING DOWN NOW!
OKAY-- ≈SIGH≈
WOOSH
COME...
...TO ME!

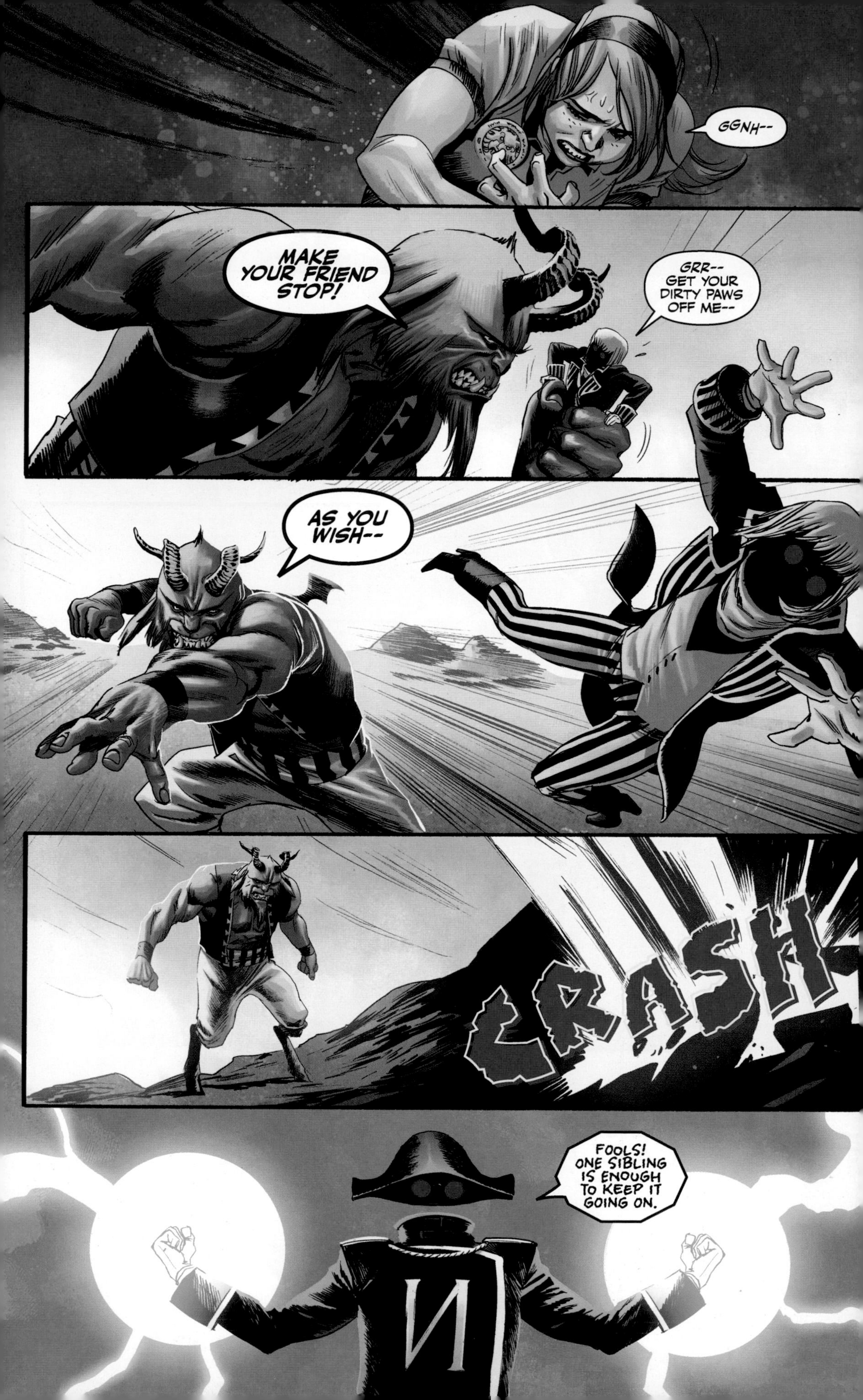
GGNH--
MAKE YOUR FRIEND STOP!
GRR-- GET YOUR DIRTY PAWS OFF ME--
AS YOU WISH--
CRASH
FOOLS! ONE SIBLING IS ENOUGH TO KEEP IT GOING ON.

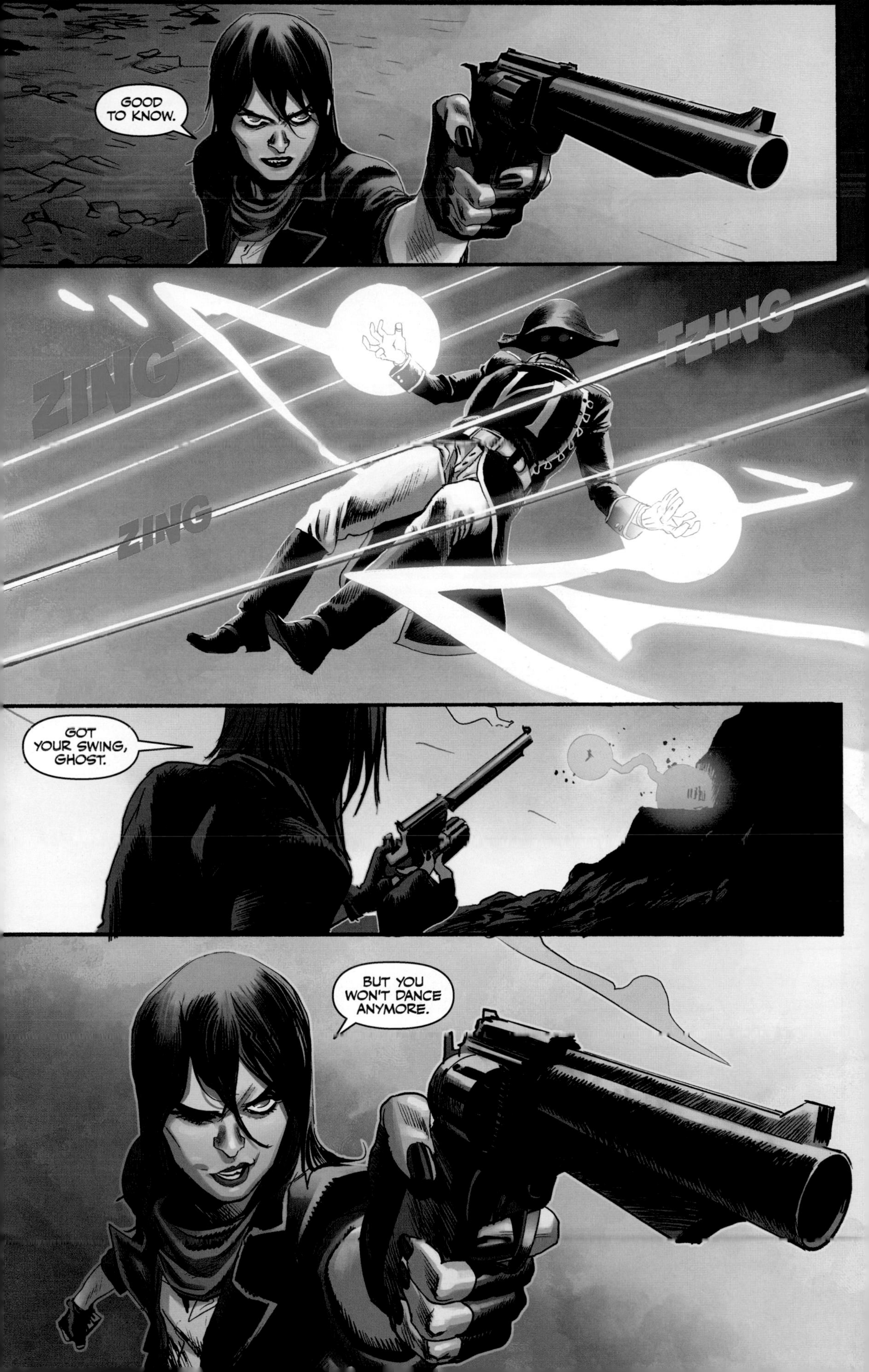
GOOD TO KNOW.
ZING
TZING
ZING
GOT YOUR SWING, GHOST.
BUT YOU WON'T DANCE ANYMORE.

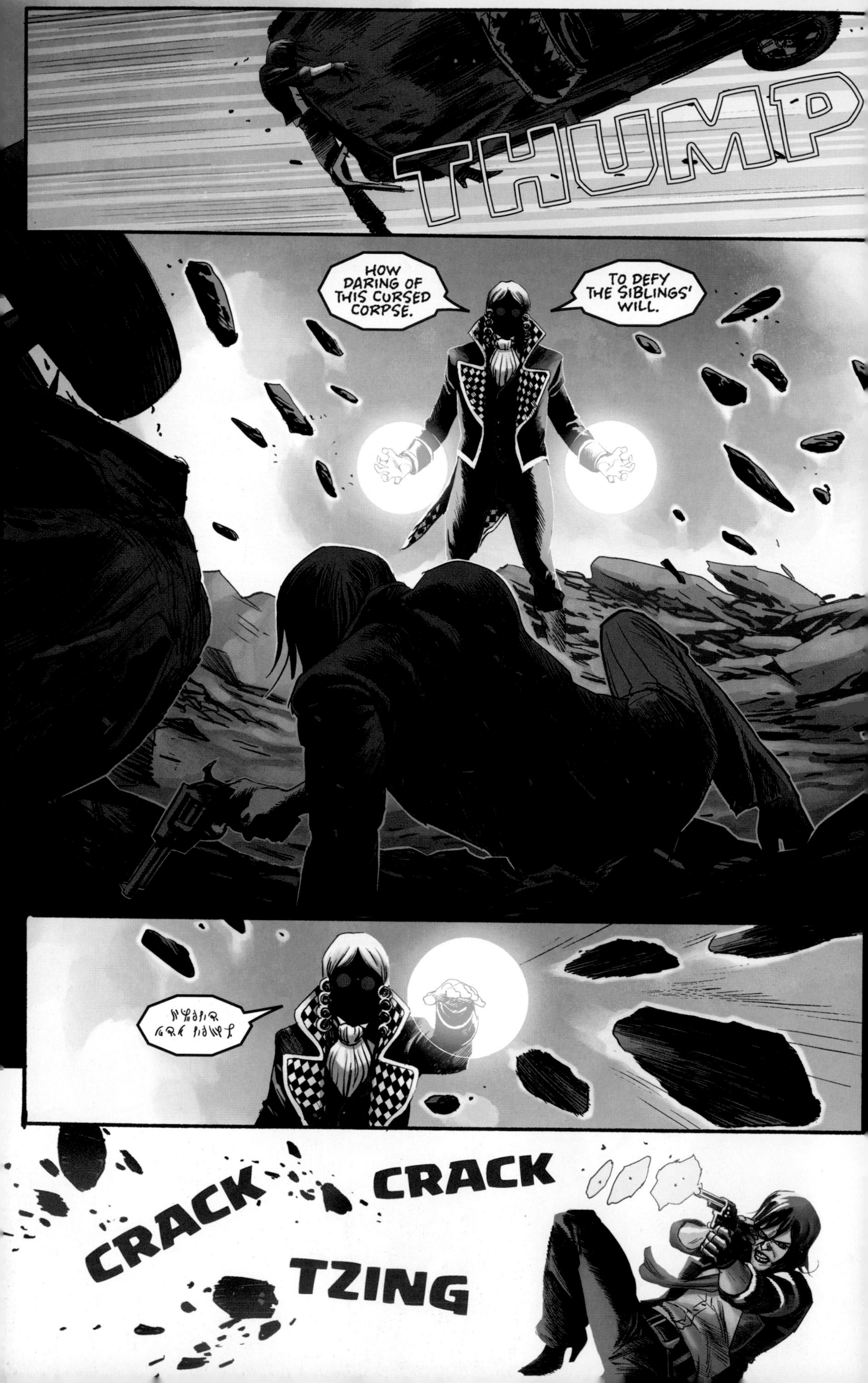
THUMP
HOW DARING OF THIS CURSED CORPSE.
TO DEFY THE SIBLINGS' WILL.
CRACK
CRACK
TZING

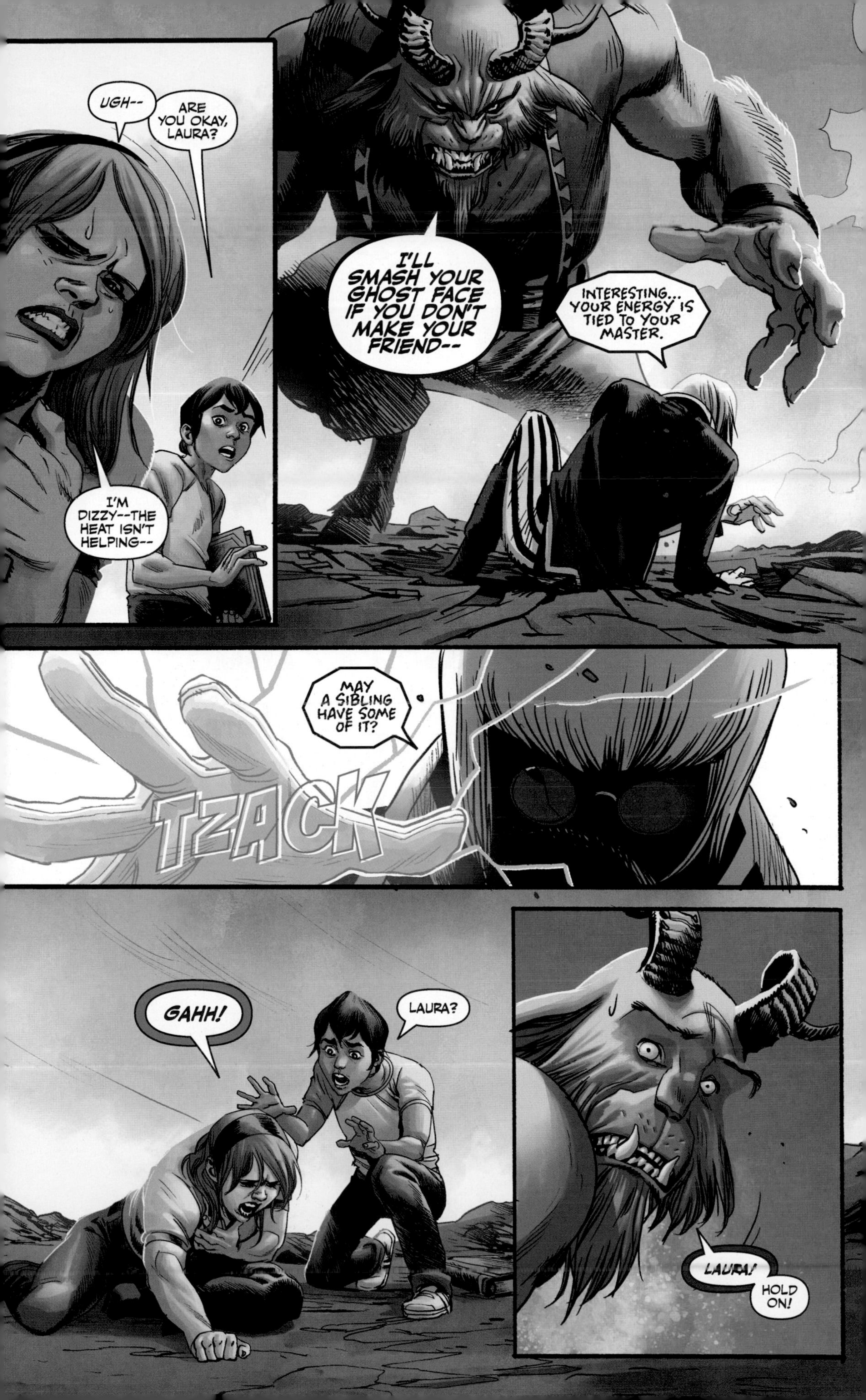
UGH--
ARE YOU OKAY, LAURA?
I'M DIZZY--THE HEAT ISN'T HELPING--
I'LL SMASH YOUR GHOST FACE IF YOU DON'T MAKE YOUR FRIEND--
INTERESTING... YOUR ENERGY IS TIED TO YOUR MASTER.
MAY A SIBLING HAVE SOME OF IT?
TZACK
GAHH!
LAURA?
LAURA!
HOLD ON!

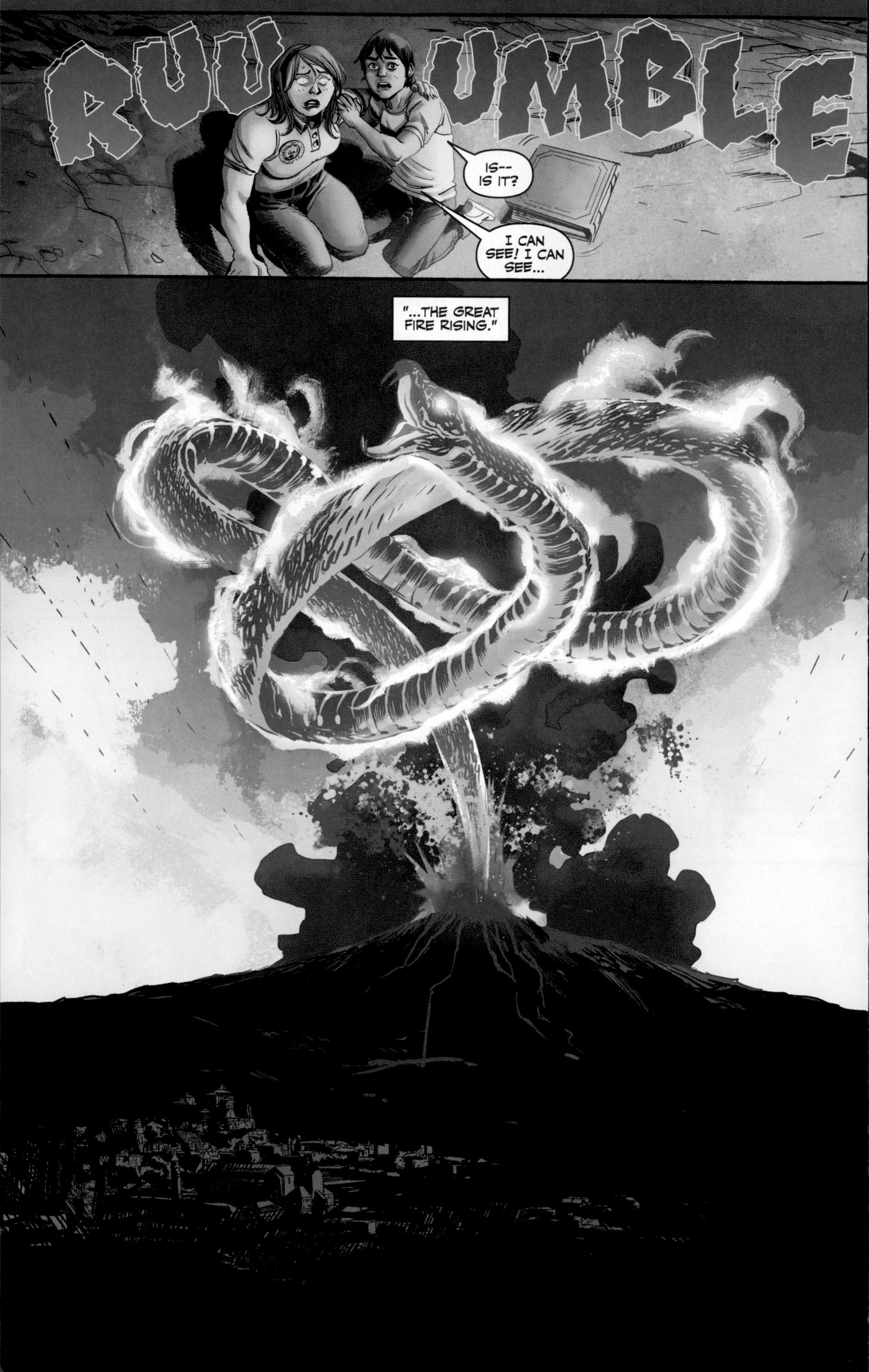
RUUUMBLE
IS--
IS IT?
I CAN
SEE! I CAN
SEE...
"...THE GREAT
FIRE RISING."

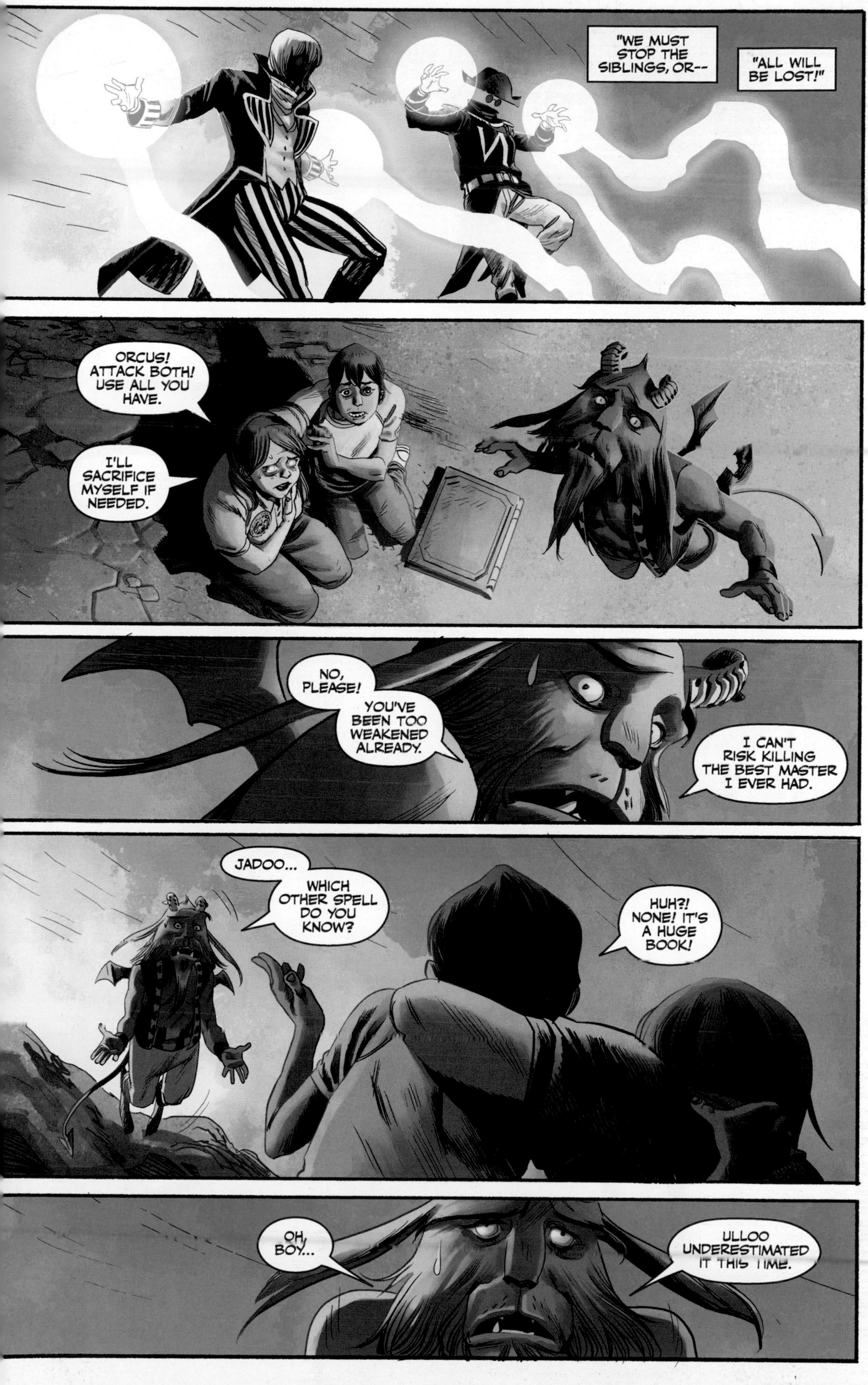
"WE MUST STOP THE SIBLINGS, OR--
"ALL WILL BE LOST!"
ORCUS! ATTACK BOTH! USE ALL YOU HAVE.
I'LL SACRIFICE MYSELF IF NEEDED.
NO, PLEASE!
YOU'VE BEEN TOO WEAKENED ALREADY.
I CAN'T RISK KILLING THE BEST MASTER I EVER HAD.
JADOO...
WHICH OTHER SPELL DO YOU KNOW?
HUH?! NONE! IT'S A HUGE BOOK!
OH, BOY...
ULLOO UNDERESTIMATED IT THIS TIME.

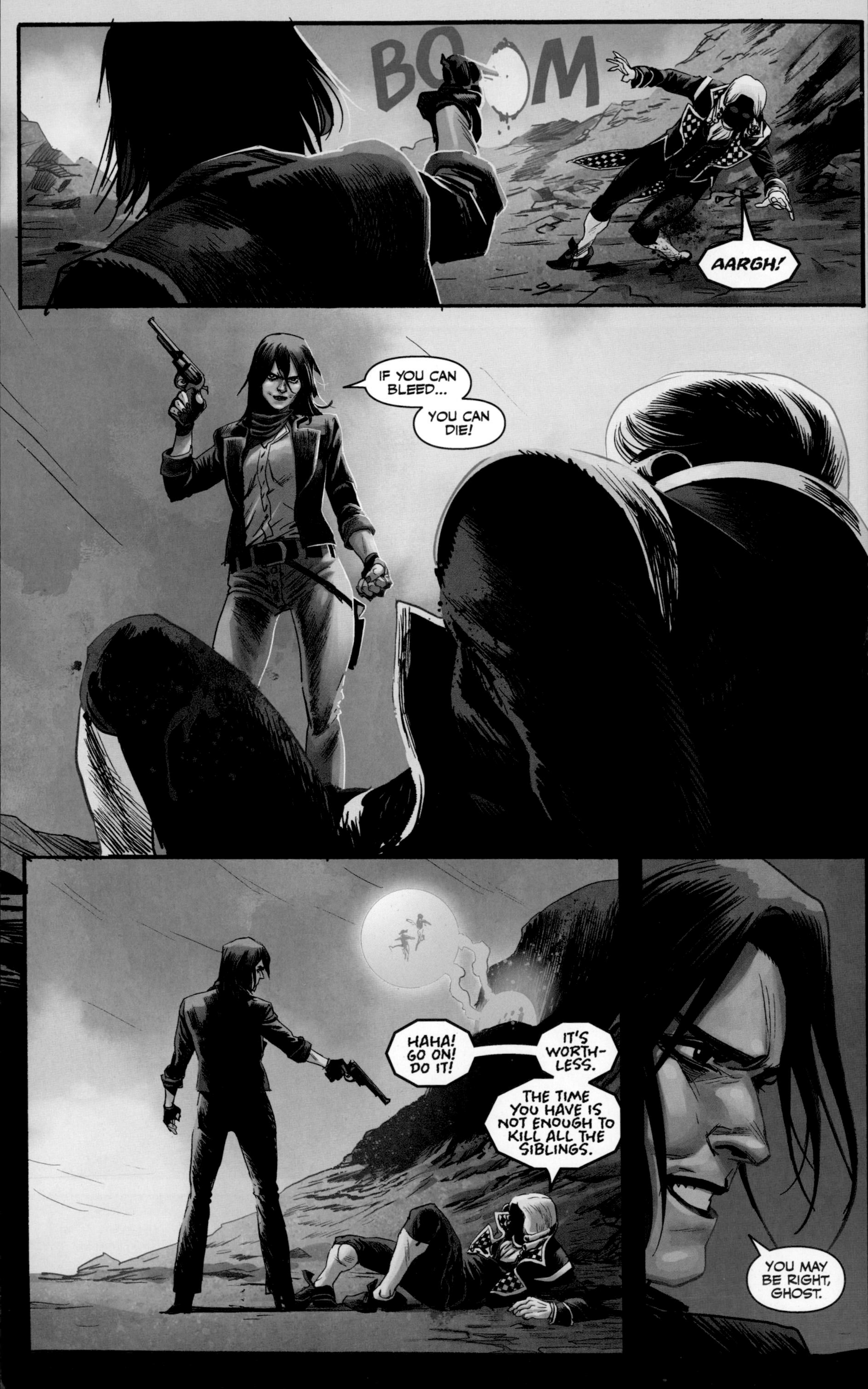
BOOM
AARGH!
IF YOU CAN BLEED...
YOU CAN DIE!
HAHA! GO ON! DO IT!
IT'S WORTH-LESS.
THE TIME YOU HAVE IS NOT ENOUGH TO KILL ALL THE SIBLINGS.
YOU MAY BE RIGHT, GHOST.

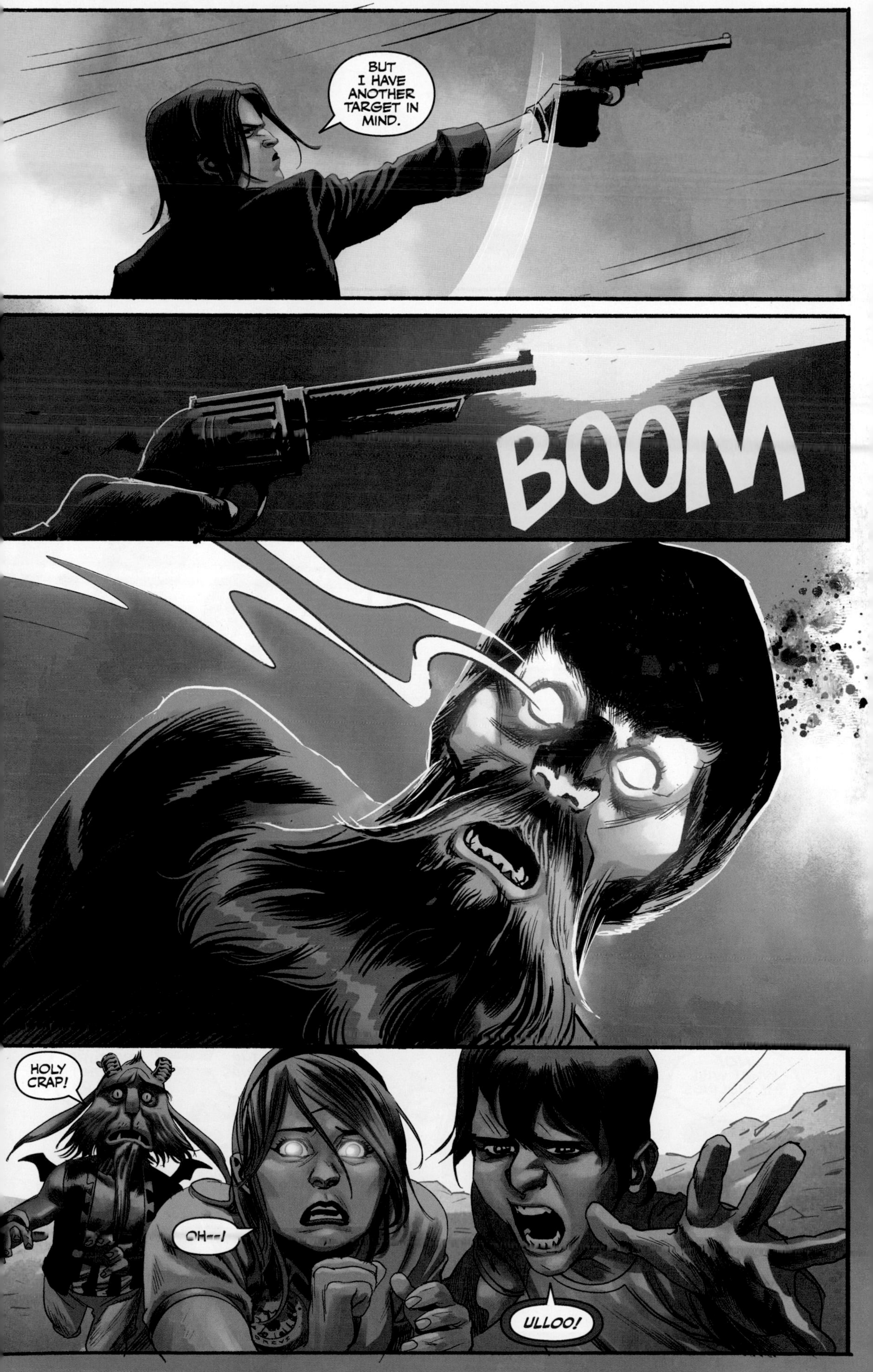
BUT I HAVE ANOTHER TARGET IN MIND.
BOOM
HOLY CRAP!
OH--!
ULLOO!

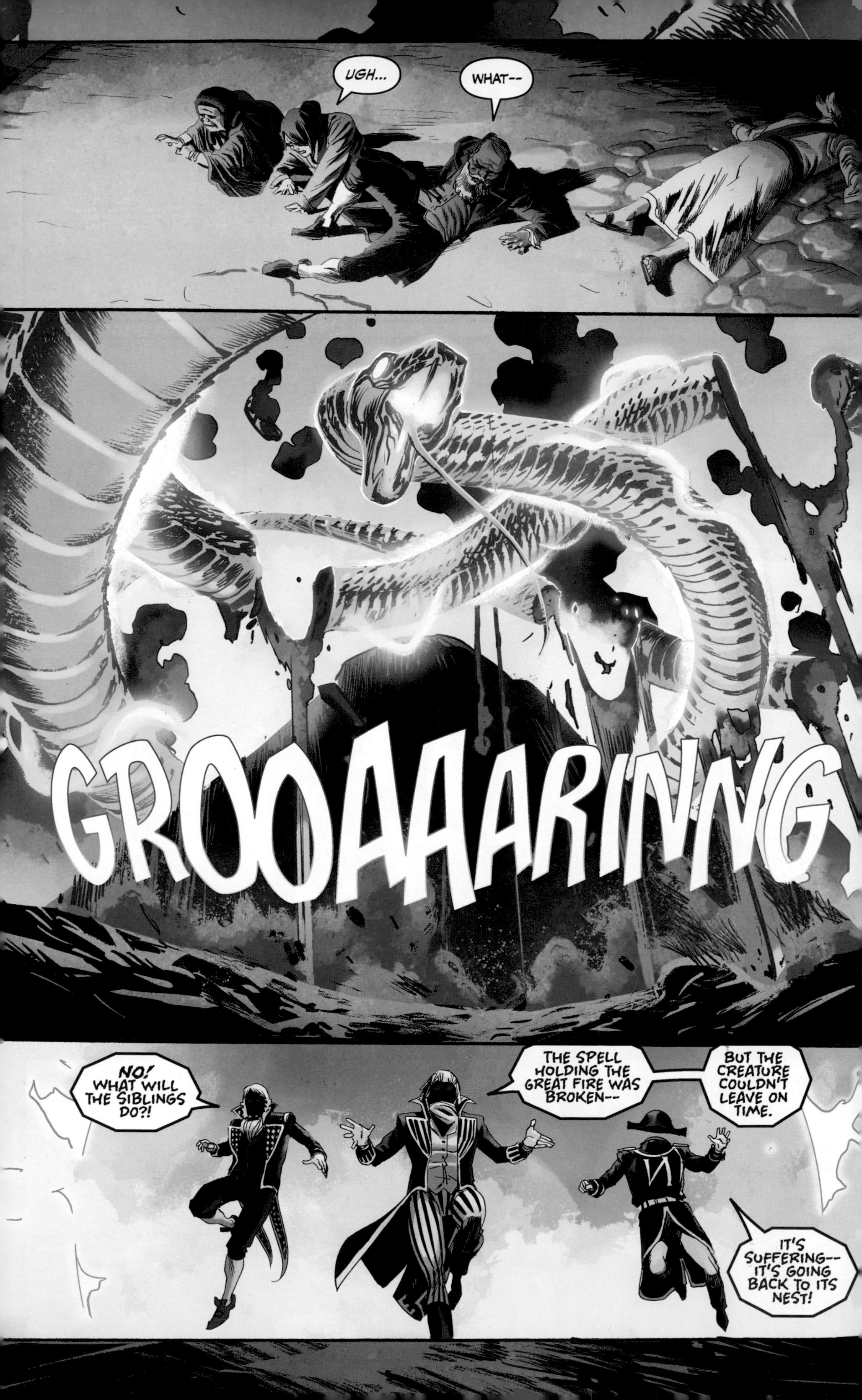
UGH...
WHAT--
GROOAAARINNG
NO! WHAT WILL THE SIBLINGS DO?!
THE SPELL HOLDING THE GREAT FIRE WAS BROKEN--
BUT THE CREATURE COULDN'T LEAVE ON TIME.
IT'S SUFFERING-- IT'S GOING BACK TO ITS NEST!

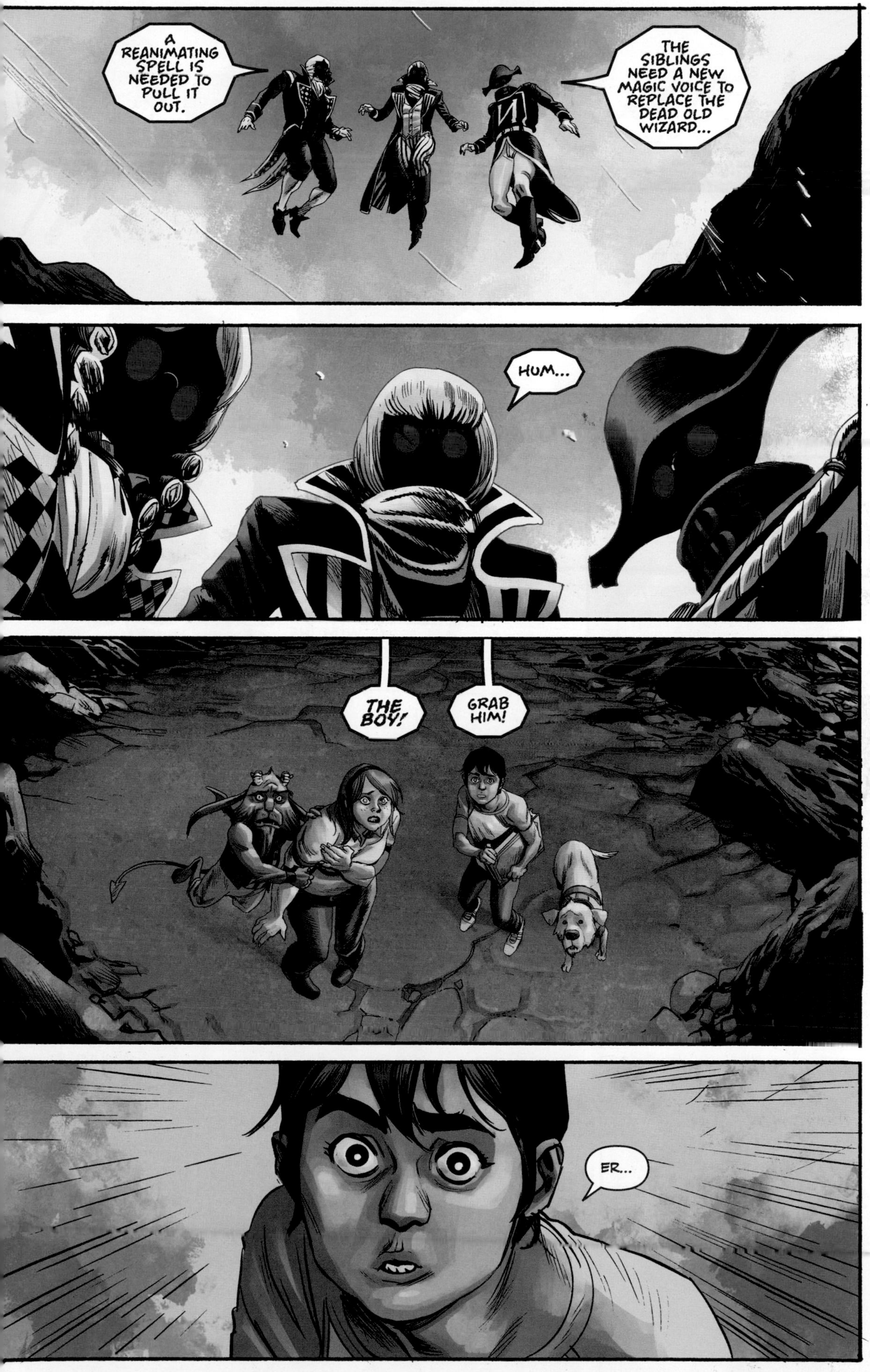
A REANIMATING SPELL IS NEEDED TO PULL IT OUT.
THE SIBLINGS NEED A NEW MAGIC VOICE TO REPLACE THE DEAD OLD WIZARD...
HUM...
THE BOY!
GRAB HIM!
ER...

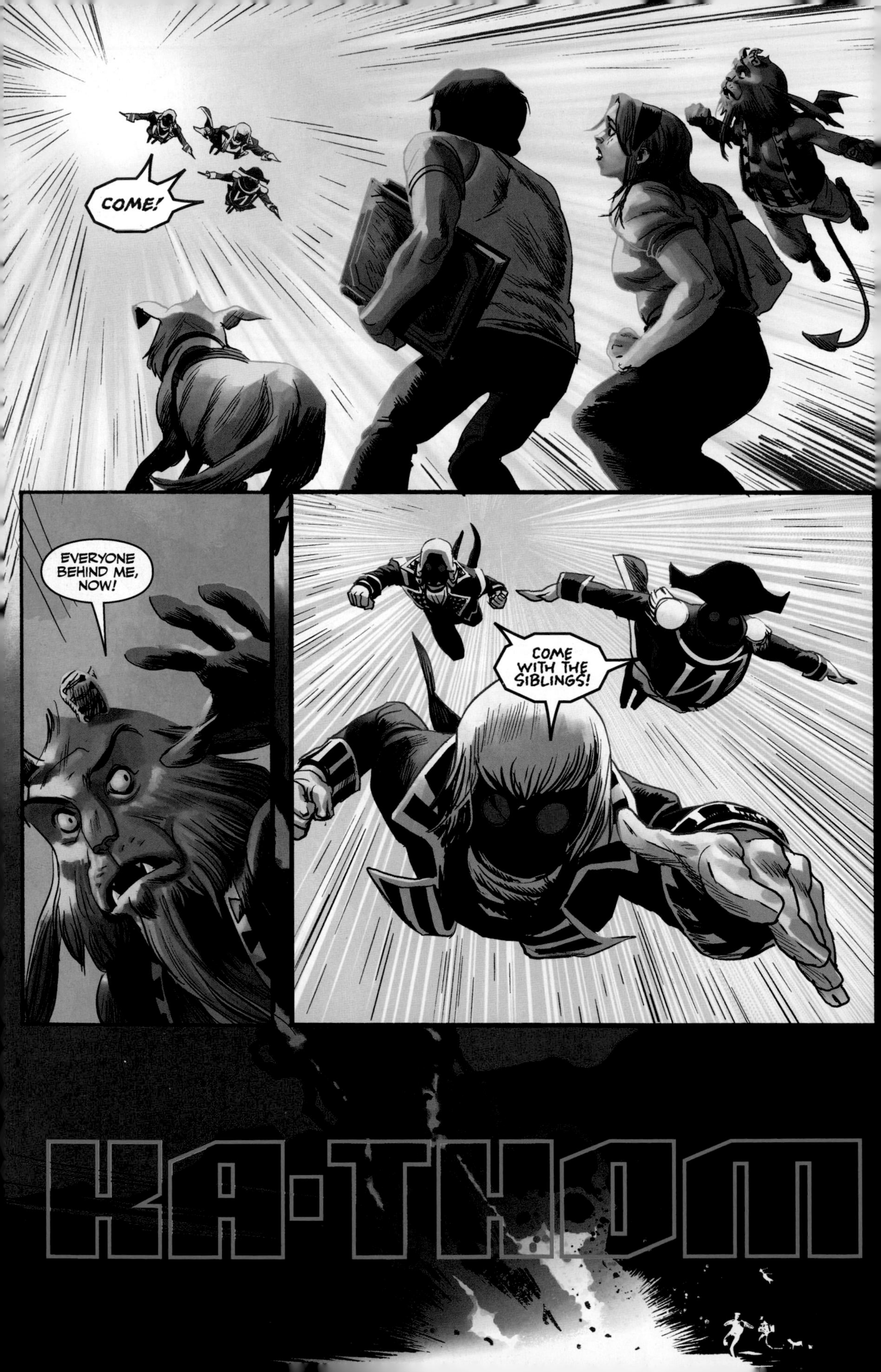
COME!
EVERYONE BEHIND ME, NOW!
COME WITH THE SIBLINGS!
KA-THOM

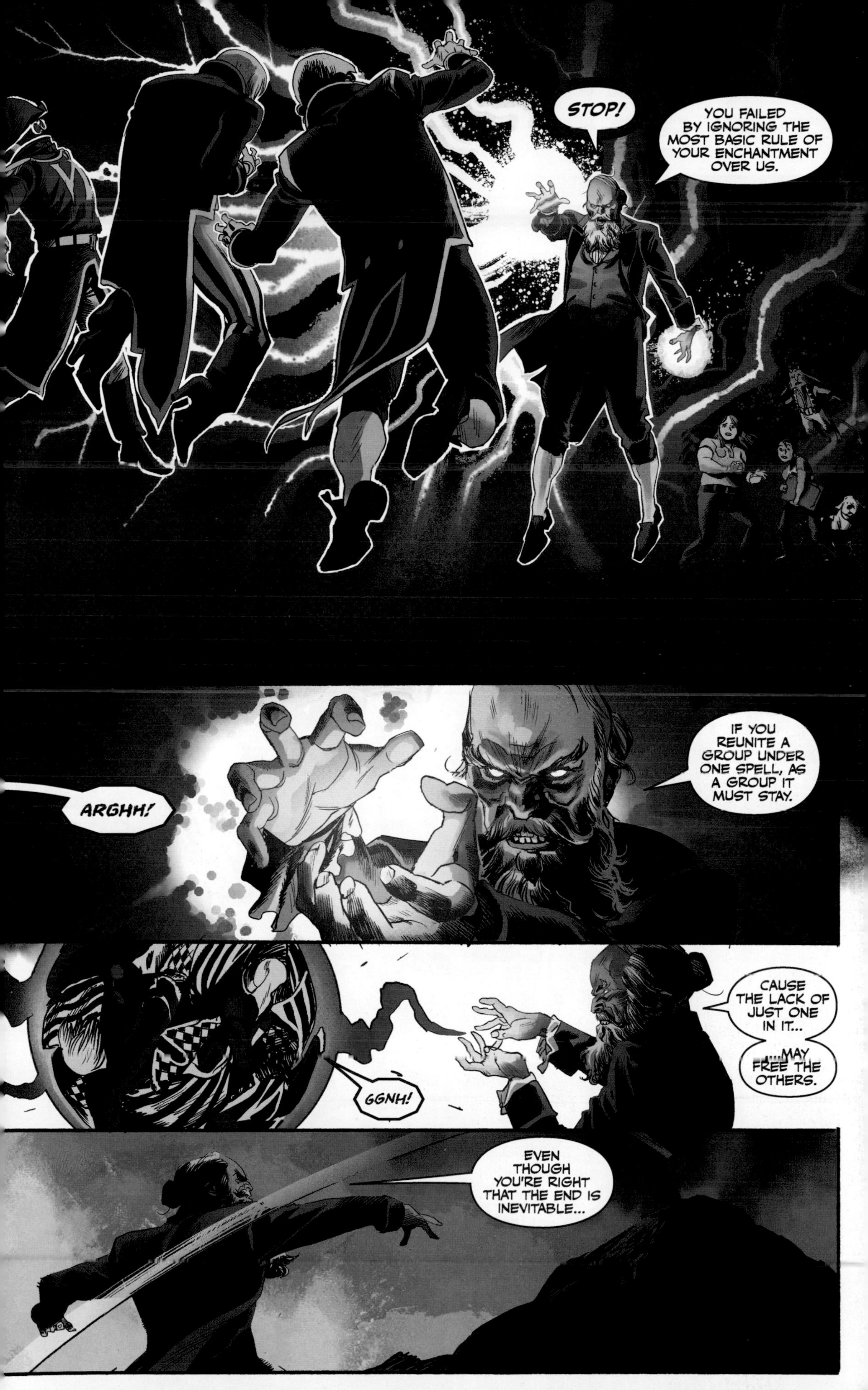
STOP!
YOU FAILED BY IGNORING THE MOST BASIC RULE OF YOUR ENCHANTMENT OVER US.
ARGHH!
IF YOU REUNITE A GROUP UNDER ONE SPELL, AS A GROUP IT MUST STAY.
CAUSE THE LACK OF JUST ONE IN IT...
...MAY FREE THE OTHERS.
GGNH!
EVEN THOUGH YOU'RE RIGHT THAT THE END IS INEVITABLE...

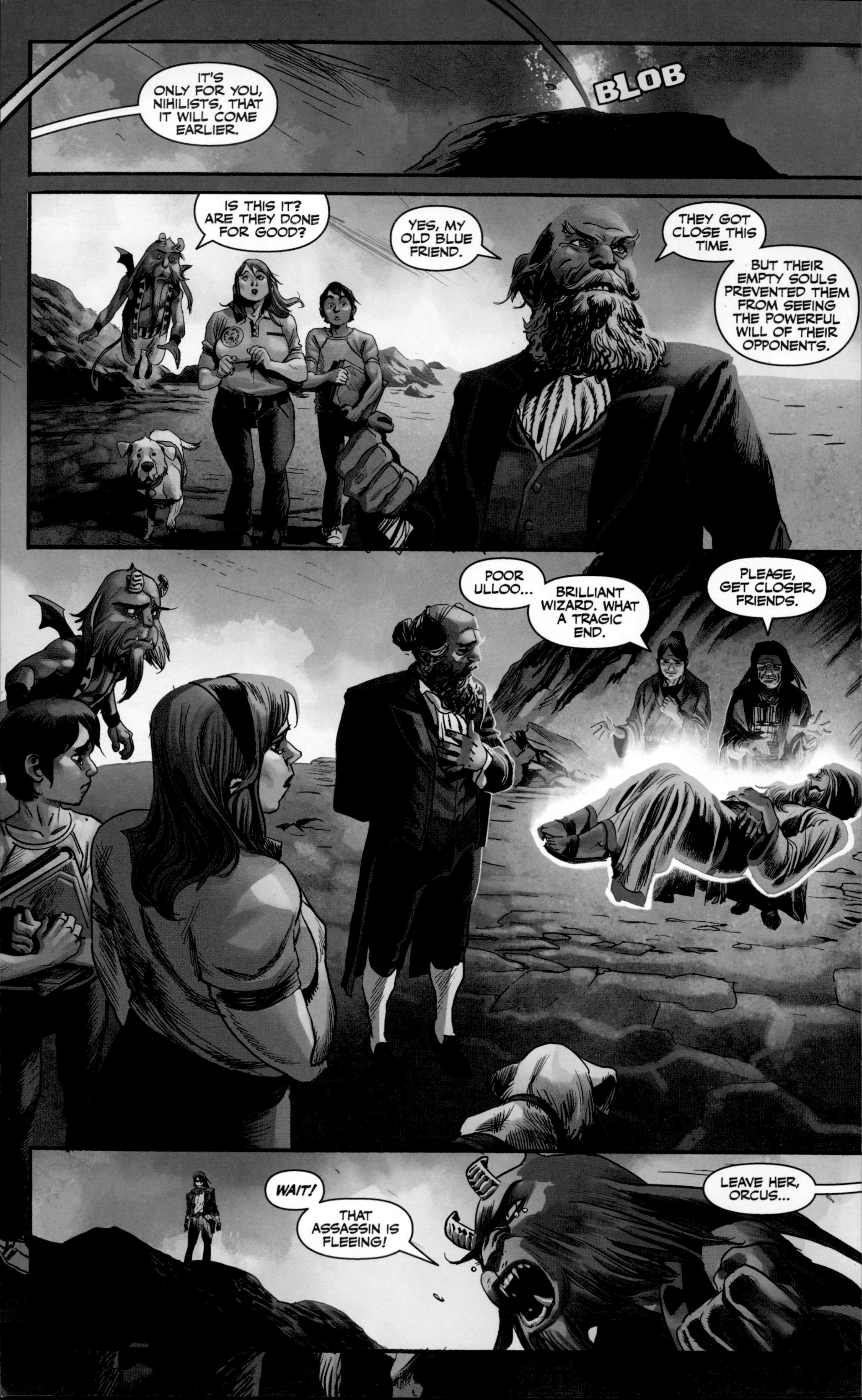
IT'S ONLY FOR YOU, NIHILISTS, THAT IT WILL COME EARLIER.
BLOB
IS THIS IT? ARE THEY DONE FOR GOOD?
YES, MY OLD BLUE FRIEND.
THEY GOT CLOSE THIS TIME.
BUT THEIR EMPTY SOULS PREVENTED THEM FROM SEEING THE POWERFUL WILL OF THEIR OPPONENTS.
POOR ULLOO...
BRILLIANT WIZARD. WHAT A TRAGIC END.
PLEASE, GET CLOSER, FRIENDS.
WAIT!
THAT ASSASSIN IS FLEEING!
LEAVE HER, ORCUS...

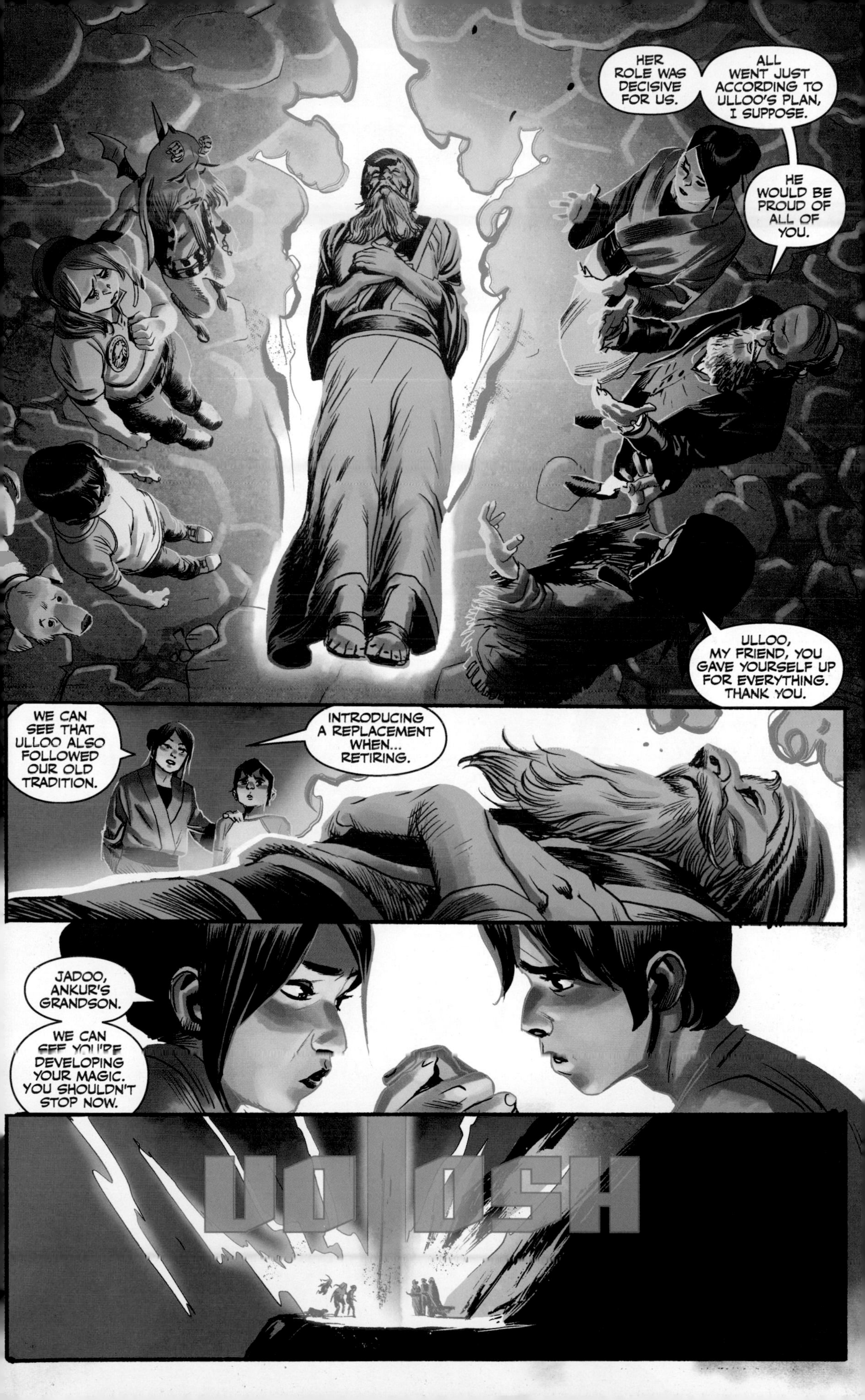
HER ROLE WAS DECISIVE FOR US.
ALL WENT JUST ACCORDING TO ULLOO'S PLAN, I SUPPOSE.
HE WOULD BE PROUD OF ALL OF YOU.
ULLOO, MY FRIEND, YOU GAVE YOURSELF UP FOR EVERYTHING. THANK YOU.
WE CAN SEE THAT ULLOO ALSO FOLLOWED OUR OLD TRADITION.
INTRODUCING A REPLACEMENT WHEN... RETIRING.
JADOO, ANKUR'S GRANDSON.
WE CAN SEE YOU'RE DEVELOPING YOUR MAGIC. YOU SHOULDN'T STOP NOW.

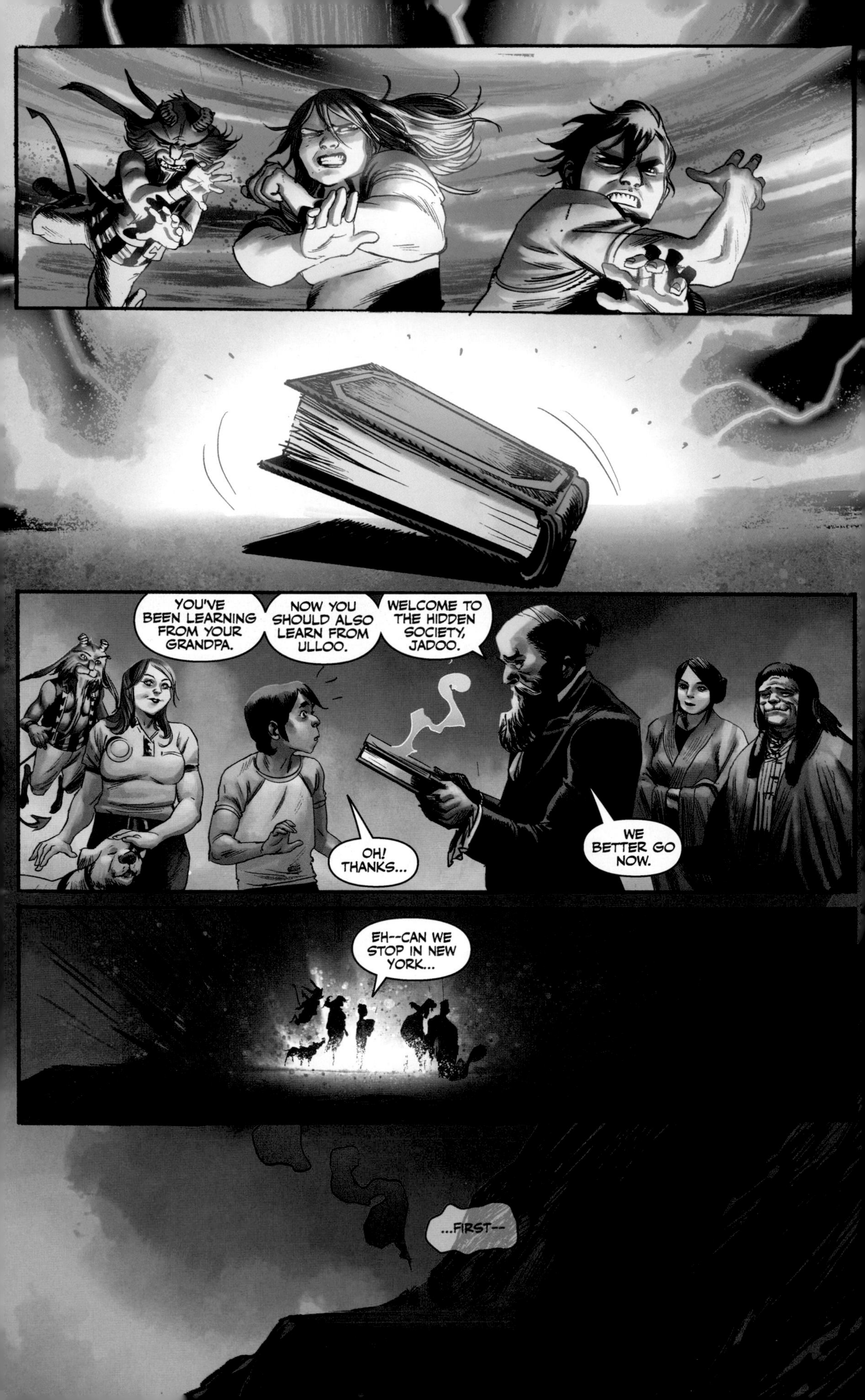
YOU'VE BEEN LEARNING FROM YOUR GRANDPA.
NOW YOU SHOULD ALSO LEARN FROM ULLOO.
WELCOME TO THE HIDDEN SOCIETY, JADOO.
OH! THANKS...
WE BETTER GO NOW.
EH--CAN WE STOP IN NEW YORK...
...FIRST--

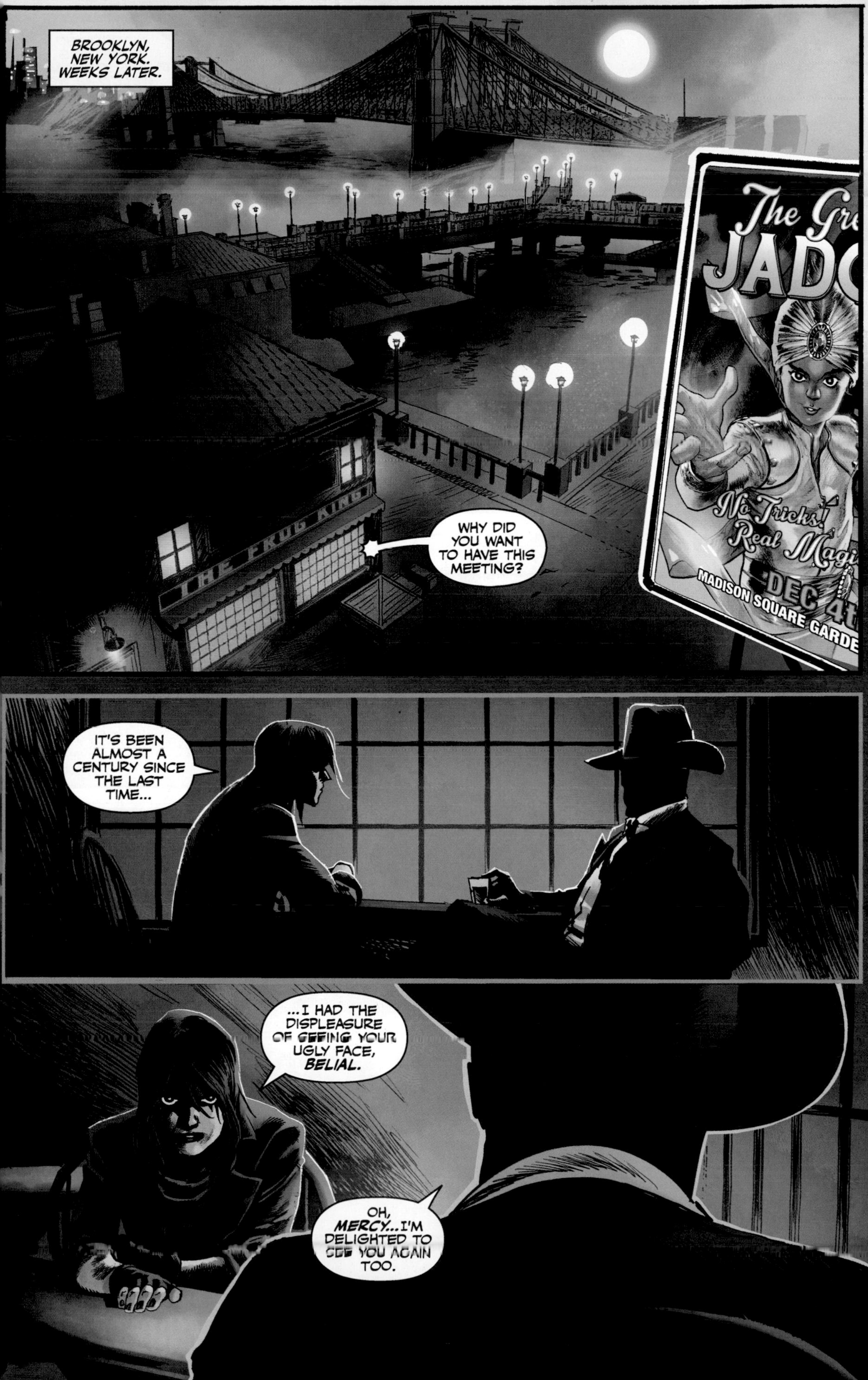
BROOKLYN, NEW YORK. WEEKS LATER.
The Great JADO
No Tricks! Real Magic
DEC 4th
MADISON SQUARE GARDE
THE FROG KING
WHY DID YOU WANT TO HAVE THIS MEETING?
IT'S BEEN ALMOST A CENTURY SINCE THE LAST TIME...
...I HAD THE DISPLEASURE OF SEEING YOUR UGLY FACE, BELIAL.
OH, MERCY...I'M DELIGHTED TO SEE YOU AGAIN TOO.

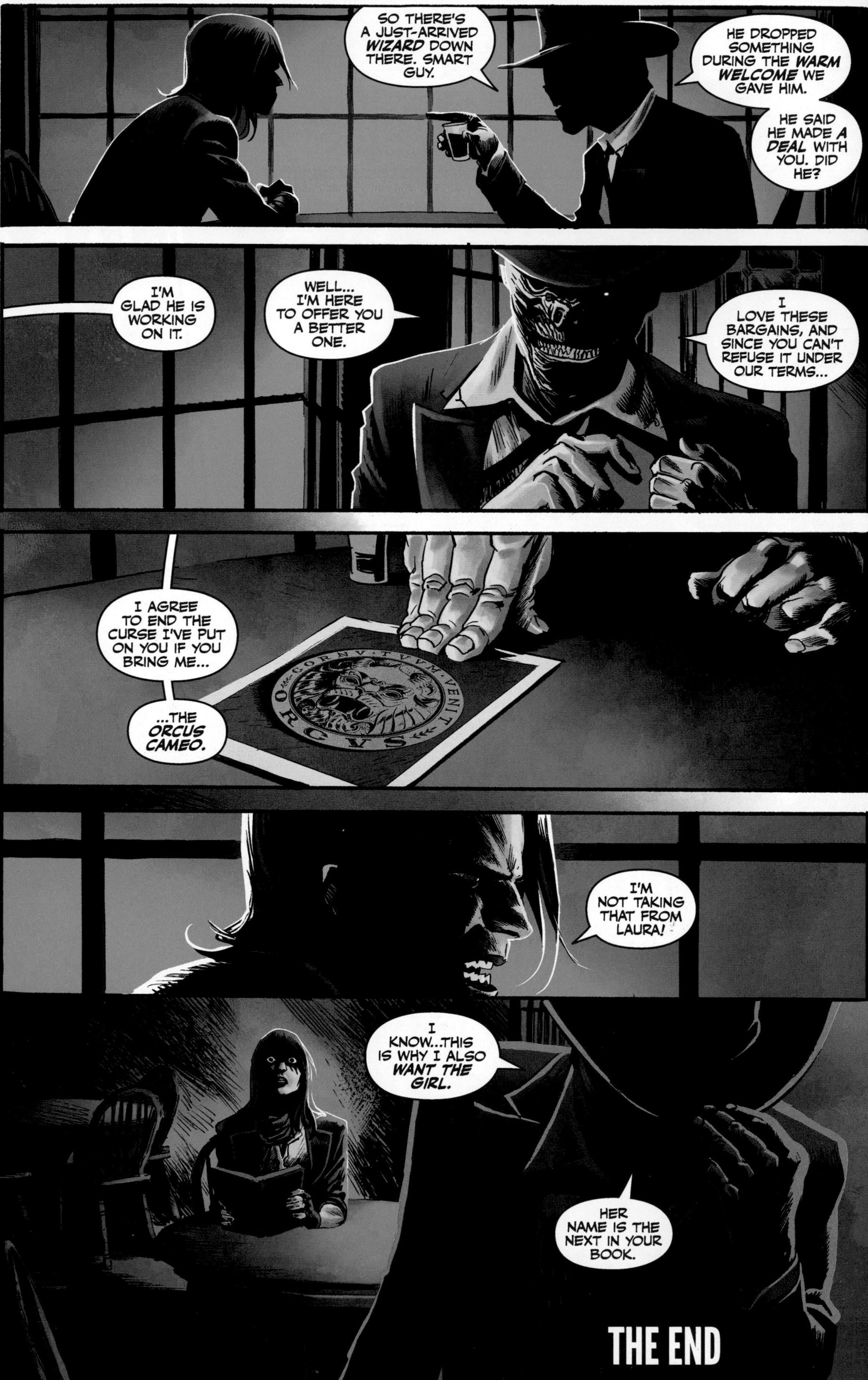
SO THERE'S A JUST-ARRIVED **WIZARD** DOWN THERE. SMART GUY.
HE DROPPED SOMETHING DURING THE **WARM WELCOME** WE GAVE HIM.
HE SAID HE MADE **A DEAL** WITH YOU. DID HE?
I'M GLAD HE IS WORKING ON IT.
WELL... I'M HERE TO OFFER YOU A BETTER ONE.
I LOVE THESE BARGAINS, AND SINCE YOU CAN'T REFUSE IT UNDER OUR TERMS...
I AGREE TO END THE CURSE I'VE PUT ON YOU IF YOU BRING ME...
...THE **ORCUS CAMEO.**
CORNV·TVVM·VENIT
ORCVS
I'M NOT TAKING THAT FROM LAURA!
I KNOW...THIS IS WHY I ALSO **WANT THE GIRL.**
HER NAME IS THE NEXT IN YOUR BOOK.
THE END

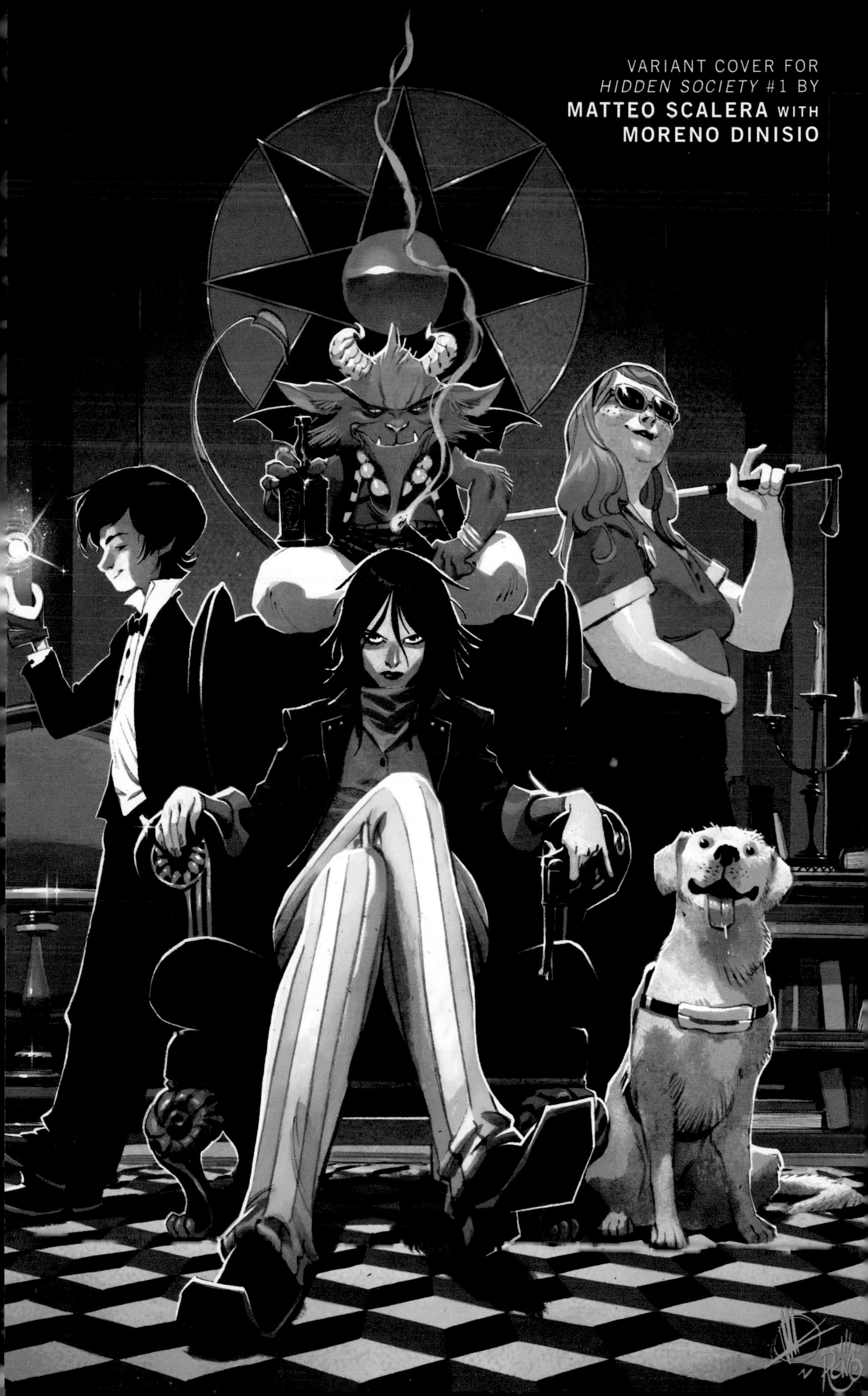

VARIANT COVER FOR
HIDDEN SOCIETY #1 BY
MATTEO SCALERA WITH
MORENO DINISIO

VARIANT COVER FOR
HIDDEN SOCIETY #4 BY
GABRIEL BÁ

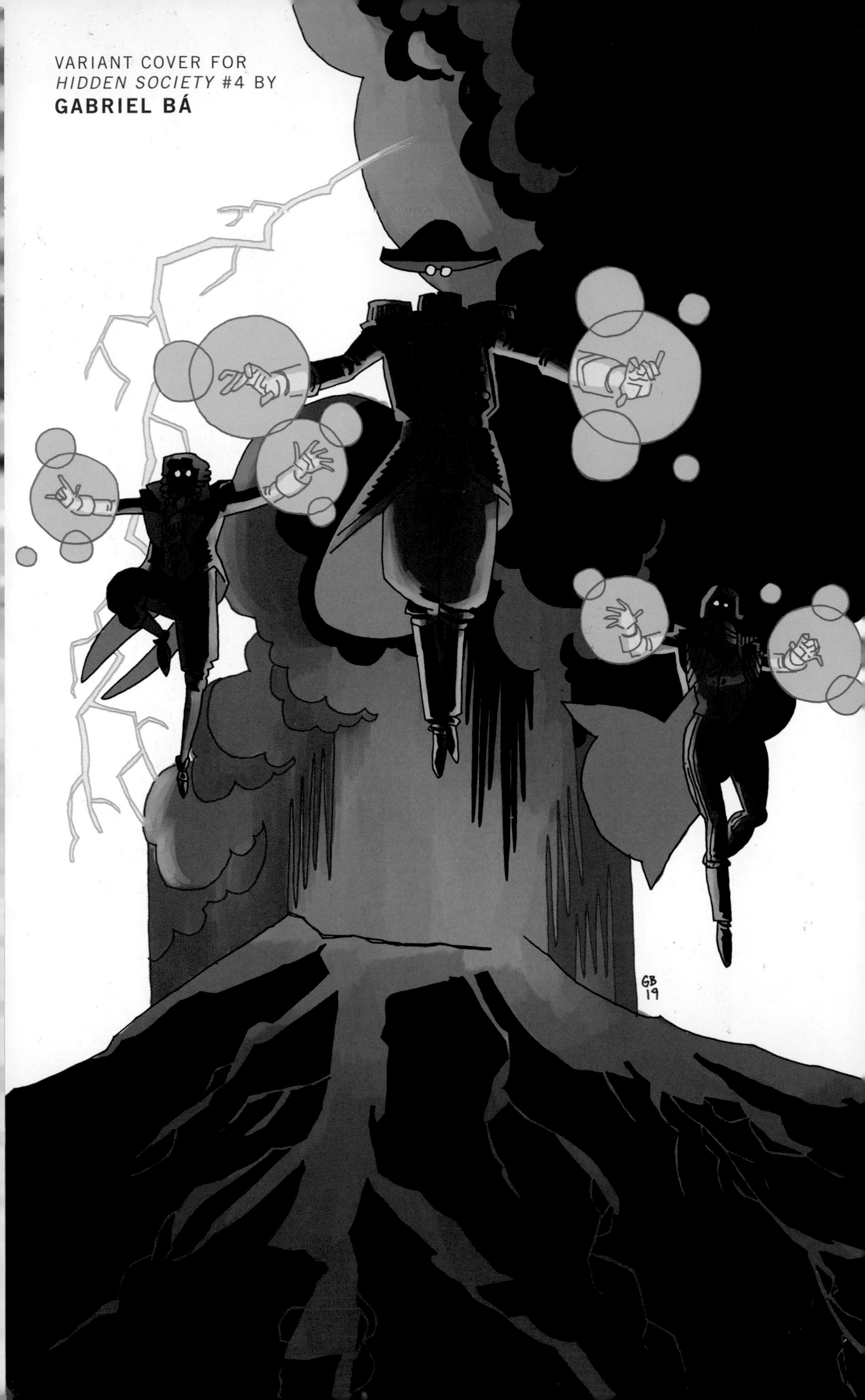
GB
19

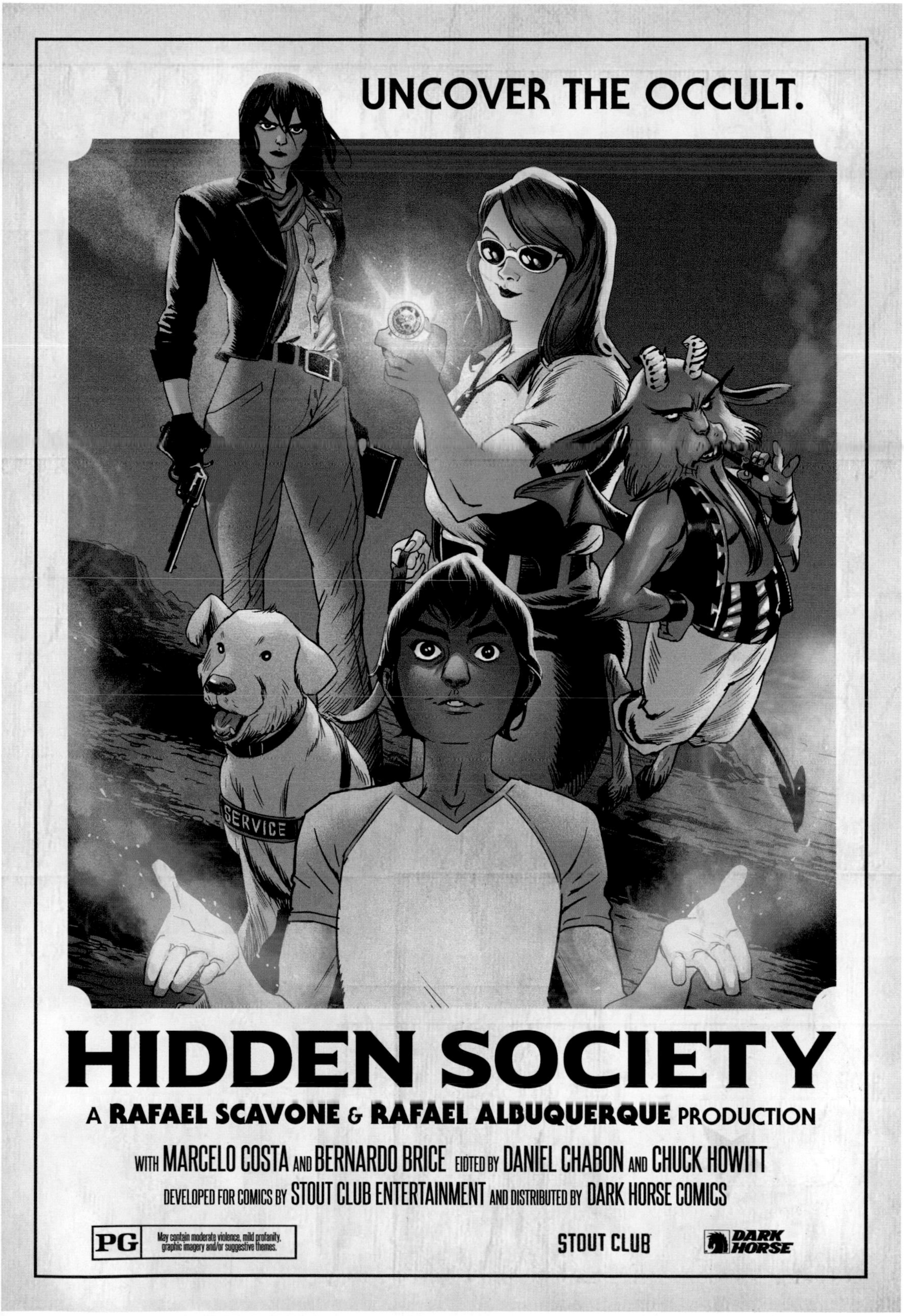

UNCOVER THE OCCULT.
SERVICE
HIDDEN SOCIETY
A RAFAEL SCAVONE & RAFAEL ALBUQUERQUE PRODUCTION
WITH MARCELO COSTA AND BERNARDO BRICE EIDTED BY DANIEL CHABON AND CHUCK HOWITT
DEVELOPED FOR COMICS BY STOUT CLUB ENTERTAINMENT AND DISTRIBUTED BY DARK HORSE COMICS
PG
May contain moderate violence, mild profanity, graphic imagery and/or suggestive themes.
STOUT CLUB
DARK HORSE

HIDDEN SOCIETY SKETCHBOOK

NOTES BY

RAFAEL SCAVONE AND RAFAEL ALBUQUERQUE

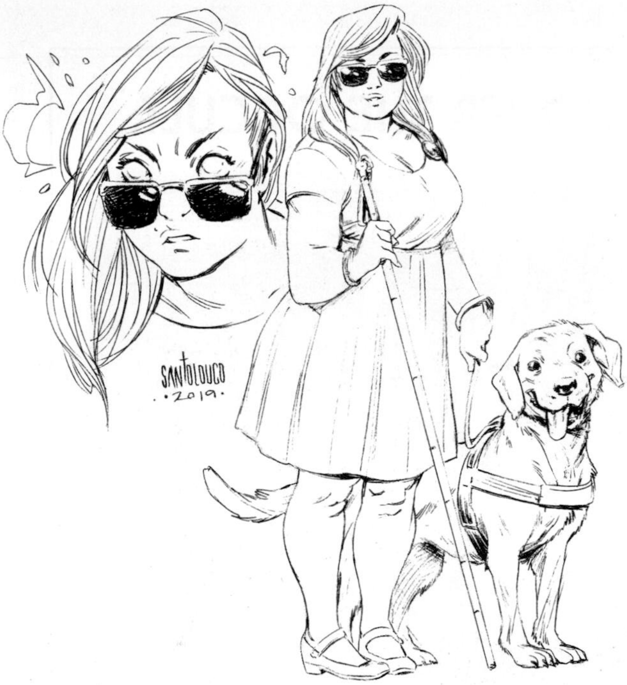
SANTOLOUCO
•2019•

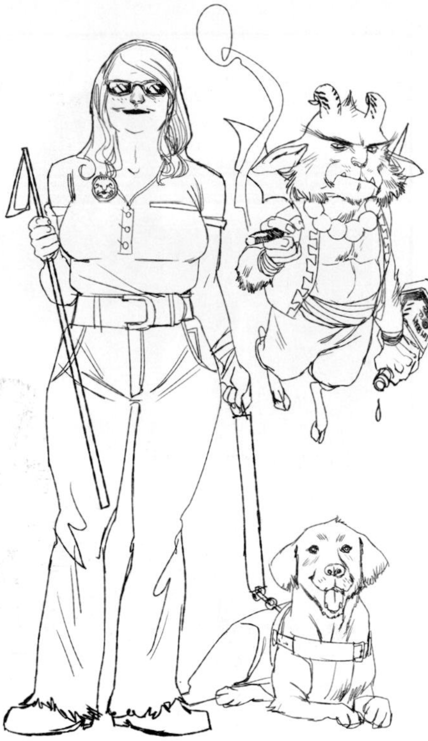

LAURA

Laura is a character avid for the thrill and adventure, and this spirit was immediately captured by the original designer Mateus Santolouco. Very few adjustments were incorporated by Albuquerque for her final look.

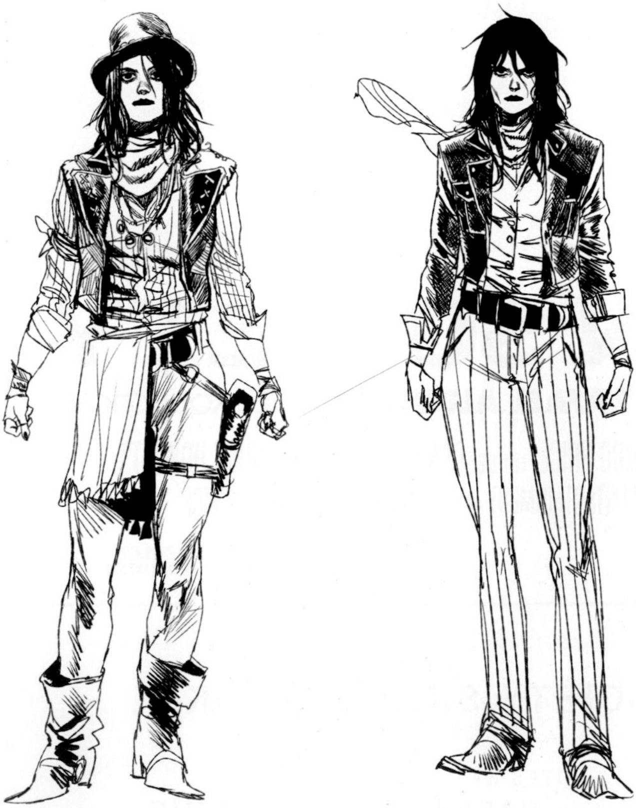

MERCY

Mercy is a character that has lived among us since the 19th century, so we wanted her look to show this immediately. Mixing a seventies Rock 'n' Roll look with some gypsy imagery, our reference was having some kind of Joan Jett old-west gunslinger living in the modern times.

ORCUS

Originally designed by Eduardo Medeiros, Orcus's design evolved to something more feline, and ironic, evoking images of ancient Roman references in Albuquerque's final interpretation.

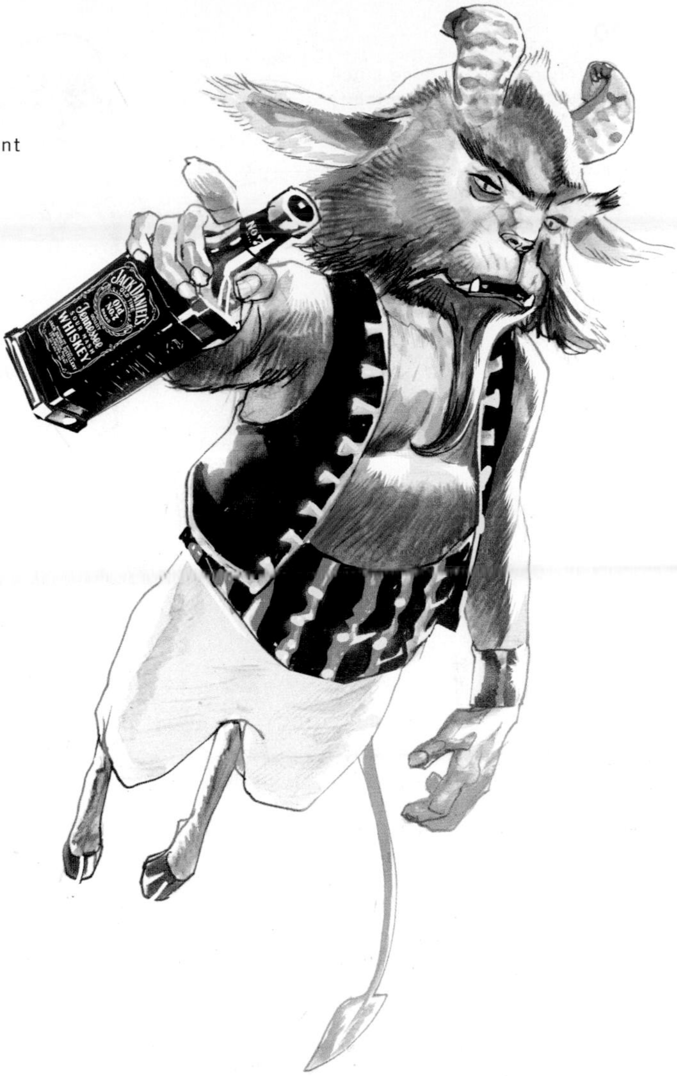
WHISKEY

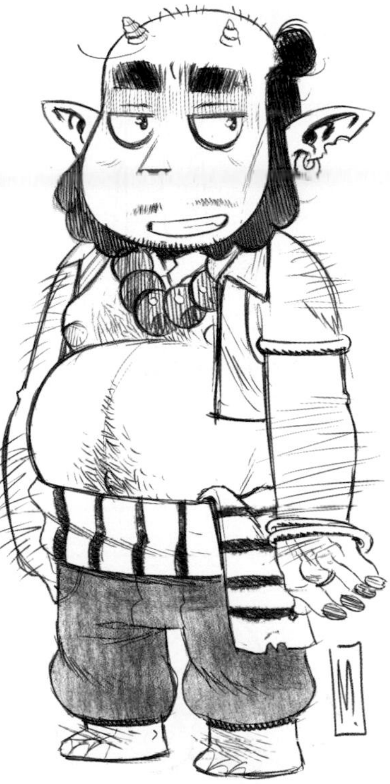

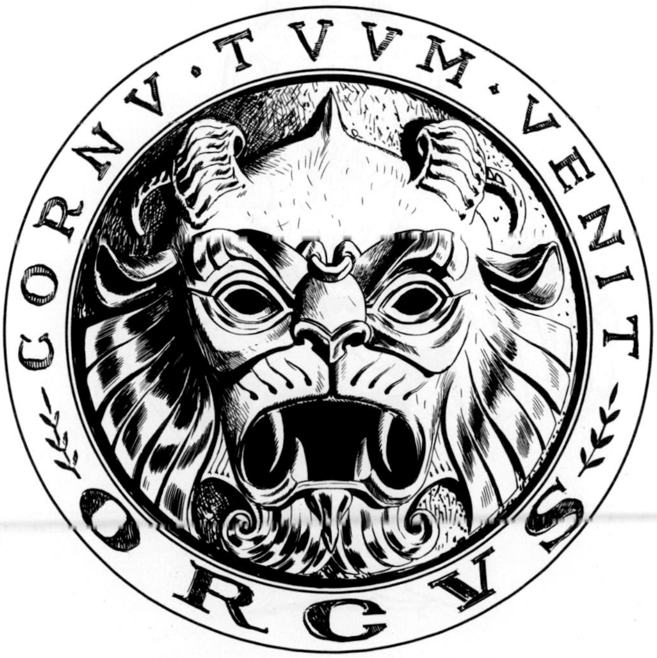
CORNV · TVVM · VENIT
ORCVS

JADOO

Not many changes were done since Albuquerque's first Jadoo sketch. The character eventually got more casual clothes, but the character's essence has been the same since the very beginning of the project.

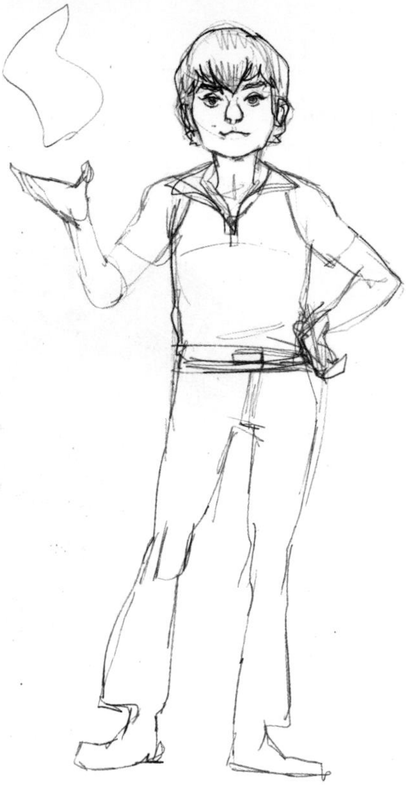

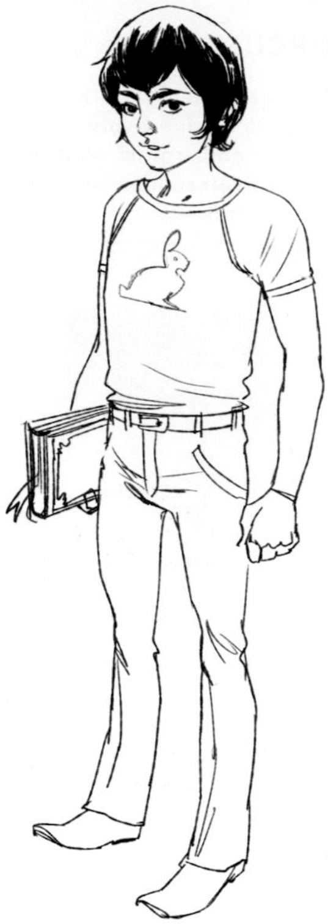

ULLOO

Ulloo was conceived at first as a much more rustic and tribal character, and with the evolution of the story we eventually needed a more regal and polite look for him. His final design was inspired by the real mystics from Mayong in Assam, India.

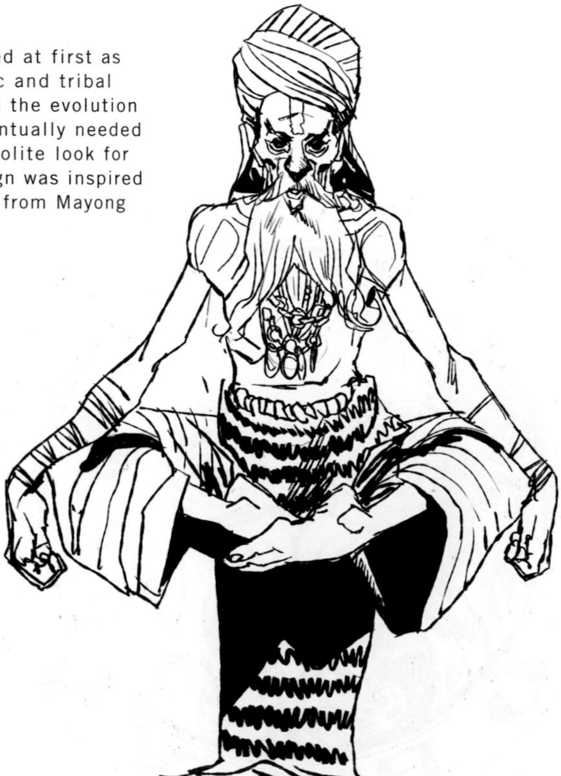

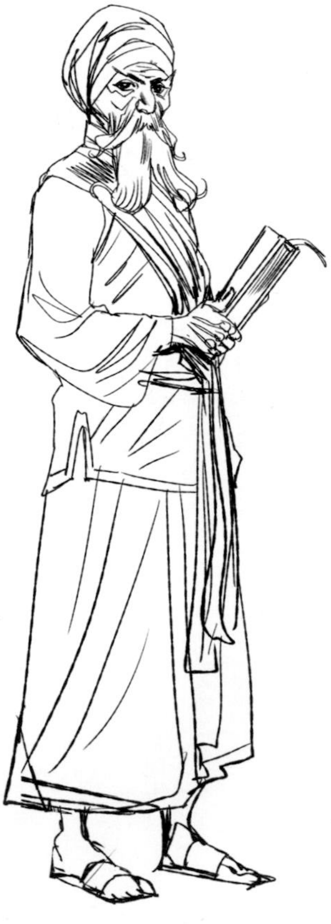

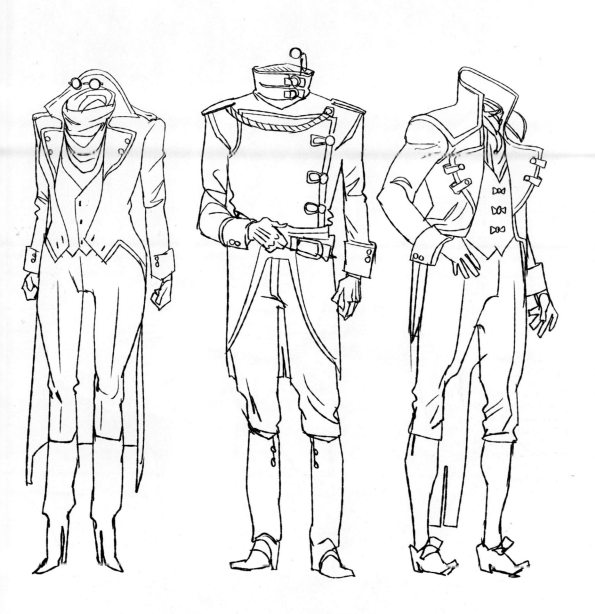

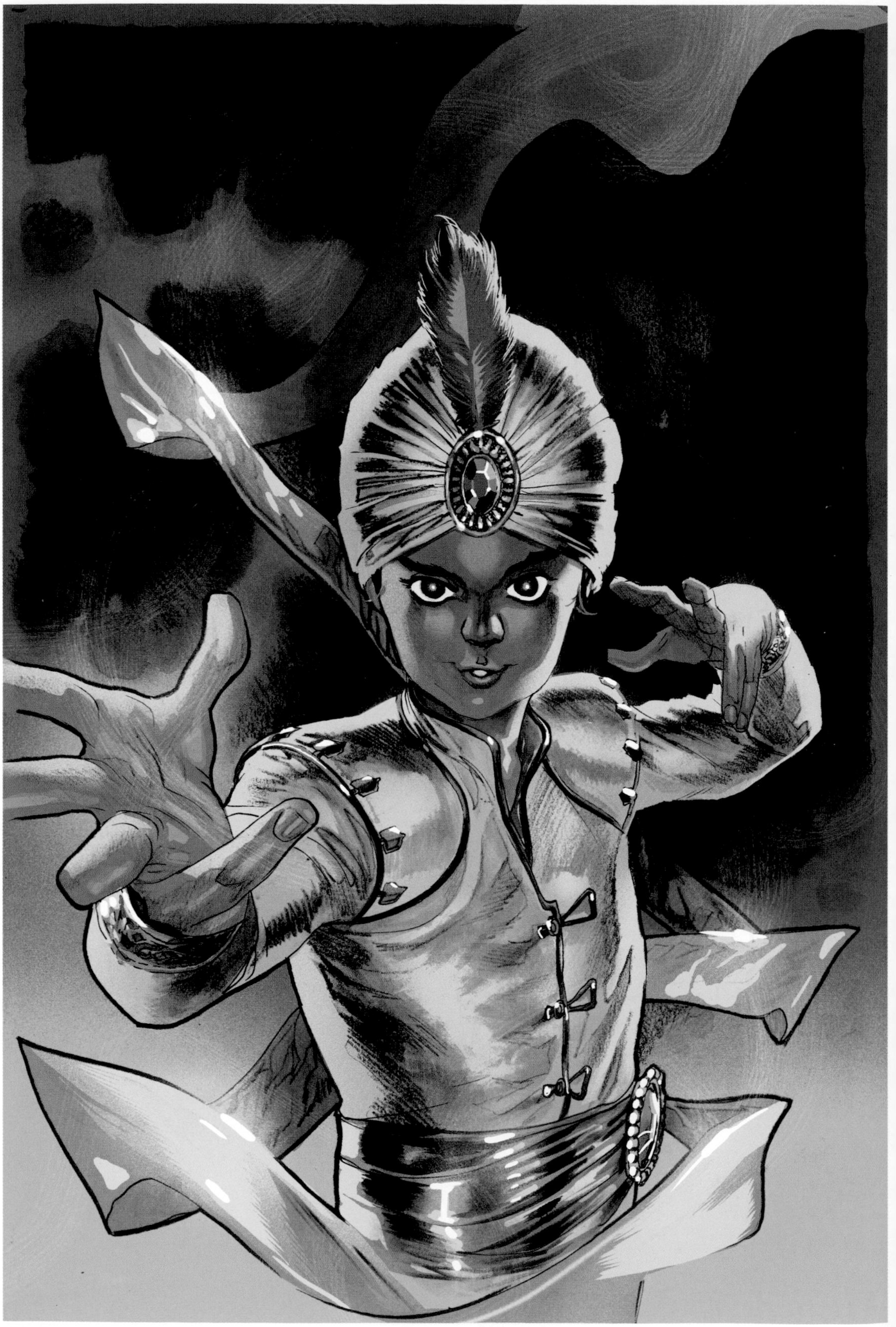

BLACK HAMMER
Jeff Lemire and Dean Ormston
BLACK HAMMER LIBRARY EDITION: VOLUME ONE
ISBN 978-1-50671-073-0 | $49.99

BLACK HAMMER LIBRARY EDITION: VOLUME TWO
ISBN 978-1-50671-185-0 | $49.99

VOLUME 1: SECRET ORIGINS
ISBN 978-1-61655-786-7 | $14.99

VOLUME 2: THE EVENT
ISBN 978-1-50670-198-1 | $19.99

VOLUME 3: AGE OF DOOM, PART I
ISBN 978-1-50670-389-3 | $19.99

VOLUME 4: AGE OF DOOM, PART II
ISBN 978-1-50670-816-4 | $19.99

QUANTUM AGE: FROM THE WORLD OF BLACK HAMMER
Jeff Lemire and Wilfredo Torres
ISBN 978-1-50670-841-6 | $19.99

SHERLOCK FRANKENSTEIN & THE LEGION OF EVIL: FROM THE WORLD OF BLACK HAMMER
Jeff Lemire and David Rubín
ISBN 978-1-50670-526-2 | $17.99

EMPOWERED VOLUME 1
Adam Warren
ISBN 978-1-59307-672-6 | $17.99

THE PAYBACKS COLLECTION
Donny Cates, Eliot Rahal and Geof Shaw
ISBN 978-1-50670-482-1 | $24.99

THE BLACK BEETLE
Francesco Francavilla
KARA BOCEK
ISBN 978-1-50670-537-8 | $12.99

THE COMPLETE ANGEL CATBIRD
Margaret Atwood and Johnnie Christmas
ISBN 978-1-50670-456-2 | $24.99

HELLBOY OMNIBUS
Mike Mignola and others
VOLUME 1: SEED OF DESTRUCTION
ISBN 978-1-50670-666-5 | $24.99

VOLUME 2: STRANGE PLACES
ISBN 978-1-50670-667-2 | $24.99

VOLUME 3: THE WILD HUNT
ISBN 978-1-50670-668-9 | $24.99

HELLBOY IN HELL
ISBN 978-1-50670-749-5 | $24.99

ORIGINAL VISIONS—THRILLING TALES!

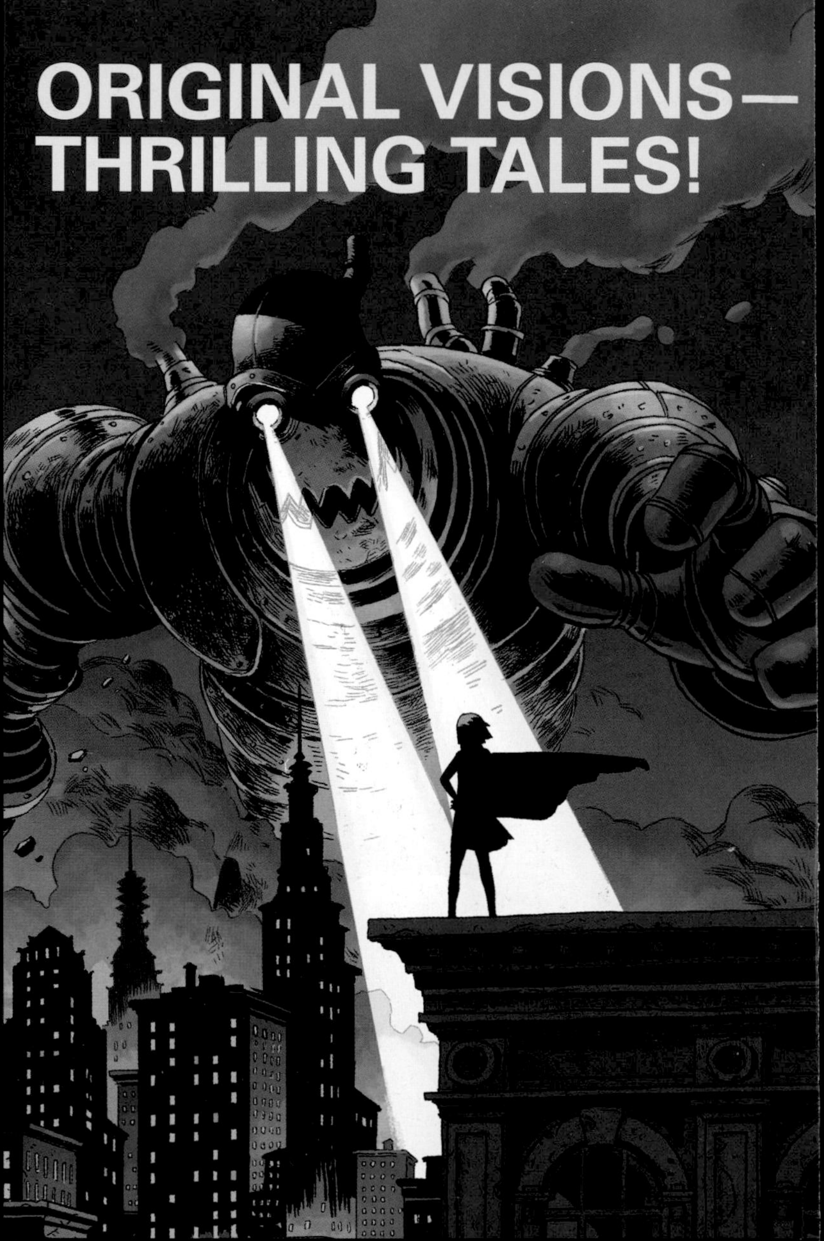

"These superheroes ain't no boy scouts in spandex. They're a high-octane blend of the damaged, quixotic heroes of pulp and detective fiction and the do-gooders in capes from the Golden and Silver Ages."
—Duane Swierczynski

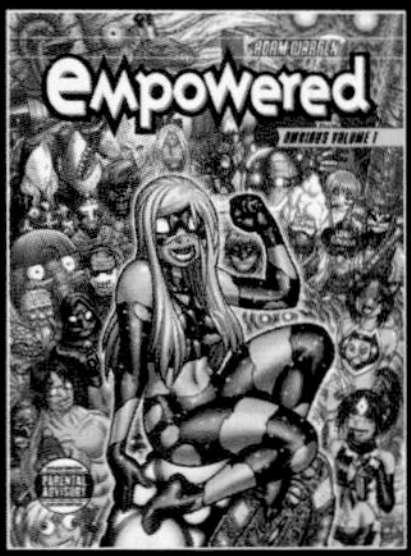
empowered
OMNIBUS VOLUME 1

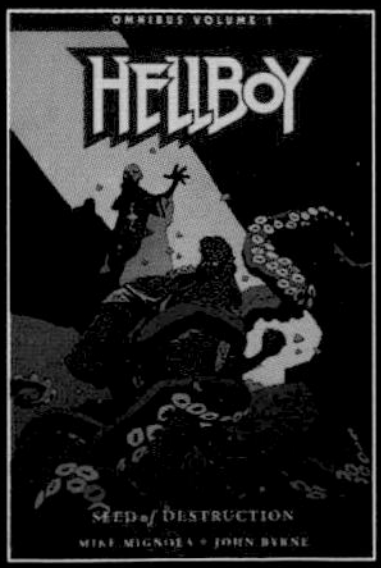
OMNIBUS VOLUME 1
HELLBOY
SEED of DESTRUCTION
MIKE MIGNOLA • JOHN BYRNE

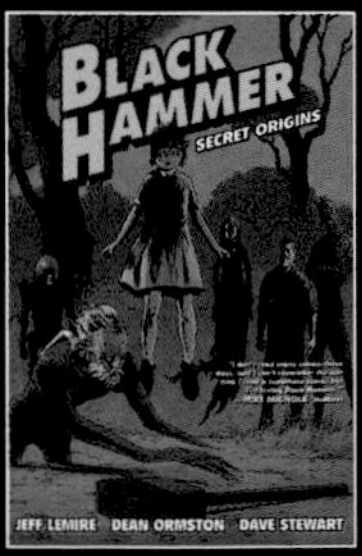
BLACK HAMMER
SECRET ORIGINS
JEFF LEMIRE DEAN ORMSTON DAVE STEWART

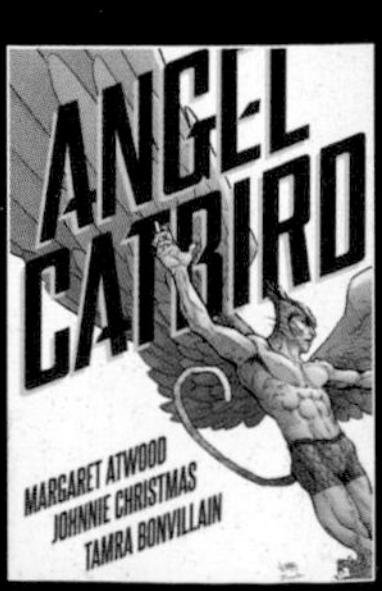
ANGEL CATBIRD
MARGARET ATWOOD
JOHNNIE CHRISTMAS
TAMRA BONVILLAIN

AVAILABLE AT YOUR LOCAL COMICS SHOP OR BOOKSTORE
To find a comics shop in your area, visit comicshoplocator.com. For more information or to order direct, visit DarkHorse.com